Talking about Detective Fiction

P. D. James was born in Oxford in 1920 and educated at Cambridge High School for Girls. From 1949 to 1968 she worked in the National Health Service and subsequently in the Home Office, first in the Police Department and later in the Criminal Policy Department. All that experience has been used in her novels. She is a Fellow of the Royal Society of Literature and of the Royal Society of Arts and has served as a Governor of the BBC, a member of the Arts Council, where she was Chairman of the Literary Advisory Panel, on the Board of the British Council and as a magistrate in Middlesex and London. She has won awards for crime writing in Britain, America, Italy and Scandinavia, including the Mystery Writers of America Grandmaster Award and The National Arts Club Medal of Honor for Literature (US). She has received honorary degrees from seven British universities, was awarded an OBE in 1983 and was created a life peer in 1991. In 1997 she was elected President of the Society of Authors.

She lives in London and Oxford and has two daughters, five grandchildren and seven great-grandchildren.

D0231322

Also by P. D. James

COVER HER FACE
A MIND TO MURDER
UNNATURAL CAUSES
SHROUD FOR A NIGHTINGALE
AN UNSUITABLE JOB FOR A WOMAN
THE BLACK TOWER
DEATH OF AN EXPERT WITNESS
INNOCENT BLOOD
THE SKULL BENEATH THE SKIN
A TASTE FOR DEATH
DEVICES AND DESIRES
THE CHILDREN OF MEN
ORIGINAL SIN
A CERTAIN JUSTICE
DEATH IN HOLY ORDERS
THE MURDER ROOM
THE LIGHTHOUSE
THE PRIVATE PATIENT

non-fiction

TIME TO BE IN EARNEST
A Fragment of Autobiography

THE MAUL AND THE PEAR TREE
The Ratcliffe Highway Murders 1811
(by P. D. James and T. A. Critchley)

Talking
about
Detective
Fiction

P. D. James

Bodleian Library
UNIVERSITY OF OXFORD

faber and faber

First published in hardback in 2009 by the Bodleian Library
Broad Street, Oxford OX1 3BG

www.bodleianbookshop.co.uk

This paperback edition first published in 2010 by Faber and Faber Ltd,
Bloomsbury House, 74–77 Great Russell Street, London WC1B 3DA

www.faber.co.uk

Cartoons used in Foreword, Chapters 4, 5 and 6: www.CartoonStock.com
Cartoons used in Chapters 1, 2 and 8 reproduced with permission of Punch
    Ltd., www.punch.co.uk
Cartoon used in Chapter 3: from author's own collection
Cartoon used in Chapter 7: David Brown/artizans.com

Every effort has been made to ascertain copyright and to trace and contact the
copyright owners for the cartoons where applicable. If any copyright owners
make themselves known a full acknowledgement will be made in future
reprints.

Designed by Dot Little
Printed and bound in England by CPI Bookmarque, Croydon

A CIP record of this publication is available from the British Library

ISBN 978-0-571-25358-6

10 9 8 7 6 5 4 3 2 1

Contents

IT'S A BLOOD CURDLING NOVEL ABOUT THE BRUTAL MURDER OF A PUBLISHER WHO REJECTED A BOOK ABOUT THE BRUTAL MURDER OF A PUBLISHER...

Foreword

This book had its beginnings in December 2006 when, at the request of the Bodleian's Publishing Department, the then Librarian invited me to write a book on British detective fiction in aid of the Library. As a native of Oxford I had known from early childhood that the Bodleian Library is one of the oldest and most distinguished in the world, and I replied that I was very happy to accept the invitation but must first finish the novel on which I was then working. The book which I was privileged to write now makes its somewhat belated appearance. I was relieved that the subject proposed was one of the few on which I felt competent to pontificate but I hope that the many references to my own methods of working won't be seen as hubris; they are an attempt to answer some of the questions most frequently asked by my readers and are unlikely to be new to audiences who have heard me speaking about my work over the years – nor, of course, to my fellow crime-writers.

Because of its resilience and popularity, detective fiction has attracted what some may feel is more than its fair share of critical attention, and I have no wish to add to, and less to emulate, the many distinguished studies of the last two centuries. Inevitably there will be some notable omissions for which I apologise, but my hope is that this short personal account will interest and entertain not only my readers, but the many who share our pleasure in a form of popular literature which for over fifty years has fascinated and engaged me as a writer.

P. D. James

THE BRITISH CHARACTER.

LOVE OF DETECTIVE FICTION.

– 1 –

What Are We Talking About and How Did It All Begin?

Death in particular seems to provide the minds of the
Anglo-Saxon race with a greater fund of innocent amusement
than any other single subject.

Dorothy L. Sayers

These words were written by Dorothy L. Sayers in her preface to a volume entitled *Great Short Stories of Detection, Mystery and Horror, Third Series*, published by Gollancz in 1934. She was, of course, talking not of the devastating amalgamation of hatred, violence, tragedy and grief which is real-life murder, but of the ingenious and increasingly popular stories of mystery and detection of which, by that time, she herself was an established and highly regarded writer. And to judge by the worldwide success of Arthur Conan Doyle's Sherlock Holmes and Agatha Christie's Poirot, it is not only the Anglo-Saxons who have an appetite for mystery and mayhem. It seems that this vicarious enjoyment in 'murder considered as a fine art', to quote Thomas De Quincey, makes the whole world kin.

In his book *Aspects of the Novel*, E.M. Forster writes:

11

'The king died and then the queen died' is a story. 'The king died, and then the queen died of grief' is a plot…. 'The queen died, no one knew why, until it was discovered that it was through grief at the death of the king.' This is a plot with a mystery in it, a form capable of high development.

To that I would add, 'Everyone thought that the queen had died of grief until they discovered the puncture mark in her throat.' That is a murder mystery, and it too is capable of high development.

Novels which enshrine a mystery, often involving a crime, and which provide the satisfaction of an ultimate solution are, of course, common in the canon of English literature, and most would never be thought of in terms of detective fiction. Anthony Trollope, who, like his friend Dickens, was fascinated by the criminal underworld and the exploits of the newly formed detective force, frequently teases us in his novels with a central mystery. Did Lady Eustace steal the family diamonds, and if not, who did? Did Lady Mason forge the codicil to her husband's will in *Orley Farm*, a codicil from which she and her son had benefited for thirty years? Perhaps Trollope gets closest to the conventions of the orthodox detective story in *Phineas Redux*, in which the hero is arrested for the murder of his political enemy, Mr Bonteen, and only escapes conviction on strong circumstantial evidence by the energetic efforts of Madame Max, the woman who loves him and obtains the vital clue which helps to convict the true murderer. Who is the mysterious woman in white in Wilkie Collins's novel of that name? In Charlotte Brontë's *Jane Eyre*, who is it that Jane hears shrieking in the night, who attacks the mysterious visitor to Thornfield Hall, and what part does the servant Grace Poole play in these dark matters? Charles Dickens provides both mystery and murder in *Bleak House*, creating in Inspector Bucket one of literature's most memorable detectives, while his unfinished novel *The Mystery of Edwin Drood* contains enough of the plot to encourage fascinating conjecture about how it was to be resolved.

A modern example of a novel which enshrines a mystery and its solution is John le Carré's *Tinker, Tailor, Soldier, Spy*. This is generally regarded as one of the most distinguished modern novels of espionage, but it is also a perfectly constructed detective story. Here the central mystery is not an act of murder but the identity of the mole at the heart of the British Secret Service. We know the names of the five suspects, and the setting gives us access to a secret esoteric and cloistered world, making us privileged participants in its mysteries. The detective called in to identify the traitor is John le Carré's sympathetic serial hero George Smiley, with the help of his junior colleague Peter Guillam, and the solution at the end of the novel is one which we the readers should be able to arrive at from evidence fairly presented.

But perhaps the most interesting example of a mainstream novel which is also a detective story is the brilliantly structured *Emma* by Jane Austen. Here the secret which is the mainspring of the action is the unrecognised relationships between the limited number of characters. The story is confined to a closed society in a rural setting, which was to become common in detective fiction, and Jane Austen deceives us with cleverly constructed clues (eight immediately come to mind) – some based on action, some on apparently

13

innocuous conversations, some in her authorial voice. At the end, when all becomes plain and the characters are at last united with their right partners, we wonder how we could have been so deceived.

So what exactly are we talking about when we use the words 'detective story', how does it differ from both the mainstream novel and crime fiction, and how did it all begin? Novels which have an atrocious crime at their heart, whose writers set out to explore and interpret the dangerous and violent underworld of crime, its causes, ramifications and effect on both perpetrators and victims, can cover an extraordinarily broad spectrum of imaginative writing extending to some of the highest works of the human imagination. These books may indeed have murder at their heart, but there is frequently no mystery about the perpetrator and therefore no detective and no clues. An example is Graham Greene's *Brighton Rock*. We know from the beginning that Pinkie is a killer and that the unfortunate Hale, desperately walking the streets and lanes of Brighton, knows, as do we, that he is going to be murdered. Our interest is not primarily in the investigation of murder, but in the tragic fate of those involved. The novel adumbrates Greene's preoccupation with the moral ambiguity of evil which is at the heart of his creativity; indeed, he came to regret the detective element in *Brighton Rock* and his own division of his novels between 'entertainments' and those presumably which he intended should be taken seriously. I'm glad that Greene later repudiated this puzzling dichotomy which picked out certain of his novels for disparagement and which helped to promote the still prevalent habit of dividing novels into those which are popular, exciting and accessible but, perhaps for these reasons, tend to be undervalued, and those in a somewhat ill-defined category which are granted the distinction of being described as literary novels. Greene surely couldn't have meant that, when writing an 'entertainment', he took less trouble with the literary style, cared less for the truth of characterisation and modified the plot and theme to accommodate what he saw as the popular taste. This is manifestly not true of a writer of whom the words of Robert Browning are particularly appropriate:

Our interest's on the dangerous edge of things.
The honest thief, the tender murderer,
The superstitious atheist.

Although the detective story at its highest can also operate on the dangerous edge of things, it is differentiated both from mainstream fiction and from the generality of crime novels by a highly organised structure and recognised conventions. What we can expect is a central mysterious crime, usually murder; a closed circle of suspects each with motive, means and opportunity for the crime; a detective, either amateur or professional, who comes in like an avenging deity to solve it; and, by the end of the book, a solution which the reader should be able to arrive at by logical deduction from clues inserted in the novel with deceptive cunning but essential fairness. This is the definition I have usually given when speaking about my work but, although not inaccurate, it now seems unduly restrictive and more appropriate to the so-called Golden Age between the wars than it is today. Not all the villains

15

are among a small group of obvious suspects; the detective may be faced with a single named or secret adversary who must be finally run down and defeated by logical deduction from observed facts and, of course, by the accepted heroic virtues: intelligence, courage and energy. This type of mystery is frequently a highly personal conflict between the hero and his prey, characterised by physicality, ruthlessness and violence, often amounting to torture, and even if the detective element is strong, the book is more appropriately described as a thriller than a detective story. The James Bond novels of Ian Fleming are the obvious example. But for a book to be described as detective fiction there must be a central mystery, and one that by the end of the book is solved satisfactorily and logically, not by good luck or intuition, but by intelligent deduction from clues honestly if deceptively presented.

One of the criticisms of the detective story is that this imposed pattern is mere formula writing, that it binds the novelist in a straitjacket which is inimical to the artistic freedom which is essential to creativity, and that subtlety of characterisation, a setting which comes alive for the reader and even credibility are sacrificed to the dominance of structure and plot. But what I find fascinating is the extraordinary variety of books and writers which this so-called formula has been able to accommodate, and how many authors have found the constraints and conventions of the detective story liberating rather than inhibiting of their creative imagination. To say that one cannot produce a good novel within the discipline of a formal structure is as foolish as to say that no sonnet can be great poetry since a sonnet is restricted to fourteen lines – an octave and a sestet – and a

16

strict rhyming sequence. And detective stories are not the only novels which conform to a recognised convention and structure. All Jane Austen's novels have a common storyline: an attractive and virtuous young woman surmounts difficulties to achieve marriage to the man of her choice. This is the age-long convention of the romantic novel, but with Jane Austen what we have is Mills & Boon written by a genius.

And why murder? The central mystery of a detective story need not indeed involve a violent death, but murder remains the unique crime and it carries an atavistic weight of repugnance, fascination and fear. Readers are likely to remain more interested in which of Aunt Ellie's heirs laced her nightly cocoa with arsenic than in who stole her diamond necklace while she was safely holidaying in Bournemouth. Dorothy L. Sayers's *Gaudy Night* doesn't contain a murder although there is an attempt at one, and the death at the heart of Frances Fyfield's *Blood from Stone* is a spectacular and mysterious suicide. But, except in those novels of espionage which are primarily concerned with treachery, it remains rare for the central crime in an orthodox mystery to be other than the ultimate crime for which no human reparation can ever be made.

So how and when did detective fiction become an accepted genre of popular fiction? To this there is no easy or generally accepted answer. The novel itself is a comparatively recent product of the human imagination, hence its name. It cannot, for example, match the ancient lineage of drama and, unlike drama and verbal storytelling, it can only appeal to a privileged minority until a community achieves a high level of literacy. Storytelling is, of course, an ancient art. Tales which combine excitement with mystery, which offer a puzzle and a solution, can be found in ancient literature and legend and were probably told even earlier by the tribal storyteller round the camp fires of our remote ancestors. Their tales were surely more likely to have dealt with heroic action, revenge and mystery than with subtle ambiguities of character and the domestic problems of the warring couple in the next cave. And novels were being written and read for decades before readers, publishers, critics and booksellers thought of defining them in such categories as Mystery, Thriller, Romantic Fiction, Fantasy or Science Fiction, divisions which are often more a matter of convenience, marketing strategy, taste or prejudice than of fact, and which can be unhelpful to both the novels and their writers.

Some historians of the genre claim that the detective story proper, which fundamentally is concerned with the bringing of order out of disorder and the restoration of peace after the destructive eruption of murder, could not exist until society had an official detective force, which in England would be in 1842 when the detective department of the Metropolitan Police came into being. A distinguished detective novelist, Reginald Hill, creator of the Yorkshire duo Andrew Dalziel and Peter Pascoe, wrote in 1978, 'Let me be clear. Without a police force there can be no detective fiction although several modern writers have, with varying degrees of success, tried to write detective stories set in pre-police days.' This opinion seems rational: detective fiction is unlikely to flourish in societies without an organised system of law enforcement or in which murder is commonplace. Mystery novelists, particularly in the Golden Age, were generally strong supporters of institutional law and order, and of the police. Individual officers might be portrayed as ineffective, plodding, slow-witted and ill-educated, but never as corrupt. Detective fiction is in the tradition of the English novel, which sees crime, violence and social chaos as an aberration, virtue and good order as the norm for which all reasonable people strive, and which confirms our belief, despite some evidence to the contrary, that we live in a rational, comprehensible and moral universe. And in doing this it not only provides the satisfaction of all popular literature, the mild intellectual challenge of a puzzle, excitement, confirmation of our cherished beliefs in goodness and order, but also entry to a familiar and reassuring world in which we are both involved in violent death and yet remain personally inviolate both from responsibility and from its terrors. Whether we should expect this detachment from vicarious responsibility is, of course, another question and one which bears on the difference between the books of the years between the wars and the detective novels of today.

One strand of the tangled skein of detective fiction goes back to the eighteenth century and includes the gothic tales of horror written by Ann Radcliffe and Matthew 'Monk' Lewis. Those gothic novelists were chiefly concerned to enthral readers with tales of terror and the horrific plight of the heroine, and although these books embodied puzzles and riddles, they were concerned far more with horror than with mystery. We recall the scene in Jane Austen's *Northanger Abbey* where the heroine, Catherine Morland, and her friend Isabella meet to discuss their current reading. Isabella says:

> 'I will read you their names directly; here they are, in my pocket-book. Castle of Wolfenbach, Clermont, Mysterious Warnings, Necromancer of the Black

Forest, Midnight Bell, Orphan of the Rhine, and
Horrid Mysteries. Those will last us some time.'

'Yes, pretty well; but are they all horrid, are you
sure they are all horrid?'

They were indeed, but since the detective story deals with
rational terror, their influence on the later development of
the genre has been limited, although there are echoes of
half-supernatural terror in some of Conan Doyle's stories.
Some critics might argue that horror plays a far greater part
than ratiocination in the modern psychological mysteries
which deal primarily with atrocious serial murders by
psychopaths. The most effective are those by writers with
personal involvement in the investigation of serial murder,
the Americans Patricia Cornwell and Kathy Reichs and, in
this country, Val McDermid, whose central character, Tony
Hill, is a psychological profiler, and whose novels show evidence of the careful research necessary both for mood and
for credibility. These novels, which are becoming increasingly popular, could be said to constitute a separate genre
in crime fiction as they do in films.

If we are looking for the origins of detective fiction
most critics are agreed that the two novelists who vie for
the distinction of writing the first full-length classical
detective story are William Godwin, Shelley's father-in-
law, who in 1794 published *Caleb Williams*, and Wilkie
Collins, whose best-known novel, *The Moonstone*, appeared
in 1868. Neither writer would have been gratified at this
posthumous distinction. Wilkie Collins in particular saw
himself as a mainstream novelist, albeit one who worked
within the category which Victorians described as sensa-

tional. These works of mystery, suspense and danger with an overlay of horror had an increasingly strong hold on the popular imagination, and there was much argument among critics, both about their literary merit and about their social desirability. Did these sensational outpourings even deserve the name of novel, or were they a new and inferior form of fiction provided to meet a rapacious public demand focused on W.H. Smith railway station bookstalls? This debate has, of course, continued but in the mid-nineteenth century it was a new and particular concern. In 1851 *The Times* complained:

> Every addition to the stock [of the bookstalls] was positively made on the assumption that persons of the better class who constitute the larger portion of railway readers lose their accustomed taste the moment they enter the station.

In 1863 a leading review in the *Quarterly Review* stated:

> A class of literature has grown up around us ... playing no inconsiderable part in moulding the minds and forming the habits and tastes of its generation; and doing so principally, we had almost said exclusively, by 'preaching to the nerves.' ... Excitement, and excitement alone, seems to be the great end at which they aim ... Various causes have been at work to produce this phenomenon of our literature. Three principal ones may be named as having had a large share in it – periodicals, circulating libraries, and railway bookstalls.

By 1880 Matthew Arnold was describing these novels as 'cheap ... hideous and ignoble of aspect ... tawdry novels which flare in the bookshelves of our railway stations, and which seem designed, as so much else that is produced for the use of our middle-class, for people with a low standard of life.' The unfortunate Mr W.H. Smith, whose bookstalls did so much to promote reading, had apparently much to answer for.

But in my view the final and accurate words about the controversy were written by Anthony Trollope in his *Autobiography*, published posthumously in 1883.

> A good novel should be both [realistic and sensational], and both in the highest degree.... Truth let there be – truth of description, truth of character, human truth as to men and women. If there be such truth, I do not know that a novel can be too sensational.

Trollope was undoubtedly categorised by his contemporaries as a sensational novelist and was here defending his own work, but these words are as true of the sensational novel of today as they were when they were written.

Both *Caleb Williams* and *The Moonstone* could be described as sensational. Hazlitt, the theatre critic and essayist (1778-1830), thought that nobody who began *Caleb Williams* could fail to finish it and that nobody who read it could possibly forget it, yet I have to admit that in adolescence I found it difficult to get through and now have only the vaguest memory of its long and complicated plot. Certainly the novel has at its heart a murder, an amateur detective – Caleb Williams – who tells the story, a pursuit, disguise, clues to the truth of the murder for which two innocent men were hanged, and at the end a deathbed confession. But Godwin was using this dramatic and complicated adventure story to promote his belief in an ideal anarchism and, so far from justifying the rule of law, *Caleb Williams* was intended to show that to trust in social institutions is to invite betrayal. The novel is important both to English fiction generally and to the history of the detective story because Godwin was the first writer to use what he hoped would be a popular form as propaganda on behalf of the poor and exploited, and in particular to expose the injustice of the legal system. This was not a path followed by writers of the interwar years, who were more interested in puzzling and entertaining their readers than in the defects of contemporary society, and I would argue that, with a very few exceptions, it is mainly the modern detective writers who have set out not only to provide an exciting and credible mystery, but to examine and criticise the world which their characters inhabit. Today, however, this is done with less didacticism and more detachment and subtlety than was shown by William Godwin, and arises from the reality of the characters and their world rather than from any ostensible desire to promote a particular social doctrine.

But if one is to award the distinction of being the first detective story to one single novel, my choice – and I think the choice of many others – would be *The Moonstone*, which T.S. Eliot described as 'the first, the longest and the best' of modern English detective novels. In my view no other single novel of its type more clearly adumbrates what were to become the main characteristics of the genre. The

Moonstone is a diamond stolen from an Indian shrine by Colonel John Herncastle, left to his niece Rachel Verrinder and brought to her Yorkshire home to be handed over on her eighteenth birthday by a young solicitor, Franklin Blake. During the night it is stolen, obviously by a member of the household. A London detective, Sergeant Cuff, is called in, but later Franklin Blake takes over the investigation, although he himself is among the suspects. *The Moonstone* is a complex and brilliantly structured story told in narrative by the different characters involved directly or indirectly in the story. The varied styles, voices and viewpoints not only add variety and interest to the narrative, but are a powerful revelation of character.

Collins is meticulously accurate in his treatment of medical and forensic details. There is an emphasis on the importance of physical clues – a bloodstained nightdress, a smeared door, a metal chain – and all the clues are made available to the reader, foreshadowing the tradition of the fair-play rule whereby the detective must never be in possession of more information than the reader. The clever shifting of suspicion from one character to another is done with great adroitness and this emphasis on physical evidence and the cunning manipulation of the reader were both to become common in succeeding mysteries. But the novel has other and more important virtues as a detective story. Wilkie Collins is excellent at describing the physical appearance and the atmosphere of the setting, particularly the contrast between the secure and prosperous Victorian Verrinder household and the eerie loneliness of the shivering sands; between the exotic and accursed jewel that has been stolen and the outwardly respectable privileged lives of upper-class Victorians. The novel provides an interesting insight into many aspects of its age, particularly through the truth and variety of its characterisation, and since clue-making is largely concerned with the minutiae of everyday life, this reflection of contemporary social mores was to become one of the most interesting features of the detective story. The innovative importance of *The Moonstone* was recognised at the time. Henry James acknowledged its influence in an article in *The Nation*.

> To Mr Collins belongs the credit of having introduced into fiction those most mysterious of mysteries, the mysteries which are at our own doors. This innovation ... was fatal to the authority of Mrs Radcliffe and her everlasting castle in the Apennines. What are the Apennines to us or we to the Apennines? Instead of the terrors of 'Udolpho', we were treated to the terrors of the cheerful country-house and the busy London lodgings.

Wilkie Collins was innovative in more than the setting. In the rose-growing detective Sergeant Cuff, Wilkie Collins created one of the earliest professional detectives, eccentric but believable, shrewdly knowledgeable about human nature and based on a real-life Scotland Yard inspector, Jonathan Whicher. *The Moonstone* is the only detective novel as far as I know in which the hero is so obviously based on a real-life police officer; the case to which he was summoned to investigate, the murder at Road Hill House in Wiltshire, caused a country-wide sensation at the time and became one of the most intriguing and written-about

25

murders of the nineteenth century. The year was 1860, the place was the detached, impressive home of a prosperous factory inspector, Samuel Kent, and his second wife Mary, and the victim their three-year-old son, Francis Saville. On the night of 29 June he was taken from his cot in the room next to the marital bedroom, and carried from the house while the family and servants slept. His body with its throat slashed was found next morning in a privy in the garden. There could be no doubt that the killer was either a member of the family or one of the domestic staff, and the atmosphere of fascinated horror and conjecture spread from the neighbourhood to the whole country, while the local police tried to cope with a crime which, from the first, proved well beyond their powers.

In June 1842 the Home Office had approved the setting up of an elite detective force to investigate particularly atrocious crimes, and Whicher was its most famous and successful member, lauded by Dickens, friend of the famous and something of a national hero. When the local police proved ineffective, Whicher was called in to take over the investigation. The horror of the deed, the age and innocence of the victim, the prosperous upper-class setting, the rumours of sexual scandal and the near certainty that the murderer was one of the household provoked a nationwide heady mixture of revulsion and fascination. It seemed that the whole country, uninhibited by considerations of family grief or privacy, was composed of amateur detectives both in the press and in personal gossip. Whicher was convinced from the start that Constance, the sixteen-year-old half-sister of the child, was guilty, but the arrest of the daughter of a respectable upper-class family provoked outrage. When

Constance was released by the magistrates and the case remained unsolved, Whicher's reputation never recovered. Five years later Constance confessed that, alone and unaided, she had murdered her half-brother.

I think it would be going too far to see the Road Hill House case itself as directly influencing the development of detective fiction, but the national reaction to the crime at the time certainly confirmed the Victorian interest in sensational murders and in the process of detection. Largely because Constance Kent's confession, although accepted by the court, could not possibly have been completely true, interest in the case has never ceased and there have been a number of well-documented accounts.

The crime also inspired later novelists, including Dickens, and as late as 1983 Francis King transferred the story to India during the period of the British Raj in his novel *Act of Darkness*. The most recent account is by Kate Summerscale in *The Suspicions of Mr Whicher*, which concentrates on the investigation of the murder and provides fascinating details of the extraordinary public response to the crime and the subsequent lives of those concerned. Kate Summerscale also provides a solution to the mystery which I find convincing.

It seems now that all the participants in the tragedy and the general public were enacting in advance and in real life the storyline of detective novels which were to become common in the interwar years: the mysterious murder, the closed circle of suspects, the isolated rural community, the respectable and prosperous setting and the brilliant detective called in from outside to solve the crime when the local police are baffled. An age so fascinated by violence, both in real life and in literature, so ready to involve itself with relish in the process of detection, was certainly ready for the advent of the man who is commonly regarded as the first great British fictional detective and who was to appear in 1887 with the publication of Arthur Conan Doyle's *A Study in Scarlet*.

"I must say, Mr. Baskerville, we had expected something larger."

The Tenant of 221B Baker Street and the Parish Priest from Cobhole in Essex

You mentioned your name, as if I should recognize it,
but I assure you that, beyond the obvious facts that you are a
bachelor, a solicitor, a Freemason, and an asthmatic, I know
nothing whatever about you.

Arthur Conan Doyle, 'The Adventure of the Norwood Builder'

It is a safe assumption that enthusiasts for detective fiction, whatever their country or nationality, if asked to name the three most famous fictional detectives, will begin with Sherlock Holmes. In the long list of amateur sleuths down the last nine decades, he remains unique, the unchallenged Great Detective whose brilliant deductive intelligence could outwit any adversary, however cunning, and solve any puzzle, however bizarre. In the decades following his creator's death in 1930 he has become an icon.

When Arthur Conan Doyle published *A Study in Scarlet* he was a newly married general practitioner living in Southsea with ambitions to become a writer, but so far with better success in medicine than in fiction, despite being both prolific and hard-working. Then, in 1886, came the idea which was to bear fruit beyond his imagination. He decided to try his luck with a detective story, but one markedly different from the tales then being published, which he thought unimaginative, unfair in their denouement, and whose detectives were mere stereotypes who depended for success more on luck and the stupidity of the criminal than their own cleverness. His detective would employ scientific methods and logical deduction. *A Study in Scarlet* was first published in 1887 as one contribution in *Beeton's Christmas Annual*, priced at one shilling. The annual was hugely popular and quickly sold out, but the story was not widely reviewed, gaining only a few mentions in the national press. A year later *A Study in Scarlet* was published as a separate volume, and reprinted in 1889. Conan Doyle, however, gained very little from this attempt at detective fiction, having relinquished all rights in his story for £25. But it is here in his first detective story, seen through the eyes of his friend and flatmate Dr Watson, that the great detective is brought clearly before us in an image which, with the addition of his deerstalker hat and pipe, has remained fixed in the public imagination.

> In height he was rather over six feet, and so excessively lean that he seemed to be considerably taller. His eyes were sharp and piercing, save during those intervals of torpor to which I have alluded; and his thin hawk-like nose gave his whole expression an air of alertness and decision. His chin, too, had the prominence and squareness which mark the man of determination. His hands were invariably blotted with ink and stained with chemicals, yet he was possessed of extraordinary delicacy of touch,

as I frequently had occasion to observe when I watched him manipulating his fragile philosophical instruments.

And it is in *A Study in Scarlet* that Holmes himself gives proof of his deductive powers.

'There has been murder done, and the murderer was a man. He was more than six feet high, was in the prime of life, had small feet for his height, wore coarse, square-toed boots and smoked a Trichinopoly cigar. He came here with his victim in a four-wheeled cab, which was drawn by a horse with three old shoes and one new one on his off foreleg. In all probability the murderer had a florid face, and the fingernails of his right hand were remarkably long. These are only a few indications but they may assist you.'

Lestrade and Gregson glanced at each other with an incredulous smile.

'If this man was murdered, how was it done?' asked the former.

'Poison,' said Sherlock Holmes curtly, and strode off.

Despite the amount of detailed information about Holmes and his habits provided by Watson in the short stories, the core of the man remains elusive. He is obviously clever with a practical, rational, non-threatening intelligence, patriotic, compassionate, resourceful and brave – qualities which mirror those of his creator. This is not surprising since writers who create a serial character inevitably endow him or her with their own interests and preoccupations. Conan Doyle admitted that 'a man cannot spin a character out of his own inner consciousness and make it really life-like unless he has some possibilities of that character within him.' Even so, I would have expected him to have been more attached to the valiant Dr Watson, wounded hero of the second Afghan war, than to this unsentimental, neurotic and co-caine-injecting genius of deduction. Holmes is a violinist so he is not without a cultural interest, but we are probably unwise to accept Watson's partial view of the measure of his talent. Although the call to a new case provokes in Holmes a surge of enthusiasm and physical and mental energy, he has a doubting and pessimistic streak, and more than a touch of modern cynicism. 'What you do in this world is a matter of no consequence. The question is, what you can make people believe you have done' (*A Study in Scarlet*). 'We reach. We grasp. And what is left in our hands at the end? A shadow. Or worse than a shadow – misery' ('The Adventure of the Retired Colourman'). In this, too, Holmes could be reflecting a dichotomy in his own character, and indeed one aspect of Victorian sensibility. He is of his age but, curiously, also of ours, and this too may be part of the secret of his lasting appeal.

The inspiration for Sherlock Holmes was Dr Joseph Bell, a consultant surgeon at the Edinburgh Royal Infirmary whose reputation as a brilliant diagnostician was based on his ability to observe closely and interpret the apparently insignificant facts presented by the appearance and habits of his patients. Conan Doyle also acknowledged the influ-ence of Edgar Allan Poe, who was born in 1809 and died in 1849, and whose detective, Chevalier C. Auguste Dupin, was the first fictional investigator to rely primarily on deduction from observable facts. Many critics would argue that the main credit for inventing the detective story and influencing its development should be shared by Conan Doyle and Poe. Poe is chiefly remembered for his tales of the macabre, but in four short stories alone he introduced what were to become the stock plot devices of early detective stories. 'The Murders in the Rue Morgue' (1841) is a locked room mystery. In 'The Mystery of Marie Rogêt' (1842) the detective solves the crime from newspaper cuttings and press reports, making this the first example of armchair detection. In 'The Purloined Letter' (1844) we have an example of the perpetrator being the most unlikely suspect, a ploy which was to become common with Agatha Christie and in danger of becoming a cliché, so that readers whose main interest in the story was correctly to identify the murderer had only to fix on the least likely suspect to be sure of success. 'The Gold-Bug' makes use of cryptography in solving the crime; so too did Dorothy L. Sayers, both in *Have His Carcase* and in *The Nine Tailors*. Poe did not describe himself as a detective writer, but both he and his hero, C. Auguste Dupin, have their rightful importance in the history of the genre, although Dupin cannot challenge the dominance of Sherlock Holmes and has little in common with Holmes except for their deductive skills. Sherlock Holmes remains unique. We may not feel personally drawn to his eccentricities, but generations have entered into his world and have shared the excitement, entertainment and pure reading pleasure of his adventures. Conan Doyle was a superb storyteller, the Sherlock Holmes canon is still in print and the stories are being read by new generations nearly eighty years after Conan Doyle's death.

No writer who achieves spectacular success does so without a modicum of good luck. For Conan Doyle this occurred when he was invited to contribute a series of self-contained short stories for *Strand Magazine*, founded by George Newnes in 1880. *The Strand* broke new ground, attracting readers with such innovations as interviews with celebrities, general articles, photographs and free gifts, foreshadowing the popular magazines which were to prosper in the next century. With a readership of over 300,000 it provided Conan Doyle with a double bonus: not only could he be assured of a huge and growing public, but he was now able to concentrate on short stories, the form which suited him best. Today such good fortune could only be equated to a long-running major television series. This too, posthumously, he gained. To add to his wide exposure during his author's lifetime, the exploits of Sherlock Holmes have been a gift to radio, television and film, and millions of viewers have thrilled to *The Hound of the Baskervilles* who have never read the novel. His success was also helped by the talent of his illustrator, Sidney Paget, who created Holmes's handsome but sternly authoritative features and clothed him in the deerstalker hat and caped coat, a picture which has formed the mental image of the great detective for generations.

Conan Doyle also had the good fortune to publish when his own character, his literary talent and his hero met the needs and expectations of his age. The Sherlock Holmes saga provided for an increasingly literate society and the emergence of an upper working and middle class with leisure to read who welcomed stories which were original, accessible, exciting and with that occasional frisson of horror to which the Victorians were never averse. Conan Doyle was himself a representative of his sex and class. He was a man his fellow countrymen could understand: a stalwart imperialist, patriotic, courageous, resourceful and with the self-confidence to congratulate himself on having 'the strongest influence over young men, especially young athletic sporting men, than anyone in England, bar Kipling'. But his most attractive characteristic was undoubtedly his passion for justice, and he was indefatigable in spending time, money and energy in righting injustices wherever they came to light. He imbued Sherlock Holmes with the same passion, the same courage.

But despite the excellent qualities which Holmes shared with his creator, Watson's description of him gives a picture of a somewhat unlikely hero. In enumerating the limits of his flatmate's interests, Watson states that his knowledge of literature was nil, although he appeared to know every detail of every horror perpetrated in the century and his reading of sensational literature was immense. In the Victorian controversy between the somewhat despised 'sensational business' and the reputable straight novel, there is no doubt where Holmes's interests lay. It was his declared policy not to acquire any knowledge which was not useful to him or would not bear upon his job. He was an expert boxer and swordsman and had a good practical knowledge of the law and of poisons, including belladonna and opium. Although exhaustively energetic when engaged on a case, he spent days lying on a sofa without uttering a word, regularly injected himself with cocaine, and with his erratic lifestyle and habit of firing off his revolver in the sitting-room to pattern the wall with bullet holes must have been an uncomfortable and sometimes dangerous companion for his friend and flatmate Dr Watson. Mrs Hudson was certainly a most accommodating landlady.

A moment of Holmes-like deduction suggests that, if there is a 221B, there must be a 221A, and possibly a 221C. What did the tenants above and below think of having their peace disturbed by Sherlock Holmes's patriotic shooting practice or the mysterious and odd people who regularly came to his door? And why did such a brilliant and successful investigator, called on by the rich and famous, able to afford a special train to take Dr Watson and himself to the scene of crime, need to share lodgings in what seems to be essentially a rooming house? We are told by Dr Watson in *A Study in Scarlet* that the accommodation at 221B Baker Street 'consisted of a couple of comfortable bedrooms and a single large airy sitting-room, cheerfully furnished and illuminated by two broad windows'. So desirable in every way were the apartments, and so moderate the terms when divided between the two men, 'that the bargain was concluded upon the spot'. We also learn that the sitting-room was Sherlock Holmes's office and the place where he received his visitors, which meant that Watson had to be banished to his bedroom when anyone arrived on business, which was not infrequently. It hardly seems a satisfactory arrangement and I am not surprised that eventually, despite the moderate cost, Watson moved out. And was this really a feasible arrangement for Sherlock Holmes, who couldn't have been a poor man? One of his clients was the King of Sardinia, and noblemen as well as the humble workers of the world came to that sitting-room for help. In 'The Adventure of the Priory School', Holmes finds Lord Saltire, the son of the Duke of Holdernesse, who was missing from his preparatory school, and receives as his fee a cheque for ten thousand pounds – in those days a small fortune. He folds up the cheque and places it carefully in his notebook with the comment, 'I am a poor man.' But poor he certainly was not. Was he perhaps a secret philanthropist who used his income from prosperous clients to subsidise the poor? He couldn't have spent money on a main and more luxurious home since his frequent absences to return to it would undoubtedly have been commented upon by Dr Watson. And what happened to Dr Watson's dog? Before moving into 221B he confesses that he keeps a bull pup, but we never hear again about this animal. Did Mrs Hudson put down her foot, or was the unfortunate puppy a victim of Sherlock Holmes's revolver practice? But for me the greater mystery has to be the missing money. I have no doubt, however, that all will later be explained to me by members of the worldwide Sherlock Holmes societies, by whom no detail of Holmes's life or cases, and no discrepancies in the plots, have been left unexamined.

In addition to his four full-length novels – *A Study in Scarlet*, *The Sign of Four*, *The Hound of the Baskervilles* and *The Valley of Fear* – Conan Doyle published five collections of short stories featuring his hero. With such a large output, the quality is inevitably sometimes uneven. A number of the stories are frankly incredible, an example being one of the most popular and best known, 'The Speckled Band'. It is also among the most terrifying. Here we encounter the most evil of Holmes's adversaries, Dr Rylott, who from his first entrance in 221B Baker Street reveals his strength and brutality. As a doctor, he surely had the means to dispose of his step-daughter with expedience and safety, but the method he employed somehow seems a wanton wish on his part to make the investigation as complicated as possible for Holmes, rather than a rational plan to commit a successful murder. There are other inconsistencies in a number of the stories, but I have some sympathy with the judgement of the late novelist and critic Julian Symons that we should not fall into the error of preferring technical perfection to brilliant storytelling, and that if one were choosing the best twenty short detective stories ever written, at least half a dozen would feature Sherlock Holmes.

Holmes's lasting attraction also derives from the setting and atmosphere of the stories. We enter into that Victorian world of fog and gaslight, the jingle of horses' reins, the grind of wheels on cobblestones and the shadow of a veiled woman climbing the stairs to that claustrophobic sanctum at 221B Baker Street. Such is the power of the writing that it is we, the readers, who conjure up this enveloping miasma of mystery and terror. *The Sign of Four* mentions a dense, drizzly fog, but the weather is rarely described except briefly in phrases like 'a bleak windy day towards the end of March', or 'a close rainy day in October'. We provide what our imaginations need, including the detail of the small sitting-room, the untidiness, the initials VR in bullet marks in the wall and the smell of Holmes's pipe. We may not always believe in the details of the plot, but we always believe in the man himself and the world he inhabits.

And the magic has remained. We readers, in our fidelity to Holmes, have a greater respect for him than had his creator. Conan Doyle was a man of high literary ambition and, although he was too good a craftsman not to take care over the Holmes stories, he didn't take them seriously and had every intention of killing off his hero when the first series ended so that he could devote himself to what he saw as more prestigious literature. It was at the end of the second series of stories that he decided to kill both Holmes and his adversary, Moriarty, by plunging them over the Reichenbach Falls. But Holmes was not so easy to kill and by public demand was reinstated, although some readers may feel that the great detective was never quite the same man after the Reichenbach experience. Conan Doyle could not resist the public clamour for Holmes to be saved, nor say no to the enormous fees he was earning. But he still deplored the egregious success of his detective and wrote to his friend, 'I have had such an overdose of him that I feel towards him as I do towards *pâté-de-foie-gras*, of which I once ate too much, so that the name of it gives me a sickly feeling to this day.' But the readers did, and indeed still do, feast on the Holmes short stories not with nausea but with renewed appetite.

Another Victorian whose influence and reputation have been almost as great, in my view deservedly, was as prolific as Conan Doyle but very different both as a man and as a writer. Gilbert Keith Chesterton, who was born on Campden Hill in London in 1874 and died in 1936, can be described in terms which are hardly ever used of a writer today: he was a man of letters. All his life he earned his living by his pen and he was as versatile as he was prolific, gaining a reputation as a novelist, essayist, critic, journalist and poet. Much of this output, particularly on social, political and

41

religious subjects, has proved ephemeral, but a few of his poems, including 'The Donkey' and 'The Rolling English Road', continue to appear in anthologies of popular verse. But he is chiefly remembered as one of the most brilliant writers of the short detective story and for his serial detective, the Roman Catholic priest Father Brown. *The Innocence of Father Brown* was published in 1911 and was followed by four further volumes; the last, *The Scandal of Father Brown*, appeared in 1935. G.K. Chesterton converted to Roman Catholicism in 1922, and his faith became central to his life and work. His fictional priest was based on his friend Father John O'Connor, to whom *The Secret of Father Brown*, published in 1927, was dedicated.

We first meet Father Brown in the story 'The Blue Cross', and see him through the eyes of Valentin, described as the head of the Paris police. Valentin found himself sharing a railway carriage with a very short Roman Catholic priest going up from a small Essex village, who seemed to Valentin to be 'the essence of those Eastern flats with a face as round and dull as a Norfolk dumpling and eyes as empty as the North Sea'. He had several brown-paper parcels which he was quite incapable of managing, a large shabby umbrella which constantly fell on the floor, and did not seem to know which was the right part of his return ticket. Valentin was not the only person to be taken in by this seeming innocence and simplicity.

Father Brown could not be more different from the Golden Age heroes of detective fiction. He worked alone with no routine police support as had Lord Peter Wimsey with Inspector Parker, no Watson to provide an admiring audience and to ask questions on behalf of the less

42

perspicacious readers, and without even Holmes's limited scientific knowledge. He solved crimes by a mixture of common sense, observation and his knowledge of the human heart. As he says to Flambeau, the master thief whom he outwits in 'The Blue Cross' and whom he restores to honesty, 'Has it never struck you that a man who does next to nothing but hear men's real sins is not likely to be wholly unaware of human evil?' There were, of course, other advantages of being a priest: he was never required to explain precisely why he was present because it was assumed that he was occupied with his priestly function, and he was a man in whom many might naturally confide.

Although we are told that Father Brown was parish priest in Cobhole in Essex before moving to London, we meet him in other and very different places, in England and overseas, and in a variety of settings and company across the whole social and economic spectrum. Nothing and no one is alien to him. We rarely encounter him in the daily routine of his pastoral duties at Cobhole, never learn where exactly he lives, who housekeeps for him, what kind of church he has or his relationship with his bishop. We are not told his age, whether his parents are still living or even his Christian name. In each of the stories he makes his quiet appearance unannounced, as much at home with the poor and humble as he is with the rich and famous, and applying to all situations his own immutable spirituality. But he is always a rationalist with a dislike of superstition, which he sees as inimical to his faith. Like the other characters in the stories – and like us, the readers – he sees the physical facts of the case, but only he, by a process of deduction, interprets them correctly. In this he resembles, in his methods, Sherlock Holmes and Hercule Poirot. We see what is apparently obvious however bizarre; he sees what is true. Chesterton loved paradox and, because we encounter Father Brown often in incongruous company and he comes unencumbered by his past, the little priest is himself a paradox, at once endearingly human, but also a mysterious and iconic harbinger of death.

G.K. Chesterton's output was prodigious and it would be unreasonable to expect all the short stories to be equally successful but the quality of the writing never disappoints. Chesterton never wrote an inelegant or clumsy sentence. The Father Brown stories are written in a style richly complex, imaginative, vigorous, poetic and spiced with paradoxes. He had been trained as an artist and he saw life with an artist's eye. He wanted his readers to share that poetic vision, to see the romance and numinousness in commonplace things. He brought two things in particular to detective fiction. He was among the first writers to realise that it could be a vehicle for exploring and exposing the condition of society, and for saying something true about human nature. Before he even planned the Father Brown stories, Chesterton wrote that 'the only thrill, even of a common thriller, is concerned somehow with the conscience and the will'. Those words have been part of my credo as a writer. They may not be framed and on my desk but they are never out of my mind.

In *Bloody Murder*, published in 1972, revised in 1985 and again in 1992, a book which has become essential reading for many aficionados of crime fiction, Julian Symons suggests that because of their richness, no more than a few Father Brown short stories should be read at a time. Certainly to settle down for an evening with Father Brown would be like facing a meal composed entirely of very rich *hors d'œuvres*, but I have never suffered from literary indigestion when reading the stories, partly because of Chesterton's imaginative power and his all-embracing humanity. At the end of the short story 'The Invisible Man' we are told that Flambeau and the other participants in the mystery went back to their ordinary lives. 'But Father Brown walked those snow-covered hills under the stars for many hours with a murderer, and what they said to each other will never be known.' We can be sure that, whatever was spoken, it had little or nothing to do with the criminal justice system.

"Your red herring. My Lord."

– 3 –

The Golden Age

*When one looks at the Golden Age in retrospect the developing
rebellion against its ideas and standards is clearly visible, but
this is the wisdom of hindsight, for during the thirties the
classical detective story burgeoned with new and
considerable talents almost every year.*

Julian Symons, *Bloody Murder*

A Victorian critic of the Sherlock Holmes stories, writing in *Blackwood's Magazine* in the late 1800s, while not altogether dismissive of the saga, concluded with the words: 'Considering the difficulty of hitting on any fancies that are decently fresh, surely this sensational business must shortly come to a close.' No prophecy could have been more misjudged. Not only did the sensational business continue, but the new century saw an outburst of creative energy directed towards detective fiction, the emergence of new talented writers and a public which greeted their efforts with an avid enthusiasm which contemporary cartoons suggest amounted to a craze. Although short stories continued to be written, gradually they gave way to the detective novel. One reason for this change was probably because the writers and their increasingly enthusiastic readers preferred a longer narrative which gave opportunities for even more complicated plotting and more fully developed characters. In the words of G.K. Chesterton, 'The long story is more successful, perhaps, in one not unimportant point: that it is possible to realise that a man is alive before he is dead.' Novelists, too, if visited by a powerful idea for an original method of murder, detective or plotline, were unwilling – and indeed still are – to dissipate it on a short story when it could both inspire and form the main interest of a successful novel.

The well-known description 'Golden Age' is commonly taken to cover the two decades between the First and Second World Wars, but this limitation is unduly restrictive. One of the most famous detective stories regarded as falling within the Golden Age is *Trent's Last Case* by E.C. Bentley, published in 1913. The name of this novel is familiar to many readers who have never read it, and its importance is partly due to the respect with which it was regarded by practitioners of the time and its influence on the genre. Dorothy L. Sayers wrote that it 'holds a very special place in the history of detective fiction, a tale of unusual brilliance and charm, startlingly original.' Agatha Christie saw it as 'one of the three best detective stories ever written.' Edgar Wallace described it as 'a masterpiece of detective fiction', and G.K. Chesterton saw it as 'the finest detective story of modern times'. Today some of the tributes of his contemporaries seem excessive but the novel remains highly readable, if hardly as compelling as it was when first published, and its influence on the Golden Age is unquestionable. E.C. Bentley, who wrote the book between 1910 and 1912, was a lifelong friend and fellow-journalist of G.K. Chesterton and probably wrote the novel with Chesterton's encouragement. But what Bentley produced was hardly what his friend would have expected. Seeing himself as a modernist, Bentley disliked the conventional straitjacket of the orthodox detective story and had little respect for Sherlock Holmes. He planned a small act of sabotage, a detective story which was to satirize rather than celebrate the genre. It is ironic that although his hero, Trent, doesn't solve the murder – nor of course did Sergeant Cuff in *The Moonstone* – Bentley is seen as an innovator not a destroyer of the detective story.

The victim in *Trent's Last Case* is an American multimillionaire, an exploiter of the poor and a ruthless financial buccaneer who is found dead in the grounds of his country house with a bullet through the eye. The detective is an amateur sleuth and a painter, Philip Trent, and only at the end of the book do we know why this is his last case. The clues are fairly presented and there is at the end not one surprising disclosure, but two. The novel is unusual in that Trent falls in love with the victim's widow, Mabel Manderson, and unlike many of the novelists of the Golden Age Bentley was as concerned with the portrayal of character, particularly that of Manderson, as he was with providing a coherent and exciting puzzle. The dominance of the love interest was also unusual. Subsequent writers tended to agree with Dorothy L. Sayers that their detectives should concentrate their energy on clues and not on chasing attractive young women. The book is also original in that Trent's solution to the mystery, although based on the clues available, proves erroneous. The fact that the detective hero doesn't solve the crime, though offending against what many see as the prime unwritten rule of detective fiction, certainly makes *Trent's Last Case* innovative.

Writing about the novel in *Bloody Murder*, Julian Symons struggles to understand the regard in which many hold the novel, largely because of the dichotomy between the opening paragraphs, which deal with an ironic savagery with Manderson's murder, and the change of mood in the second part. There is also an uncertainty in Bentley's characterisation of Trent, who at times is almost a figure of fun, and yet whose love affair is treated with great seriousness and so far from being a diversion to the detective element is cleverly integrated with the plot. Nevertheless, instead of being later regarded as an iconoclastic or ironic novel, *Trent's Last Case* was seen as perhaps the most significant and successful immediate precursor of the Golden Age.

The writers of the Golden Age attracted to this fascinating form were as varied as their talents. It must at times have seemed as if everyone who could put together a coherent narrative was compelled to have a go at this challenging and lucrative craft. Many writers who made a reputation for detective fiction already had successful careers in other fields. Nicholas Blake, whose detective is Nigel Strangeways, was the poet Cecil Day-Lewis (1904–1972). Edmund Crispin was the pseudonym of Robert Bruce Montgomery (1921–1978), a musician, composer and critic. Cyril Hare was Judge Alfred Alexander Gordon Clark (1900–1958). Monsignor Ronald Knox (1888–1957) wrote under his own name, as did G.D.H. Cole (1889–1959) and his wife Margaret (1893–1980), who were both economists. These novelists, already successful in other fields, produced books which have a liveliness, humour and distinction of style which places them well above what Julian Symons categorises as 'the humdrums'. They seem, indeed, to have been written as much for the amusement of the author as for the entertainment of his readers. Michael Innes, the pseudonym of John Innes Mackintosh Stewart (1906–1994), was an Oxford don and Professor of English at the University of Adelaide for ten years. His detective, Sir John Appleby of Scotland Yard, is one of the earliest, possibly the first, of that group of academic sleuths who are sometimes referred to as 'dons' delights'. Appleby is, however, very far from an amateur, having begun his career in the police and progressed naturally through the ranks from inspector to the highest rank, Commissioner of the Metropolitan Police, a promotion which I find somewhat hard to believe. Innes produced in Appleby probably the most erudite of all fictional detectives in books which are witty, literate, larded with quotations chosen to be unfamiliar to all but learned academics and with plots which are sometimes more bizarre than credible. One of the most interesting aspects of Appleby is the way in which he ages and matures so that readers who fall under his spell can have the satisfaction of vicariously living his life. From his first case, the murder of Dr Umbleby in 1936, to that of Lord Osprey in 1986, no other detective writer has produced for his hero such a well-documented life, including Appleby's retirement. This is very rare. Although I admire Ian Rankin's temerity in allowing Detective Inspector John Rebus to retire, most of us with a serial hero are content to take refuge in the fashionable illusion that our detectives are immutably fixed in the first age we assigned to them; although in a moment of disillusion they may talk of retiring, they seldom actually do so.

Other prominent academics joined in the game, perhaps intrigued by the challenge set by the rules which were laid down by Ronald Knox in the preface to *Best Detective Stories 1928–29*, which he edited. The criminal must be mentioned in the early part of the narrative but must not be anyone whose thoughts the reader has been allowed to follow. All supernatural agencies are ruled out. There must not be more than one secret room or passage. No hitherto undiscovered poisons should be used or, indeed, any appliance which needs a long scientific explanation. No Chinamen must figure in the story. No accident must help the detective, nor is he allowed an unaccountable intuition. The detective himself must not commit the crime or alight on any clues which are not instantly produced for the reader. The stupid friend of the detective, the Watson, should be slightly, but no more than slightly, less intelligent than the average reader and his thoughts should not be concealed. And, finally, twin brothers and doubles generally must not appear unless the reader has been duly prepared for them.

These rules, if accepted as mandatory, would have reduced the detective story to a quasi-intellectual puzzle in which the reader would be exercising his intelligence, not only against the fictional murderer, but against the writer, whose quirks and cunning ploys aficionados set out to recognise and confute. Rules and restrictions do not produce original, or good, literature, and the rules were not strictly adhered to. The Watson became superfluous relatively soon and, having a tendency, indeed an obligation, to be boring, was rarely missed. But writers obviously felt the need to have a character to whom the detective could communicate, however slightly, the progress of his investigation, as much for the reader's benefit as for his own, and commonly a servant provided this convenient expedient. Dorothy L. Sayers's Lord Peter Wimsey had Bunter and could of course discuss the progress of the case with his brother-in-law, Chief Inspector Parker. Margery Allingham's Albert Campion had his cockney manservant, Magersfontein Lugg, but Lugg seems designed more as comic relief than a sounding board for his master's theories, and Campion, who frequently worked with the police, could rely more rationally on Inspector Stanislaus Oates and Charlie Luke. After the departure of Captain Hastings, Agatha Christie's Poirot made something of a confidant of Chief Inspector Japp, but otherwise both he and Miss Marple preferred to work in isolation, their reticence broken only by their occasional enigmatic hints and comments.

One rule was brilliantly broken by Agatha Christie, arch-breaker of rules, in her long-running play *The Mousetrap*. She perpetrated an even more audacious deception on the reader in *The Murder of Roger Ackroyd*, where the narrator proves to be the murderer, an ingenious if defensible defiance of all the rules, and although she provided perfectly fair clues, some readers have never forgiven her. The prohibition against Chinamen is difficult to understand. Or was it perhaps the general view that Chinamen, if inclined to murder, would be so clever and cunning in their villainy that the famous detective would be unfairly hampered in his investigation? It is possible that Monsignor Knox was obliquely referring to Dr Fu Manchu, that oriental genius of crime created by Sax Rohmer, who for nearly fifty years between 1912 and 1959 pursued his evil purposes while no doubt contributing to racial prejudice and fear of the menacing Yellow Peril.

The first rule is interesting. Certainly a proper regard to structure and balance would suggest that the murderer should make an appearance comparatively early in the story, but a demand that this should be no later than two-thirds of the way through the narrative seems unduly restrictive. Some novelists like to begin either with a murder or with the discovery of the body, an exciting and shocking beginning that not only sets the mood of the novel but involves the reader immediately in drama and action. Although I have used this method with some of my novels, I have more commonly chosen to defer the crime and begin by establishing the setting and by introducing my readers to the victim, the murderer, the suspects, and the life of the community in which the murder will take place. This has the advantage that the setting can be described with more leisure than is practicable once the action is under way, and that many of the facts about the suspects and their possible motives are known and do not have to be revealed at length during the course of the investigation. Deferring the actual murder, apart from the build-up of tension, also ensures that the reader is in possession of more information than is the detective when he arrives at the scene. It is an inviolable rule that the detective should never know more than the reader but there is no injunction against the reader knowing more than the detective – including, of course, when a particular suspect is lying.

With his rule that the reader should not be allowed to follow the murderer's thoughts, Monsignor Knox raises one of the main problems in writing mystery fiction. In an introduction to an anthology of short stories published in 1928, Dorothy L. Sayers confronted this difficulty, which still challenges detective novelists today. Miss Sayers did nothing in her life by halves. Having decided to earn some much-needed money by writing detective fiction, she applied her mind to the history, technique and possibilities of the genre. Being highly intelligent, opinionated and combative, she had no hesitation in giving other people the advantage of her views. Not surprisingly it is Sayers to whom we frequently look for an expert view on the problems and challenges of writing detective fiction in the Golden Age. She wrote:

> It does not – and by hypothesis never can – attain the loftiest level of literary achievement. Though it deals with the most desperate effects of rage, jealousy and revenge, it rarely touches the heights and depths of human passion. It presents us only with a *fait accompli* and looks upon death and mutilation with a dispassionate eye. It does not show us the inner workings of the murderer's mind; it must not, for the identity of the murderer is hidden until the end of the book.

If the detective story is to be more than an ingenious puzzle, the murderer must be more than a conventional cardboard stereotype to be knocked down in the last chapter, and the writer who can solve the problem of enabling the reader at some point to share the murderer's compulsions and inner life, so that he becomes more than a necessary character to serve the plot, will have a chance of writing a novel which is more than a lifeless if entertaining conundrum.

The majority of the Golden Age novels are at present out of print, but the names of the most popular still resonate; their crumbling paperbacks can still be seen on the racks of second-hand bookstores or in private libraries where their owners are reluctant finally to dispose of old friends who have given so much half-remembered pleasure. Those writers who are still read have provided something more than an exciting and original plot: distinction in the writing, a vivid sense of place, a memorable and compelling hero and – most important of all – the ability to draw the reader into their highly individual world.

The omni-talented amateur with apparently nothing to do with his time but solve murders which interest him has had his day, partly because his rich and privileged lifestyle became less admirable, and his deferential acceptance by the police less credible, in an age when men were expected to work. Increasingly the private eye had a profession, or occasionally some connection with the police. Doctors were popular and were usually provided with some idiosyncratic hobby or habit, an interest for which they had plenty of time since we rarely saw them with a patient. Among the most popular was H.C. Bailey's detective Reggie Fortune MA, MB, BSc, FRCS, who first appeared in 1920 in *Call Mr Fortune*. Reggie is a weighty character in both senses of the word, a gourmet, the husband of an exceptionally beautiful wife and a doughty defender of the weak and vulnerable, particularly children. Occasionally his concern as a social reformer in these fields tended to override the detective element. His whimsicality and distinctly odd elliptical style of speaking could be irritating, but the fact that he featured in ninety-five detective stories, the last published in 1946, is a measure of his readers' loyalty.

Perhaps the most eccentric doctor detective of the inter-war years is Dame Beatrice Adela Lestrange Bradley, Gladys Mitchell's psychiatrist who first appeared in 1929 in *Speedy Death*. Thereafter Miss Mitchell published a book a year, sometimes two, until 1984. Dame Beatrice was a true original: elderly, bizarre in dress and appearance, with the eyes of a crocodile. Professionally she was highly regarded, despite the fact that her methods seemed more intuitive than scientific, and although we are told she was consultant to the Home Office it is not clear whether this entailed treating any home secretary whose peculiarities were causing concern, or involving herself with convicted criminals, which seems equally unlikely. In either case she had plenty of time to be driven round the country in style by George, her chauffeur, and to involve herself in such interests as Roman ruins, the occult, ancient Greek mysticism and the Loch Ness Monster. There are frequent allusions to her mysterious past – a distant ancestor was apparently a witch – and she was much given to conclusions which seem to owe more to her esoteric knowledge than to logical deduction. Like Reggie Fortune, she had a maverick attitude to authority. I remember enjoying the best of the novels because of Miss Mitchell's style, although I frequently found the stories confusing and occasionally yearned for the rationality which surely lies at the heart of detective fiction.

Three writers whose books have deservedly lasted beyond the Golden Age and can still be found in print are Edmund Crispin, Cyril Hare and Josephine Tey. Each had a profession apart from writing and each produced one book which has generally proved the favourite among their work. Edmund Crispin, following his time at St John's College, Oxford, where he was part of the generation which included Kingsley Amis, spent two years as an organ scholar and choirmaster. Like many other detective writers, he made excellent use of his personal experience, both of Oxford and of his career as a musician. His hero is Gervase Fen, Professor of English Language and Literature at St Christopher's College, who made his appearance in 1944 with *The Case of the Gilded Fly*. Gervase Fen is a true original, a ruddy-faced man with unruly hair, much given to witticisms and, appropriately enough, quotations from the classics, who romps through his cases with infectious *joie de vivre* in books which are genuinely very funny. We meet his wife, Dolly, a placid comfortable lady who sits peacefully knitting, apparently undisturbed by her husband's propensity for investigating murder, and who takes no part in his adventures, contenting herself by reminding him not to wake the children when he returns home. We learn nothing of the sex of these children and are only surprised that Professor Fen has found the time and energy to father them. He seems to be rarely inconvenienced by academic duties and in one book, *Buried for Pleasure* (1948), he becomes a parliamentary candidate, narrowly escaping what for him would have been the inconvenience of being elected. Crispin's most ingenious book is generally regarded as *The Moving Toyshop* (1946), which begins when the young poet Richard Cadogan, arriving late at night in Oxford, casually opens an unlocked door and finds himself in a toyshop with the dead body of a woman on the floor. Reasonably, he summons the police, but they arrive to find no toyshop and no corpse. Fen joins forces with Cadogan and they clatter through Oxford in Fen's old car, 'Lily Christine', causing maximum damage and disturbance to the populace in their determination to solve the mystery.

Crispin's books are always elegantly written with a cast of engaging, witty characters. Most readers at some point in the story will laugh aloud. Crispin is a farceur, and the ability successfully to combine this less-than-subtle humour with murder is very rare in detective fiction. One modern writer who comes to mind is Simon Brett, whose hero – if the word can be regarded as appropriate – Charles Paris is an unsuccessful and hard-drinking actor separated from his wife. Like Edmund Crispin, Simon Brett makes use of his own experience – in his case as a playwright for radio and television – and, like Crispin, he can combine humour with a credible mystery solved by an original and believable private eye.

Cyril Hare was a barrister who became a county court judge; he took his writing name from his London home, Cyril Mansions in Battersea, and his chambers in Hare Court. Like Edmund Crispin, he made effective use of his professional experience and expertise, creating in his hero, Francis Pettigrew, a humane, intelligent but not particularly successful barrister who, unlike Professor Fen, is a reluctant rather than avid amateur detective. Like Crispin he has a felicitous style and his humour, although less laughter-provoking, has wit and subtlety. His best-known book – and, I would argue, by far the most successful – is *Tragedy at Law*, published in 1942. This novel, which is happily in print, is also something of a period piece since we the readers move with the Honourable Sir William Hereward Barber, a judge of the High Court of Justice, as he travels round the towns of the South West Circuit. This perambulation in great state of an assize judge has now been abolished with the creation of the Crown Court; as the book is set in the early days of the Second World War, we have the interest both of fairly recent history and of a now dead tradition. The plot is well worked out, credible and, as with the majority of his books, rests on the provisions of the law. Like Crispin's, the writing is lively, the dialogue convincing, the characters interesting and the plot involving. The book opens with a loud complaint by the judge that, because of the economies of war, his appearance is not being celebrated as it should be with a flourish of trumpets. The man, the time and the place are immediately set in an opening paragraph which is as arresting as if the trumpets had indeed sounded.

Jospehine Tey, the pseudonym of the Scottish writer Elizabeth Mackintosh (1896–1952), was better known in her lifetime for her play *Richard of Bordeaux* than she was for her detective fiction. Her detective is Inspector Alan Grant, who is very much in the gentlemanly mould, notable for his intuition, intelligence and Scottish tenacity. He first appeared in *The Man in the Queue* (1929) and was still on the job when, in 1952, Tey published her eighth and last crime novel, *The Singing Sands*. But with the two novels which many readers regard as among her best, *Brat Farrar* (1949) and *The Franchise Affair* (1948), she moved further from the conventional plot of the detective story and with such success that she might not now be regarded as a detective novelist had she not created Inspector Grant. Novelists who prefer not to be so designated should beware of introducing a serial detective.

Brat Farrar is a mystery of identity set on the estate and the riding stables of Latchetts on the south coast. If Patrick Ashby, heir to the property, has really committed suicide, who is the mysterious young man calling himself Brat Farrar who returns to claim the family inheritance, who not only looks like Patrick but is familiar with details of the family history? We, the readers, know that he is an impostor, although we quickly come to sympathise with him. This, then, is a mystery of identification, common in English fiction, and the fact that *Brat Farrar* is also a murder mystery only becomes apparent late in the novel. In what is probably Tey's best-known book, *The Franchise Affair*, two eccentric newcomers to the village, an elderly widow and her spinster daughter, are accused by a young woman of imprisoning her in their isolated house, The Franchise, and making her work as their slave, a plot based on the real-life Elizabeth Canning case of 1753–4. The story conforms more closely to the conventional mystery, although there is no murder. A local solicitor, who is consulted by the women, is convinced of their innocence and sets out to prove it. The mystery is, of course, centred on the girl. If her story is false from start to finish, how did she obtain the facts which enabled her to lie so convincingly? An uncomplicated structure and the first-person narrative – the tale is told by the solicitor – engage the reader both with the characters, who are exceptionally well-drawn, and with the social and class prejudices of the small-town community – prejudices which the author to some extent undoubtedly shared.

Josephine Tey has not only retained her hold on readers of detective fiction, but is now being resurrected in the novels of Nicola Upson, who sets her mysteries in the years between the wars and peoples them with real-life characters of the time, Josephine Tey being her serial protagonist. Famous detectives have from time to time been resurrected on film or in print – Jill Paton Walsh is continuing the Wimsey saga – but Nicola Upson is the first writer to choose a previous real-life crime novelist as an ongoing character.

The great majority of detectives in the Golden Age were men – and, indeed, if they were professional police officers, had to be male, since women at that time had a very limited role in policing. In general women characters who dabbled in detection were either sidekicks or cheerful crusaders-in-arms to the dominant male hero, serving either as a Watson or a love interest, or both. One obvious exception is Agatha Christie's Miss Marple, who is not only unique in working entirely alone without the help of a Watson, but in being invariably cleverer than the police detectives she encounters, and whose sex life, if any, is mercifully shrouded in mystery. But as time progressed it was thought necessary that even the women who played a subsidiary part in the triumphs of the male hero should have some kind of job in their own right rather than sit at home ministering to the needs of their spouse. In the Campion novels by Margery Allingham, Lady Amanda Fitton, who finally marries Albert Campion and who, if the author's hints are to be believed, presumably becomes at least a viscountess, is blessed not only with a title of her own, but with a job as an aircraft designer – although we never hear her discussing her job, nor is she ever seen at her drawing board. Lord Peter Wimsey's Harriet Vane is a successful novelist, as was the author, but in the four murder investigations in which she features it is Wimsey who plays the dominant part. In *Strong Poison* he saves her from execution, and in *Have His Carcase*, the novel in which Harriet discovers the bloodless body on Flat Iron Rock, he arrives, partly because he can't resist the challenge of a corpse, but principally to save Harriet from the embarrassment of being regarded as a suspect. In *Gaudy Night* Harriet actually calls him in to investigate a mystery which she should have been able to solve herself if her mind hadn't been preoccupied with the difficulty for a woman of reconciling the emotional and intellectual life, and in particular her own relationship with Lord Peter. Georgia Cavendish, the wife of Nicholas Blake's hero Nigel Strangeways, is a celebrated traveller and explorer with a flamboyant taste in fashion and a highly original and strong personality. It is interesting that neither Harriet Vane nor Georgia Cavendish is described as beautiful although both, particular Georgia, are sexually attractive, and so of course is Lady Amanda.

Although women detectives play little part in the novels of the Golden Age, somewhat surprisingly they appeared very early in the history of crime writing. To discuss their exploits and examine their significance to the genre requires a whole book – which has, indeed, been written by Patricia Craig and Mary Cadogan in their fascinating *The Lady Investigates* (1981). I am particularly sorry not to have encountered Lady Molly of Scotland Yard, the creation of Baroness Orczy, more famous for the

Scarlet Pimpernel stories. The majority of Baroness Orczy's detective stories were written before the full flowering of the Golden Age, but in 1925 she published *Unravelled Knots*, which foreshadowed later English armchair detectives who, physically disabled and unable to sally forth, solved crimes by a mixture of intuition and clues brought to them by a peripatetic colleague, of which Josephine Tey's *The Daughter of Time* is probably the best-known English example. Lady Molly appeared in 1910 and one can only agree with the 'high-born Frenchwoman' who describes her as 'a true-hearted English woman, the finest product on God's earth, after all's said and done'. Baroness Orczy was probably aware that none of her readers in 1910 would think that consorting with the police in a criminal investigation was a proper job for a lady, even for a true-hearted English woman, but Lady Molly, like others of her time, is sacrificing herself to vindicate her husband who is languishing in Dartmoor prison, wrongly convicted of murder. Needless to say, Scotland Yard officers are at Lady Molly's feet and adulation is inspired in everyone she encounters. The story is told by her sidekick, Mary Granard, who used to be her maid and who idolises her dear lady's beauty, charm, brains and style, and the marvellous intuition which, in Mary's opinion, made her the most wonderful psychologist of her time. The relationship between them is one of sickening sentimentality. Mary, who obviously serves the function of a Watson, complained while on a case that there was something she didn't understand. '"No, and you won't until we get there," Lady Molly replied, running up to me and kissing me in her pretty engaging way.' I suspect that

Lady Molly's husband was in no hurry to be liberated from Dartmoor prison.

Not surprisingly, given the talents of many of the writers, the Golden Age detective stories were competently and sometimes very well written, and some of the best will endure. Nevertheless, subtlety of characterisation, a setting which came alive for the reader and credibility of motive were often subjugated, particularly in the humdrums, to the demand to provide an intriguing and mysterious plot. Writers vied with each other in their search for an original method of murder and for clues of increasing ingenuity and complexity. Webster has written that death has ten thousand doors to let out life, and it seems that most of them have at one time or another been used. Unfortunate victims were dispatched by licking poisoned stamps, being battered to death by church bells, stunned by a falling pot, stabbed with an icicle, poisoned by cat claws and not infrequently found dead in locked and barred rooms with looks of appalling terror on their faces. This world was summed up by William Trevor, the Anglo-Irish novelist and short story writer, when he spoke of reading detective stories as a child in his acceptance speech on winning a literary award in 1999.

> All over England, it seemed to me, bodies were being discovered by housemaids in libraries. Village poison pens were tirelessly at work. There was murder in Mayfair, on trains, in airships, in Palm Court lounges, between the acts. Golfers stumbled over corpses on fairways. Chief Constables awoke to them in their

gardens.

We had nothing like it in West Cork.

Nor in West Kensington either.

These novels are, of course, paradoxical. They deal with violent death and violent emotions, but they are novels of escape. We are required to feel no real pity for the victim, no empathy for the murderer, no sympathy for the falsely accused. For whomever the bell tolls, it doesn't toll for us. Whatever our secret terrors, we are not the body on the library floor. And in the end, by the grace of Poirot's little grey cells, all will be well – except of course with the murderer, but he deserves all that's coming to him. All the mysteries will be explained, all the problems solved and peace and order will return to that mythical village which, despite its above-average homicide rate, never really loses its tranquillity or its innocence. Rereading the Golden Age novels with their confident morality, their lack of any empathy with the murderer and the popularity of their rural settings, readers can still enter nostalgically this settled and comfortable world. 'Stands the church clock at ten to three?' And is there arsenic still for tea?

It was a tough case. Plenty of
witnesses, but no one was talking.

– 4 –

Soft-centred and Hard-boiled

It was about eleven o'clock in the morning, mid-October,
with the sun not shining and a look of hard wet rain in the
clearness of the foothills.... I was neat, clean, shaved
and sober, and I didn't care who knew it.
I was everything the well-dressed private detective ought to be.
I was calling on four million dollars.

Raymond Chandler, *The Big Sleep*

While the well-born and impeccably correct detectives of the Golden Age were courteously interviewing their suspects in the drawing rooms of country houses, the studies of rural clergymen and the rooms of Oxford academics, across the Atlantic crime writers were finding their material and inspiration in a very different society and writing about it in prose that was colloquial, vivid and memorable. Although this book is primarily about British detective novelists, the commonly described hard-boiled school of American fiction, rooted in a different continent and in a different literary tradition, has made such an important contribution to crime writing that to ignore its achievements would be seriously misleading. The two most famous innovators, Dashiell Hammett and Raymond Chandler, have had a lasting influence beyond the crime genre, both in their own country and abroad.

No writer, whatever form his fiction takes, can distance himself entirely from the country, civilization and century of which he is a part. A reader coming from Dashiell Hammett or Raymond Chandler to Agatha Christie or Dorothy L. Sayers could reasonably feel that these writers were living not only on different continents but in different centuries. So what England were these predominantly middle-class, well-educated novelists and their devoted readers portraying, what traditions, beliefs and prejudices were the purveyors of popular literature consciously or unconsciously reflecting?

As I was born in 1920 it was an England I knew, a cohesive world, overwhelmingly white and united by a common belief in a religious and moral code based on the Judeo-Christian inheritance – even if this belief was not invariably reflected in practice – and buttressed by social and political institutions which, although they might be criticised, attracted general allegiance, and were accepted as necessary to the well-being of the state: the monarchy, the Empire, the Church, the criminal justice system, the City, the ancient universities. It was an ordered society in which virtue was regarded as normal, crime an aberration, and in which there was small sympathy for the criminal; it was generally accepted that murderers, when convicted, would hang – although Agatha Christie, arch-purveyor of cosy reassurance, is careful not to emphasise this disagreeable fact or allow the dark shadow of the public hangman to fall upon her essentially comfortable pages. The death penalty is mentioned by Margery Allingham, and Dorothy L. Sayers in *Busman's Honeymoon* actually has the temerity to confront Lord Peter Wimsey with the logical end to his detective activities, when he crouches weeping in his wife's arms on the morning when Frank Crutchley hangs. Some readers may feel that, if he couldn't face the inevitable outcome of his detective hobby, he should have confined himself to collecting first editions.

Despite the turbulent antagonisms of post-war Europe and the growth of fascism, the 1930s were years of remarkable freedom from domestic crime and although there must have been areas, particularly of the inner cities, which were at least as violent as they are today, pictures of this disruption were not being brought daily into people's sitting-rooms by television and the Internet. It was therefore possible to live in a country town or in a village and feel almost entirely secure. We can read an Agatha Christie novel set in what seems a mythical village, in which the inhabitants are happily reconciled to their allotted rank and station, and we feel that this is an exaggerated, romanticised or idealised world. It isn't, not altogether. Dorothy L. Sayers describes it in *Busman's Honeymoon*. Harriet is speaking of her husband, Lord Peter:

> She understood now why it was that, with all his masking attitudes ... he yet carried about with him that permanent atmosphere of security. He belonged to an ordered society and this was it. More than any of the friends in her own world he spoke the familiar language of her childhood. In London anybody at any moment might do or become anything, but in a village, no matter what village, they were all immutably themselves, parson, organist, sweep, duke's son and doctor's daughter, moving like chessmen upon their allotted squares.

71

It is precisely this view of England that in general the 1930s' detective writers, particularly women, were portraying: middle-class, hierarchical, rural, peaceable. But it was an age of underlying anxiety. Before the institution of the welfare state, the dread of unemployment, of sickness, of economic failure was very real and the growing power of the fascist dictators abroad threatened the possibility of a further war before the country had recovered from the appalling carnage, social upheaval and personal tragedies of the 1914–18 conflict. Already the posturing of home-grown fascism was provoking violent clashes, particularly in London's East End. It was small wonder that people longed for that 'permanent atmosphere of security' and were able to find it, at least temporarily, in a popular form which was both ordered and reassuring.

The differences between the hard-boiled school and such Golden Age writers as Agatha Christie, Dorothy L. Sayers and Michael Innes, are so profound that it seems stretching a definition to describe both groups under the same category. If the British detective story is concerned with bringing order out of disorder, a genre of reconciliation and social healing, restoring the mythical village of Mayhem Parva to prelapsarian tranquillity, in the United States Hammett and Chandler were depicting and exploring the great social upheavals of the 1920s – lawlessness, prohibition, corruption, the power and violence of notorious gangsters who were close to becoming folk heroes, the cycle of boom and depression – and creating detectives who were inured to this world and could confront it on their own terms.

Dashiell Hammett (1894–1961) had a tough and underprivileged youth working on the railway, then as a Pinkerton detective, and as a soldier in the First World War. He was discharged as tubercular, married his hospital nurse and had two children, supporting his family by writing short stories for the pulp magazines that were extremely popular during the 1920s. The editors demanded violent action, vividly portrayed characters and a prose style ruthlessly pruned of all inessentials; all this Hammett provided.

Hammett's stories are not about restoring the moral order, nor are they set in a world in which the problem of evil can be solved by Poirot's little grey cells or Miss Marple's cosy homilies, a world as innocuous as flower-arranging. Hammett knew from traumatic personal experience how precarious is the moral tightrope which the private investigator daily walks in his battle with the criminal. The first of his detectives has worked for fifteen years as an operative for the Continental Detective Agency and is known only as 'Continental Op'. It is appropriate that the Op is unnamed. There is nothing subtle about him and little we expect to know – except his age, thirty-five, that he is short and fat, and that his only loyalty is to the Continental Detective Agency and his job. But there is an honesty and directness about this personal code, limited as it may be.

'I like being a detective, like the work. And liking work makes you want to do it as well as you can. Otherwise there'd be no sense to it.'

The Op tells his own story, but flatly, without explanations, excuses or embellishments. He is as ruthless as the world in which he operates, a violent gun-carrying dispenser of the only justice he recognises. Short and fat he may be, but in *Red Harvest* (1929) he takes on the combined strength of the police, corrupt politicians and gangsters to cleanse the city of Personville, meeting violence with violence. His loyalty to the job means that he doesn't take bribes; indeed he seems impervious to the lure of money – in this, at least, he is superior to the company he keeps. He is naturally solitary, and how could he be otherwise with such a job in a corrupt and lawless world? When a woman attempts to seduce him, his response is a brutal rejection; later, to get rid of her, he shoots her in the leg, but not without a certain compunction: 'I had never shot a woman before. I felt queer about it.' There is not much that the Op feels queer about.

Hammett's most famous detective, Sam Spade, whose hunting-ground is San Francisco, appears only in one full-length novel, *The Maltese Falcon* (1930), but this book, his best known, and the film in which Humphrey Bogart portrayed the detective, have ensured that Spade has become the archetypical hard-boiled private eye. Like the Op, Spade's only loyalty is to his work and to his colleagues. He is classless, younger and more physically attractive than the Op, but there is a cruelty in his ruthlessness and he is the more immoral of the two, capable of falling in love with a woman but never putting love above the demands of the job.

After the success of *The Maltese Falcon*, Hammett was offered a job as a screenwriter in Hollywood. There he met the playwright Lillian Hellman and began a love affair which lasted until his death. After this move to the highly lucrative and hedonistic world of Hollywood, he began drinking heavily and lived in a way which a friend described as making sense 'only if he had no expectations of being alive much beyond Thursday'. During the Hollywood years he became involved with left-wing political causes and in 1951 was sentenced to six months in prison because he would not give evidence against Communists who had jumped bail. After his release his books were proscribed and during his final ten years he lived on the charity of others. He would not be the only writer whose talent was destroyed by money, self-indulgence and the egregious temptations of fame, but perhaps for him the temptations were the more irresistible because of the penury and struggles of those early years.

Might Hammett have written another novel as good as *The Maltese Falcon* if he had resisted that invitation to move to Hollywood? I think it doubtful. It may be that by then he had said all he wanted to and that his talent was exhausted. Nevertheless, his achievement remains remarkable. In a writing career of little more than a decade he raised a commonly despised genre into writing which had a valid claim to be taken seriously as literature. He showed crime writers that what is important goes beyond an ingenious plot, mystery and suspense. More important are the novelist's individual voice, the reality of the world he creates and the strength and originality of the writing.

The early life of Raymond Chandler, born in 1888, was markedly different from that of Hammett. He was educated in England at Dulwich College and returned to the United States in 1912, where he had a successful business career before retiring in 1933 to devote himself to writing. Like Hammett, he learned his craft by contributing to the pulp magazines but wrote later that he rejected the editor's insistence in cutting out all descriptions on the grounds that the readers disliked anything that held up the action.

I set out to prove them wrong. My theory was that the readers just *thought* they cared about nothing but the action; that really, although they didn't know it, the thing they cared about, and that I cared about, was the creation of emotion through dialogue and description.

And that was what, superbly, Chandler provided. In this he reminds me of a very different writer but one who was also brilliant at writing dialogue, Evelyn Waugh. When asked why he never described what his characters were thinking, Waugh replied that he didn't know what they were thinking, he only knew what they said and did. The hard-boiled detectives are not introspective; it is through action and dialogue that their story is told.

Chandler's hero, Philip Marlowe, accepts that he is earning a precarious and dangerous living in a world which is lawless, tawdry and corrupt but, unlike Spade, he has a social conscience, personal integrity and a moral code beyond unquestioning loyalty to his job and colleagues. He is discriminating about the kind of work he will accept, never takes tainted money or betrays a friend, and is totally loyal even to undeserving clients. More personally vulnerable than Spade, he is a more reluctant private eye, troubled and repelled by the corrupt and heartless world in which he earns his living and uncomfortably sensitive to the suffering of its victims. In the words of a character in *The Long Goodbye*,

'There ain't no clean way to make a hundred million bucks .... somewhere along the line guys got pushed to the wall, nice little businesses got the ground cut out from under them .... decent people lost their jobs .... Big money is big power and big power gets used wrong. It's the system.'

Marlowe tells his story in the first person in prose that is terse but richly descriptive and larded with wisecracks.

I wasn't wearing a gun .... I doubted if it would do me any good. The big man would probably take it away from me and eat it.

The story may at times be incoherent but the writing never disappoints in what Chandler cared most about, the creation of emotion through dialogue and description.

Both Sam Spade and Philip Marlowe are licensed investigators and, unlike the British amateur detectives, have to some extent a recognised function and authority. But their attitude to the police is ambivalent, ranging from a wary and reluctant co-operation to open enmity. The police are seen by both as brutal and corrupt. Captain Gregorius of *The Long Goodbye* 'solves crimes with the bright light, the soft sap, the kick to the kidneys, the knee to the groin, the fist to the solar plexus, the night stick to the base of the spine'. Even after a beating from Gregorius, Marlowe, unyielding to his brutality, has the courage to hurl his contempt in Gregorius's face. 'I wouldn't betray an enemy into your hands. You're not only a gorilla, you're an incompetent.' How different from the honest and paternal Superintendent Kirk in Dorothy L. Sayers's *Busman's Honeymoon*, unable to speak grammatical English when discussing the case of the body in the cellar with Peter Wimsey, but always ready to compete with Lord Peter in dredging up an appropriate quotation to demonstrate his literary credentials.

In a famous passage from his critical essay *The Simple Art of Murder*, Chandler describes his detective in words which were more appropriate to a work of high romance:

> In everything that can be called art there is a quality of redemption.... But down these mean streets a man must go who is not himself mean, who is neither tarnished nor afraid. The detective in this kind of story must be such a man. He is the hero, he is everything.... He must be the best man in his world and a good enough man for any world.

This is surely too romantic and unrealistic a view to be credible. The vision of Continental Op, Sam Spade, or even the compassionate Marlowe, riding forth like a knight errant to redress the evils of the world of which he is a part, does violence both to the ethos of the hard-boiled school and to the character, and surely makes Marlowe as much a figure of fantasy as Lord Peter Wimsey.

Very different, too, is the hard-boiled detectives' response to women. The Op and Spade generally preserve their emotions as inviolate as the secrets they uncover and only Marlowe is susceptible to love. Here are no brave and cheerful comrades-in-arms, no devoted non-interfering wives at home with their knitting, no successful professional women with interesting lives of their own, no carefully crafted figures of wish-fulfilment. The women in the hard-boiler are sexually alluring temptresses seen by the hero as inimical both to their masculine code and to the success of the job. They may not all get shot in the leg, but if guilty they are likely to be handed over to the police without compunction.

We have, of course, always had the most notable detective stories of America and Canada available in this country, including the hard-boiled school. I came to the American hard-boiled school in the 1960s through the work of Ross Macdonald, the pseudonym of Kenneth Millar (1915–1983), and he remains my favourite of the triumvirate of the best-known hard-boiled writers. His childhood was a tragic odyssey of poverty and rejection. His mother, deserted by her husband when Macdonald was three, dragged him round Canada depending on the charity of relatives and Macdonald narrowly escaped the appalling fate of being consigned to an orphanage. Such pain in childhood is never forgotten and seldom forgiven, and all his writing life Macdonald's fiction was influenced by the inescapable heritage of the past. His detective, Lew Archer, is in the tradition of Philip Marlowe and, like Marlowe, he casts a critical eye on society, concerned particularly with the searing damage to the human spirit caused by the ruthlessness, greed and corruption of big business. Although Macdonald's complicated plots are not without violence, he is more a detached observer than a participator, somewhat resembling a secular Father Brown in his empathy for human suffering. Less romantic than Chandler, his style has the vigour and imaginative richness of a man confident of his mastery of epithets and, particularly in his later novels, he attains a standard which places him first among those novelists who raised the genre from its roots in pulp fiction to serious literature. In an influential review in 1969 the writer Eudora Welty described his work as 'the finest series of detective novels ever written by an American', a verdict with which I feel few critics would disagree.

For me the most remarkable of the moderns is Sara Paretsky. When she created her private eye, V.I. Warshawski, it was in conscious emulation of the myth of the solitary private eye and his lone campaign against the corruption of the powerful, but her Polish-American heroine has a humility, a humanity and a need for human relationships which the male hard-boilers lack. Her territory is Chicago, not the Chicago of the dramatic city centre or the prosperous suburbs, but the city's southeast side, the neighbourhood of the poor who live in shanties on the contaminated marshland known as Dead Stick Pond. Paretsky creates a powerful vision of the Chicago where V.I. Warshawski grew up and where she operates as a courageous, sexually liberated female investigator. Through her heroine and in her private life of speaking and journalism, Paretsky conducts her campaign against injustice and, in particular, the right of women to control their lives and their sexuality. No other female crime writer has so powerfully and effectively combined a well-crafted detective story with the novel of social realism and protest. And here, too, we see the influence of Raymond Chandler.

Chandler despised the English school of crime writing, stating that, 'the English may not always be the best writers in the world, but they are incomparably the best dull writers', his most vituperative criticism being directed at Dorothy L. Sayers. In 1930, the year in which Hammett published *The Maltese Falcon*, the Golden Age in England was at the height of its popularity. Agatha Christie brought out *The Murder at the Vicarage*, Dorothy L. Sayers *Strong Poison*, Margery Allingham *Mystery Mile* and, four years later, Ngaio Marsh was to make her debut with *A Man Lay Dead*. These four highly successful women are among the relatively few whose books are still in print and read today, a longevity undoubtedly sustained, in the case of Christie and Sayers, by television. All four consolidated and affirmed the structure and conventions of the classical detective story, inventing detectives who have entered into the mythology of the genre. Three of the women aspired to, and achieved, a standard of writing and characterisation which helped to raise the reputation of the detective story from a harmless but predictable literary diversion into a popular form that could be taken as seriously as a well-written mainstream novel.

For me they have an additional interest. To read the detective novels of these four women is to learn more about the England in which they lived and worked than most popular social histories can provide, and in particular about the status of women in the years between the wars. For this reason, if no other, they should have a chapter to themselves.

" Check with our legal people if we can publish a detective story in which the murderer turns out to be the author. "

– 5 –

Four Formidable Women

Agatha's best work is, like P.G. Wodehouse and Noel Coward's best work, the most characteristic pleasure-writing of this epoch and will appear one day in all decent literary histories. As writing it is not distinguished, but as story it is superb.

Robert Graves, letter, 15 July 1944

Reams of paper have been expended on attempts to explore the secret of Agatha Christie's success. Writers who explore the phenomenon not uncommonly begin with the arithmetic of her achievements: outsold only by the Bible and Shakespeare, translated into over one hundred foreign languages, author of the longest running play ever seen on the London stage and, in addition, recipient of awards that success usually affords only to the highest literary talent – a Dame of the British Empire and an honorary degree of Doctor of Literature from Oxford University. The perennial question remains, how did this gently reared, essentially Edwardian lady do it?

Certainly Christie's universal appeal doesn't lie in blood or violence. Not for her the bullet-ridden corpses down Raymond Chandler's mean city streets, the urban jungle of the wisecracking, fast-shooting, sardonic private eye or the careful psychological examination of human depravity.

Although both her best-known detectives, Poirot and Miss Marple, occasionally investigated murder overseas, her natural world as perceived by her readers is a romanticised cosy English village rooted in nostalgia, with its ordered hierarchy: the wealthy squire (often with a new young wife of mysterious antecedence), the retired irascible colonel, the village doctor and the district nurse, the chemist (useful for the purchase of poison), the gossiping spinsters behind their lace curtains, the parson in his vicarage, all moving predictably in their social hierarchy like pieces on a chessboard. Her style is neither original nor elegant but it is workmanlike. It does what is required of it. She employs no great psychological subtlety in her characterisation; her villains and suspects are drawn in broad and clear outlines and, perhaps because of this, they have a universality which readers worldwide can instantly recognise and feel at home with. Above all she is a literary conjuror who places her pasteboard characters face downwards and shuffles them with practised cunning. Game after game we are confident that this time we will turn up the card with the face of the true murderer, and time after time she defeats us. And with a Christie mystery no suspect can safely be eliminated, even the narrator of the story. With other mystery writers of the Golden Age we can be reasonably confident that the murderer won't be one of the attractive young lovers, a policeman, a servant or a child, but Agatha Christie has no favourites either with murderer or victim. Most mystery writers jib, as do I, at killing the very young, but Agatha Christie is tough, as ready to murder a child, admittedly a precocious unappealing one, as she is to despatch a

84

blackmailer. With Mrs Christie, as with real life, the only certainty is death.

Perhaps her greatest strength was that she never over-stepped the limits of her talent. She knew precisely what she could do and she did it well. For over fifty years this shy and conventional woman produced murder mysteries of extraordinarily imaginative duplicity. With her immense output the quality is inevitably uneven – some of the later books in particular show a sad falling-off – but at her best the ingenuity is dazzling. Her prime skill as a storyteller is the talent to deceive, and it is possible to identify some of the tricks, often verbal, by which she gently seduces us into self-deception. In time we almost match the cunning of the author. We beware of entering that most lethal of rooms, the country house library, we become suspicious of the engaging n'er-do-well returning from foreign parts and take careful note of mirrors, twins and androgynous names. She is particularly fond of a version of the eternal triangle in which a couple, apparently happily engaged or married, are menaced by a third person, sometimes predatory and rich. When the victim is murdered there is little mystery about the chief suspect. Only at the end of the book does Miss Christie turn the triangle round and we recognise that it was that way up all the time. And her clues are brilliantly designed to confuse. The butler goes over to peer closely at a calendar. She has planted in our mind the suspicion that a crucial clue relates to dates and times, but the clue is, in fact, that the butler is short-sighted.

Both the trickery and the final solution are invariably more ingenious than believable. The books are mild intel-lectual puzzles, not credible blueprints for real murder. In

Death on the Nile, for example, the murderer is required to dash round the deck of a crowded river-steamer, acting with split-second precision and depending on not being observed either by passengers or by crew. In another book we are told that the murderer unscrews the digits of a number on the door of a hostel room, so luring the victim to the wrong room. In real life we never go unerringly to the room we want; we identify it by the floor and by the numbers on adjoining doors. In *Dumb Witness* the clue is that a brooch made of initials is glimpsed in a mirror at night. But the brooch is worn by a woman in a dressing-gown – the last garment on which a heavy brooch would normally be pinned. But to the Christie aficionado this is mere quibbling. And indeed it does seem ungracious to point out inconsistencies or incredulities in books which are primarily intended to entertain – a far from ignoble aim – and in which the reader is in general treated fairly and falls more often than not into a pit of his own devising.

The moral basis of the books is unambiguous and simple, epitomised by Poirot's declaration: 'I have a bourgeois attitude to murder: I disapprove of it.' But even the horror of murder is sanitised; the necessary violence is perfunctorily described, there is no grief, no loss, an absence of outrage. We feel that at the end of the book the victim will get up, wipe off the artificial blood and be restored to life. The last thing we get from a Christie novel is the disturbing presence of evil. Admittedly Poirot and Miss Marple occasionally used the word, but with no more relevance than if they were referring to the smell of bad drains. One of the secrets of her universal and enduring appeal is that it excludes all disturbing emotions; those are for the real world from which we are escaping, not for St Mary Mead. All the problems and uncertainties of life are subsumed in the one central problem: the identity of the killer. And we know that, by the end of the book, this will be satisfactorily solved and peace and order restored to that mythical village whose inhabitants, apparently so harmless and familiar, prove so enigmatic, so surprising in their ingenious villainy.

Agatha Christie hasn't in my view had a profound influence on the later development of the detective story. She wasn't an innovative writer and had no interest in exploring the possibilities of the genre. What she consistently provided is a strong and exciting narrative, the challenge of a puzzle, an accommodating and accessible style and original detectives in Poirot and Miss Marple, whom readers can encounter in book after book with the comfortable assurance that they are meeting old friends. Her main influence on contemporary crime writers was to affirm the popularity and importance of ingenuity in clue plotting and of surprise in the final solution, thus helping significantly to set the limited range and the conventions of what were to become the books of the Golden Age. Dorothy L. Sayers could have been thinking of Agatha Christie when she wrote:

> Just at present ... the fashion in detective fiction is to have characters credible and lively; not conventional but, on the other hand, not too profoundly studied – people who live more or less on the *Punch* level of emotion.

It seems a little unjust to classify Agatha Christie's characters as being on the *Punch* level. She is more than that. She may draw them in clear outline with none of the ambiguities of shading, but she gives us enough to enable us to feel that we know them. But do we? Are they, like the material clues, intended to deceive?

Rereading a selection of her stories to affirm or modify my existing prejudices I found some had lost even their ability to keep me reading. Others surprised me by being both better written and more ingeniously puzzling than I had remembered, among them one published in 1950, *A Murder is Announced*. For me, this story demonstrates both her strength and her weakness. Here we have the usual village setting, Chipping Cleghorn, and a cast of characters typical of Christieland, but the setting is described with more realism than in the later books, and a keener eye to the economic changes and social nuances brought about by the difficult post-war years. As usual with Christie the dialogue is particularly effective, but here it is used not merely to reveal character but to contain vital clues, one of which even the most careful reader would probably miss. The people are drawn with economy but with more subtlety than usual, and both the motive for the murders and the solution to the mystery derive directly from the characters, their unchangeable past and living present. This ability to fuse character with clues is one of the marks of a good detective story. Admittedly the end of the novel is disappointing, with over-complicated and contrived relationships and a surfeit of incredible killings. And she was over-fond of the unconvincing contrivance whereby one of the characters acts as a decoy and is on the point of being killed when the police and Miss Marple dash in to arrest the murderer. But in Chipping Cleghorn or St Mary Mead murder is only a temporary embarrassment. The vicar may find a body on his study floor but it is unlikely to interfere with the preparation of the Sunday sermon. We enter this peaceable and nostalgic world with the confident expectation of taking comfort from Miss Marple's common sense and her enigmatic comments on the crime as we move together to a satisfactory solution in the final chapter, when truth and justice will once more prevail.

And while highly regarded and prizewinning novels of the post-war era are often no longer obtainable, Agatha Christie's books are still ranged on the shelves of bookshops and libraries. Poirot and Miss Marple still appear regularly on our television screens and it is a safe bet that, whenever detection fiction is discussed, the name of Agatha Christie will be mentioned either in praise or in disparagement. Her critics sometimes exhibit vehemence close to personal outrage, seeing her books as trivial, intellectually feeble and written without distinction of style or subtlety of characterisation. But one thing is certain: Agatha Christie has provided entertainment, suspense and temporary relief from the anxieties and traumas of life both in peace and war for millions throughout the world and this is an achievement which merits our gratitude and respect. I suspect that a traveller, stranded in an airport hotel overnight and finding in the bedside cabinet two novels, the latest winner of a prestigious literary prize and an Agatha Christie, would reach for the latter to assuage the half-acknowledged fear of contemporary travel and the discomfort and boredom of a long night.

Of the four women writers I have chosen to illustrate detective stories as social history, Dorothy L. Sayers, who was born in 1893 and died in 1957, was the most versatile: novelist, poet, playwright, amateur theologian, Christian apologist, translator of Dante. It is a safe assumption that any aficionado of the classical detective story, asked to name the six best writers in the genre, would include her name. Yet paradoxically there is no other writer of the Golden Age who provokes such strong and often opposing responses. To her admirers she is the writer who did more than any other to make the detective story intellectually respectable, and to change it from an ingenious but lifeless sub-literary puzzle into a specialised branch of fiction with serious claims to be judged as a novel. To her detractors she is outrageously snobbish, intellectually arrogant, pretentious and occasionally dull. But there can be no doubt of her influence both on succeeding writers and on the genre itself. And she brought to the detective story writing that was always good and scholarly and occasionally – as in the description of the storm in *The Nine Tailors* – outstanding. Sayers wrote with intelligence, wit, humour, and she created in Lord Peter Wimsey a genuine folk hero whose vitality has ensured his survival. Readers who dislike her novels tend to concentrate their criticism on Lord Peter, finding him snobbish, unconvincing and irritating. But it is apparent that Sayers, who took an ironic and detached view of her creation, had her reading public very much in mind. Writing later to her American publishers, she told them that she would give him 'an attractive mother to whom he was much attached, and an immaculate "gentleman's gentleman" – Bunter by name'. Going on, she wrote:

Lord Peter's large income (the source of which, by the way, I have never investigated) was a different matter. I deliberately gave him that. After all, it cost me nothing, and at that time I was particularly hard up and it gave me pleasure to spend his fortune for him. When I was dissatisfied with my single unfurnished room, I took a luxurious flat for him in Piccadilly. When my cheap rug got a hole in it, I ordered an Aubusson carpet. When I had no money to pay my bus fare, I presented him with a Daimler double-six, upholstered in a style of sober magnificence, and when I felt dull I let him drive it.

It was a vicarious satisfaction in the privileges and pleasures of wealth which she could be confident her readers would share.

There is one way in which Dorothy L. Sayers was very much a writer of her own time, and that is the ingenuity of her complicated methods of death. This is one aspect of her talent which has had little influence on modern novelists, and one which we have largely outgrown. Realism and credibility have supplanted ingenuity. Despite her highly original talent and the quality of her writing, she was an innovator of style but not of form, and was content to work within the contemporary conventions of the detective story which in the Golden Age were imperatives. Readers of the 1930s expected that the puzzle would be both dominant and ingenious, and that the murderer in his villainy would exhibit almost superhuman cunning and skill. It was not sufficient that the victim should be murdered; he must be ingeniously, bizarrely and horribly murdered. Those were not the days of the swift bash to the skull followed by sixty thousand words of psychological insight. Because of this need to provide a plot that was both original and ingenious, many of the murders she devised would not have worked in practice. That does not spoil our present-day pleasure in the books, but marks them as very much of their age. *Have His Carcase*, for example, is extraordinarily complex, involving a cipher, letters posted abroad, complicated alibis and unconvincing disguises. It is hard to reconcile this ingenuity with a murderer who is shown as both stupid and brutal, even if he is given a somewhat unlikely accomplice. And how extraordinary that the victim could be a haemophiliac without his doctor, his dentist, the police surgeon or the pathologist noticing the fact within the first few minutes of the post-mortem examination. But was one ever held?

The murder in *Unnatural Death* is equally implausible. It is not really possible to kill someone by injecting air into a vein, at least not with a normal-sized syringe. I am advised that the syringe would have to be so large that the patient would be more likely to die of shock on beholding it than from any effects of the injected air! It is unlikely, too, that the victim in *The Nine Tailors* would be killed merely by the clanging of bells, however long, loud and close the peal. And I personally could have advised Mr Tallboy in *Murder Must Advertise* of many simpler and surer ways of killing his blackmailer than by climbing onto the roof and using a catapult through the skylight. Today, in choosing how to despatch our victims, we are less concerned with originality and ingenuity than with practical, scientific and psychological credibility.

But one way in which I suggest that Dorothy L. Sayers was in advance of her age is the realism with which she describes the finding of the body. She well knew the importance of this moment of high drama and she was not too squeamish to show us something of the horror of violent death. In this she was very different from her co-crime-writer Agatha Christie, who obviously felt a deep repugnance for describing physical violence. One cannot imagine Agatha Christie describing with such realism the finding by Harriet Vane of the body with its throat cut on the Flat-Iron Rock.

> It *was* a corpse. Not the sort of corpse there could be any doubt about, either.... Indeed, if the head did not come off in Harriet's hands, it was only because the spine was intact, for the larynx and all the great vessels of the neck had been severed and a frightful stream, bright red and glistening, was running over the surface of the rock and dripping into a little hollow below.
>
> Harriet put the head down again and felt suddenly sick. She had written often enough about this kind of corpse, but meeting the real thing in the flesh was quite different. She had not realised how butcherly the severed vessels would look, and she had not reckoned with the horrid halitus of blood, which steamed to her nostrils under the blazing sun.

To the thirties' writer of detective fiction death was, of course, necessary but, however ingenious or bloody, it was rarely allowed to horrify or distress. Today – and I suggest that Dorothy L. Sayers had a potent, and perhaps unacknowledged, influence – we aim for greater realism. Murder, the contaminating and unique crime, is messy, horrifying and tragic and the modern reader of crime fiction is not spared these realities.

But in the more minor expediencies of murder Sayers was typical of her time. She had a liking for maps, rough illustrative drawings, ciphers and house plans. A plan which particularly intrigues me is provided in *Clouds of Witness* where victim and suspects are guests of the Duke of Denver at his Yorkshire shooting box, Riddlesdale Lodge. A plan of the second floor shows that eight people had to make do with one small bathroom and separate lavatory, a lack which may partly explain the English obsession with the state of their bowels.

For many of Dorothy L. Sayers's readers, perhaps for most, *Gaudy Night* stands at the peak of her artistic achievement. It is unique among her novels – and rare among detective stories – in not having a mysterious death at its heart. There are, of course, two attempted murders, one of the over sensitive student Miss Newland, and one of Harriet Vane herself. The criticism made at the time by female academics was that the novel was out of date, portraying the Oxford, not of the thirties, but of Sayers's own student days. The women's college she describes with such loving recollection, with its rigid segregation of the sexes and its formal manners, is, of course, one that has passed away for ever. What relevance has the novel, therefore, for the reader of today and for today's writer of detective fiction?

For me *Gaudy Night* is one of the most successful marriages of the puzzle with the novel of social realism and serious purpose. It tells me, as a writer of today, that it is possible to construct a credible and enthralling mystery and marry it successfully to a theme of psychological subtlety and this is perhaps the most important of Dorothy L. Sayers's legacies to writers and readers. She wrote to her friend, Muriel St Clare Byrne, that *Gaudy Night* was not a detective story at all, but a novel of an almost entirely psychological kind with a mild detective interest. But here I must take issue with the author – a presumptuous and perhaps a dangerous thing to do. She did herself less than justice. *Gaudy Night* is a true detective story. We want to know who among a closed circle of suspects is responsible for the malicious disruption at Shrewsbury College and the clues to the mystery are fairly, indeed plainly, presented. I can still recall my first reading of the novel when I was sixteen, and my self-disgust at my failure to identify the culprit when all the necessary information had been so carefully, if cunningly, provided.

Margery Allingham also portrayed aspects of the age in which she wrote, but was happy to range outside territory with which she was familiar. *Flowers for the Judge* deals with publishing; *Dancers in Mourning* with the frenetic world of the theatrical star; *The Fashion in Shrouds* with the ephemeral mystique of a high fashion house. All provide a vivid picture of the community in which they are set. Her writing life was long (forty-five years) and apart from published articles, broadcasts and book reviews, she wrote twenty novels of crime and adventure between 1929 and 1966. The novels became increasingly sophisticated, concentrating more on character and milieu than on mystery, and in 1961 she wrote that the crime novel could be 'a kind of reflection on society's conscience'. This was to become increasingly true of detective fiction generally, but Allingham herself reflected rather than criticised the age in which her stories are set. She had considerable descriptive gifts, especially for places; the seedier squares of north-west London, decaying post-war streets, the salt marshes of the Essex coast. Like Dorothy L. Sayers, she created an upper-class detective (in Albert Campion) – so grand, apparently, that the name of his mother can only be whispered – but one who developed psychological subtlety and, indeed, even changed his appearance as she found the original Campion inadequate to the widening scope of her creative art.

She is notable too for the creation of eccentrics who never degenerate into caricatures, except perhaps for Magersfontein Lugg who, despite the occasional usefulness of skills developed in his criminal past, is a little too much the traditional stage comedy cockney to be convincing and who would surely be too unsuitable a manservant for even Campion to tolerate. One of the Allingham novels which, for me, best illustrates her talent is the cleverly named *More Work for the Undertaker* (Allingham was good at choosing titles), published in 1949. In this novel, set in one of the gloomier streets of post-war London, she combined the eccentric Palinode household with a vivid evocation of place and a strong and continually exciting narrative to produce what was recognised at the time as a distinguished detective story.

Ngaio Marsh has justified her own statement that 'The mechanics of a detective story may be shamelessly contrived but the writing need not be.' It has been said that the formula for a successful detective story is 50 per cent good detection, 25 per cent character and 25 per cent what the writer knows best. Ngaio Marsh, a New Zealander, made good use of her own distinguished career in the theatre by setting some of her most successful books, notably *Enter a Murderer*, *Opening Night* and *Death at the Dolphin* in the world of drama, making excellent use of backstage intrigue and giving a lively account of the problems and mechanics of running a professional company of players in the years between the wars. She is less concerned with the psychology of her characters than is Margery Allingham and the lengthy interrogations by her urbane detective, Superintendent Roderick Alleyn, have their longueurs, but both women are novelists, not merely fabricators of ingenious puzzles. Both sought, not always successfully, to reconcile the conventions of the classical detective story with the novel of social realism. But because Ngaio Marsh experienced Britain as a long-staying visitor who saw what she thought of as a second homeland through somewhat naïve and uncritical eyes, she gives a less accurate, more idealised, nostalgic and regrettably sometimes snobbish picture of England than do her crime-writing contemporaries. I have most enjoyed the books set in her native New Zealand, *Vintage Murder* (1937), *Colour Scheme* (1943) and *Died in the Wool* (1945) where landscapes, characters and plot are interrelated and she brings the people and the soil of her native county vividly before us.

None of these women, of course, would have described herself as a social historian or as having a prime responsibility either to portray contemporary mores or to criticise the age in which she worked, and it is perhaps this detachment of purpose which makes these writers so reliable as historians of their age. They were of their time and wrote for their time and their stories give a clear and, indeed, a personal account of what it was like to live and work as an educated woman in the decades between the wars.

The 1914–18 war had, of course, very greatly advanced the cause of women's emancipation. They gained the vote and already had the right to a university education but not to a degree until 1920, when in October of that year Dorothy L. Sayers was one of the first women to receive an Oxford degree. The professions were now open to them, but their lives were still extraordinarily restricted compared with today. The mass slaughter of young men in the Great War had meant that there were three million so-called surplus women and very few opportunities open to them, since married men were given priority for jobs. Dorothy L. Sayers deals with this most tellingly, particularly in her treatment of Miss Climpson and her Cattery, a small group of spinsters employed by Lord Peter to assist his detective work. He explains their function to Inspector Parker in *Unnatural Death*.

Miss Climpson is a manifestation of the wasteful way in which this country is run. Thousands of old maids, simply bursting with useful energy, forced by our stupid social system into hydros and hotels and communities and hostels and posts as companions, where their magnificent gossip-powers and units of inquisitiveness are allowed to dissipate themselves, or even become harmful to the community, while the ratepayer's money is spent on getting work for which these women are providentially fitted, inefficiently carried out by ill-equipped policemen like you.

Dorothy L. Sayers, among much in her books that is tendentious or over-romanticised, does deal realistically with the problem of the so-called superfluous women deprived of the hope of marriage by the slaughter of the 1914–18 war, women with intelligence, initiative and often with education, for whom society offered no real intellectual outlet. And those who did find intellectual satisfaction commonly achieved it at the sacrifice of emotional and sexual fulfilment. It is interesting and, I think, significant that there is no married don in *Gaudy Night* and only one married woman – and she a widow – Mrs Goodwin, who is a member of the senior common room. Women in the Civil Service and teaching were required to resign on marriage, the supposition obviously being that now they had a man to support them they should direct their energies to the proper sphere of interest for their sex. I cannot think of a single detective story written by a woman in the 1930s which features a woman lawyer, a woman surgeon, a woman politician, or indeed a woman in any real position of political or economic power.

One notable exception to the way in which women were perceived as wives, mothers, useful little helpmeets such as stenographers and secretaries, is Margery Allingham's Lady Amanda Fitton. Another Allingham heroine who has a professional job is Val Ferris, Albert Campion's sister, who has been unhappily married but now works singlemindedly to establish herself as a leading dress designer. She and the actress Georgia are in love with the same man, and the book *The Fashion in Shrouds* explores the emotional pressures on women who dedicate themselves to a career but also want fulfilment in their emotional lives, a problem which is also one of the themes of Dorothy L. Sayers's *Gaudy Night*. Val and Georgia are described in the novel as 'two fine ladies of the modern world', but both are aware of their inner dissatisfaction as they drive home alone to their bijoux, hard-earned houses. The novelist says: 'Their several responsibilities are far heavier than most men's and their abilities greater', but their femininity – 'femininity unprotected from itself' – is presented as 'a weakness, not a strength'. And when Alan, Val's future husband, proposes to her, he sets out his terms unambiguously. He wants to take 'full responsibility' for Val, including financial responsibility, and expects in turn that she will yield to him 'your independence, the enthusiasm which you give your career, your time and your thought'. She does this almost with a sigh of relief. It is very difficult to imagine a modern writer of detective stories, particularly a woman, thinking that this is a satisfactory solution to Val's dilemma. It is even more difficult to imagine a modern female reader tolerating such blatant misogyny.

Ngaio Marsh is also of her age in the ingenuity of her methods of murder and surprisingly ruthless and robust in her dispatch of victims. In *Died in the Wool*, set in a sheep station, Florence Rubrick is stunned and then suffocated in a bale of wool. The victim in *Off with His Head* is decapitated. In *Scales of Justice*, Colonel Carterette, after being struck on the temple, is killed by the point of a shooting-stick which the killer actually sits on to push it home. She knew, too, the importance to a novel of the heart-stopping moment when the body is discovered. In *Clutch of Constables* we share Troy's horror as she looks down at the body of Hazel Rickerby-Carrick bobbing and bumping against the starboard side of the river steamer, 'idiotically bloated, her mouth drawn into an outlandish rictus grinning through discoloured foam'. Death is never glamorised nor trivialised by Ngaio Marsh.

If Ngaio Marsh worked largely within the conventions of the detective novel of her age, in which way did she transcend these conventions and transcend them so successfully that her novels are still read with pleasure while so many of her contemporaries are only named in the reference books of crime? Firstly, I suggest it lay in her power of characterisation, not only in the sensitive and attractive portrayal of Alleyn and his wife Troy, but in the rich variety of characters who people her thirty-two novels. Her eccentrics are never caricatures. I remember particularly the president, The Boomer, in *Black as He's Painted*, poor deluded Florence Rubrick in *Died in the Wool*, Nurse Kettle in *Scales of Justice*, the distinctive Maori Rua Te Kahu, in *Colour Scheme*, the Lamprey family depicted in *A Surfeit of Lampreys* with love but with insight and honesty. It is because in a Ngaio Marsh novel we can believe in the people and enter for our comfort and entertainment into a real world inhabited by credible human beings, so that some critics, including Julian Symons, have deplored her need to introduce murder, a view which occasionally she appeared to share. She wrote of her characters:

I wish I could set them up in an orderly, well-planned fashion, as I'm sure my brothers and sisters-in-crime do. But no. However much I try to discipline myself as to plot and general whodunnitry, I always find myself writing about a set of people in a milieu that for one reason or another attracts me, and then, bad cess to it, I have to involve them in some crime or other. Does this mean one is a straight novelist manquée?

It is indeed the set of people in a milieu which so powerfully attracts us as readers. Perhaps the most valid criticism of Ngaio Marsh is that she was too concerned with the details of the 'whodunnitry'. The novels have great vitality and originality while the scene is being set and the characters assembled, but tend to sag in the middle, borne down by the weight of police interrogation and routine investigation. The distinction she drew between a novel and a detective story is, of course, one which finds little favour with crime writers today; we feel entitled to be judged as novelists not as mere fabricators of mystery. But it was a distinction reaching back to the Victorians and was a view shared by other crime writers of her time including, somewhat surprisingly, Dorothy L. Sayers at the start of her career.

And finally, but certainly not last, there is the quality of her writing, particularly her descriptive powers. Sometimes it is a single word which reveals her mastery. *Singing in the Shrouds* begins with a description of the London docks and the tall cranes are described as 'pontifical', an arresting and vivid image. H.R.F. Keating, who includes *Surfeit of Lampreys* in his collection of the hundred best crime novels ever written, instances one sentence from that novel, which describes the heroine, Roberta, arriving from New Zealand by boat in London. She looks out at the other ships at anchor in the early morning light, and, Ngaio Marsh writes, 'Stewards, pallid in their undervests, leant out of portholes to stare.' The picture is arresting, original and certainly described from personal experience. But for me, perhaps not surprisingly, it is the New Zealand novels which include some of her best descriptive writing: her native country seen through an artist's eyes and described with a writer's voice.

Reading the best of Ngaio Marsh, I feel that there was always a dichotomy between her talent and the genre she chose. So why did she pursue it with such regularity, producing thirty-two novels in forty-eight years? They were quickly written, principally to supply a regular and sufficient income for her to live and dress well, and to enable her to continue her main interest, which was the promotion of the theatre, particularly Shakespeare's plays, in her native New Zealand. Marsh was a deeply reserved, indeed in some respects a private person, and she may well have felt that to extend the scope of her talent would be to betray aspects of her personality which she profoundly wished to remain secret. There was, too, the complication that she lived a double life. New Zealand was her birthplace and she wrote about it with affection, but her heart was in England and some of her happiest memories were when she took the long journey from the South Island to London. Her response to New Zealand was always ambivalent. She disliked and criticised the New Zealand accent, was uncertain in her literary portrayal of the Maoris, found her chief and most lasting friendship among a family of English aristocrats and retained a romantic view of the perfect English gentleman, a species to which, of course, her detective Roderick Alleyn belonged.

When Dorothy L. Sayers finished with Lord Peter and transferred her creative enthusiasm to her theological plays, she could comfort herself that she had done well with her aristocratic sleuth, and in *Gaudy Night* had used the detective story to say something about the almost sacramental importance of work and the problems for women of reconciling the claims of heart and mind which, she wrote, had been important to her all her life. Margery Allingham widened the scope of her talent so that the later novels are markedly superior to those written earlier both in characterisation and plot, while Agatha Christie knew precisely what she could do best and did it with remarkable consistency and regularity throughout a long writing life. It seems to me that only Ngaio Marsh – popular as she was and indeed remains – could have left a more impressive legacy as a novelist.

All four women had their secrets. Dorothy L. Sayers concealed the birth of her illegitimate son from her parents and close friends until her death. Her parents never knew they had a grandson. Agatha Christie never explained or spoke about her mysterious disappearance in 1926 which became a national scandal; Margery Allingham suffered much ill-health and personal anguish at the end of her life. Both Christie and Marsh falsified their ages, Marsh by actually altering her birth certificate. The secrets of their characters' lives were finally explained by the brilliance of Hercule Poirot, Albert Campion, Lord Peter or Roderick Alleyn, but their own secrets remained inviolate until after their deaths, when all secrets, however carefully guarded or pitiable, fall prey to the insistent curiosity of the living.

Christie, Allingham and Marsh successfully continued writing detective stories well after the Second World War. *Postern of Fate* was published in 1973, Allingham's *Cargo of Eagles* in 1966 and Marsh's *Light Thickens* in 1982. Dorothy L. Sayers's last full-length detective story, *Busman's Honeymoon*, was first published in 1937 and reissued by Gollancz in 1972. But by the time it first appeared Sayers was already losing interest in her aristocratic detective and turning her attention to her theological plays, and finally to her half-completed translation of Dante's *Divine Comedy*, which was to be her creative passion for the rest of her life. But no novelist can distance herself from the social and political changes of contemporary life, and those detective writers who lasted into the new age, symbolised by that mushroom cloud over Hiroshima, necessarily had to adapt their fictional worlds to less comfortable times. Agatha Christie did so with some success but even so, when a character in her books refers to returning from the war, or his experience during the war, I have to look back to the date of publication to know whether he is referring to the Great War of 1914–18 or the 1939–45 conflict.

In the Agatha Christie novels the changes in contemporary life are mostly shown by the inconveniences suffered by the characters in obtaining servants, good service from tradesmen or maintaining their houses. Superintendent Spence, the retired policeman in *Hallowe'en Party*, published in 1969, deplores the way that girls are no longer looked after by their aunts and older sisters and that 'more girls nowadays marry wrong 'uns than they ever used to in my time'.

Mrs Drake complains that 'mothers and families generally' were not looking after their children properly any more. There are complaints that too many people who ought to be under mental restraint are allowed to wander round freely at risk to the public and that those who went to church only got the modern version of the Bible, which had no literary merit whatsoever. Altogether things are not as they were in St Mary Mead. Poirot, however, is little changed, although in *Hallowe'en Party* he admits to dyeing his hair. Strangely, however, he now speaks like an Englishman but still, to Mrs Oliver's dismay, insists on wearing patent leather shoes in the country. The limp which affected him when we first encountered him has long since disappeared.

While Roderick Alleyn shows no sign of development either for good or ill, Allingham's Albert Campion becomes more serious and Lord Peter Wimsey is elevated into a wish-fulfilment hero, the kind of man his creator would obviously have liked to marry: the scholar manqué of *Gaudy Night*, standing with the Warden of All Souls outside St Mary's Church having listened to the University sermon. But the great international changes of the immediate post-war years largely passed these writers by in their fiction, though not in their lives, as no doubt was artistically understandable. In the words of Jane Austen in *Mansfield Park*:

> Let other pens dwell on guilt and misery. I quit such odious subjects as soon as I can, impatient to restore every body, not greatly in fault themselves, to tolerable comfort, and to have done with all the rest.

Miss Marple would have approved.

It was my story. A murder mystery. A
who-done-it-and-got-away-with-it-until-
he-wrote-about-it.

6

Telling the Story:
Setting, Viewpoint, People

'It is my belief, Watson, founded upon my experience, that the lowest and vilest alleys of London do not present a more dreadful record of sin than does the smiling and beautiful countryside.'

Arthur Conan Doyle, 'The Adventure of the Copper Beeches'

Reading any work of fiction is a symbiotic act. We the readers contribute our imagination to that of the writer, willingly entering his world, participating in the lives of its people and forming from the author's words and images our own mental picture of people and places. The setting in any novel is therefore an important element of the whole book. Place, after all, is where the characters play out their tragicomedies and it is only if the action is firmly rooted in a physical reality that we can enter fully into their world. This is not to suggest that setting is more important than characterisation, narrative and structure; all four must be held in creative tension and the whole story written in compelling language if the book is to survive beyond its first month of publication. Many readers if questioned would opt for characterisation as the vital element in fiction and, indeed, if the characters fail to convince the novel is no more than a lifeless unsatisfying narrative. But the setting is where these people live, move and have their being, and we need to breathe their air, see with their eyes, walk the paths they tread and inhabit the rooms the writer has furnished for them. So important is this identification that many novels are named for the place on which the action is centred; obvious examples are *Wuthering Heights*, *Mansfield Park*, *Howard's End* and *Middlemarch*, where the setting exerts a unifying and dominant influence on both the characters and the plot. I aimed to make this true of the River Thames in my novel *Original Sin*, where the river links both the more dramatic events of the story and the mood of the people who live or work near it. To one it is a source of continual fascination and pleasure, her riverside flat a symbol of ambition achieved, while to another the dark ever-flowing stream is a terrifying reminder of loneliness and death.

Some novelists in the canon of English fiction have created imaginary places in such detail and with so much care that they become real for both writer and reader. Anthony Trollope said of Framley Parsonage that he had added to the English counties, that he knew its roads and railways, its towns and parishes, and which hunts rode over it, and that there was 'no name given to a fictitious site which does not represent to me a spot of which I know all the accessories, as though I had lived and wandered there'. Similarly Thomas Hardy created Wessex, of which one can draw a map, a dream county which has 'by degrees, solidified into a utilitarian region which people can go to, take a house in, and write to the papers from'. Writers of detective fiction seldom have space to describe a setting in such detail, but although it may be done with more economy, the place should be as real to the reader as Barchester and Wessex.

I think it important, too, that the setting, which being integral to the whole novel, should be perceived through the mind of one of the characters, not merely described by the authorial voice, so that place and character interact and what the eye takes in influences the mood and the action.

One function of the setting is to add credibility to the story, and this is particularly important with crime fiction, which often deals with bizarre, dramatic and horrific events which need to be rooted in a place so tangible that the reader can enter it as he might a familiar room. If we believe in the place we can believe in the characters. In addition the setting can from the first chapter establish the mood of the novel, whether of suspense, terror, apprehension, menace or mystery. We have only to think of Conan Doyle's *The Hound of the Baskervilles*, of that dark and sinister mansion set in the middle of the fog-shrouded moor, to appreciate how important setting can be to the establishment of atmosphere. *The Hound of Wimbledon Common* would hardly provide such a frisson of terror.

But the setting of a detective story can emphasise the terror by contrast while, paradoxically, also providing a relief from horror. The poet W.H. Auden, for whom the reading of detective stories was an addiction, examined the genre in the light of Christian theology in his well-known essay 'The Guilty Vicarage'. He states:

> In the detective story, as in its mirror image, the Quest for the Grail, maps (the ritual of space) and timetables (the ritual of time) are desirable. Nature should reflect its human inhabitants, i.e., it should be the Great Good Place; for the more Eden-like it is,

111

> the greater the contradiction of the murder ... the
> corpse must shock not only because it is a corpse but
> also because, even for a corpse, it is shockingly out
> of place, as when a dog makes a mess on a drawing
> room carpet.

He believed, as I think do most British writers of the detective story, that the single body on the drawing room floor can be more horrific than a dozen bullet-ridden bodies down Raymond Chandler's mean streets, precisely because it is indeed shockingly out of place.

I have used setting in this way to enhance danger and terror by contrast in a number of my novels. In *A Taste for Death* the two bodies, each with its head almost severed, are discovered in a church vestry by a gentle spinster and the young truant she has befriended. The contrast between the sanctity of the setting and the brutality of the murders intensifies the horror and can produce in the reader a disorientating unease, a sense that the ordained order has been overturned and we no longer stand on firm ground. In *An Unsuitable Job for a Woman*, my first book featuring the young woman detective Cordelia Gray, a particularly appalling and callous murder takes place in high summer in Cambridge, where wide lawns, sun-dappled stone and the sparkling river recall to Cordelia's mind some words by John Bunyan: 'Then I saw that there was a way to Hell, even from the gate of Heaven.' It is often these paths to hell, not the destination, which provide for a crime novelist the most fascinating avenues to explore.

Detective novelists have always been fond of setting their stories in a closed society, and this has a number of obvious advantages. The stain of suspicion cannot be allowed to spread too far if each suspect is to be a rounded, credible, breathing human being, not a cardboard cut-out to be ritually knocked down in the last chapter. And in a self-contained community – hospital, school, office, publishing house, nuclear power station – where, particularly if the setting is residential, the characters often spend more time with working colleagues than they do with their families, the irritation that can emerge from such cloistered and unsought intimacy can kindle animosity, jealousy and resentment, emotions which, if they are sufficiently strong, can smoulder away and eventually explode into the destructive finality of violence. The isolated community can also be an epitome of the wider world outside and this, for a writer, can be one of the greatest attractions of the closed communal setting, particularly as the characters are being explored under the trauma of an official investigation for murder, a process which can destroy the privacies both of the living and of the dead.

The village setting has always been popular – typically, of course, in Agatha Christie – since an English village is itself a closed society and one which, whether we live in a village or not, retains a powerful hold on our imagination, an image compounded of nostalgia for a life once experienced or imagined and a vague unfocused longing to escape the city for a simpler, less frenetic and more peaceful life. It is interesting how vividly we the readers create the rural setting for ourselves, often powerfully helped by images from television or film. I don't think Agatha Christie has anywhere described in detail St Mary Mead but we know the village street, the church, the cottage, genuinely old but untarnished by time, with its neat front garden, shining knocker and, within, Miss Marple, with her mixture of gentle authority and kindness, explaining to her latest maid that the dusting leaves something to be desired.

Settings, particularly landscapes, are often most effectively described when the writer uses a place with which he is intimately familiar. If we want to know what it is like to be a detective in twenty-first-century Edinburgh we can learn more from Ian Rankin's Rebus novels than we can from any official guidebook, as we move with Rebus down the roads and alleyways of the city and into its pubs and its public and private buildings. Ruth Rendell has used East Anglia and London, both places with which she is familiar, for some of her most admired novels written under the pseudonym Barbara Vine. East Anglia has a particular attraction for detective novelists. The remoteness of the east coast, the dangerous encroaching North Sea, the bird-loud marshes, the emptiness, the great skies, the magnificent churches and the sense of being in a place alien, mysterious and slightly sinister, where it is possible to stand under friable cliffs eaten away by the tides of centuries and imagine that we hear the bells of ancient churches buried under the sea.

Oxford has provided the setting for many detective stories by men and women who have lived or have been educated there, and who can walk with confident familiarity through its quads and down its famous streets. In the words of Edmund Crispin in his novel *The Moving Toyshop*: 'It is true that the ancient and noble city of Oxford is, of all the towns of England, the likeliest progenitor of unlikely events and persons.' The air of Oxford has indeed proved peculiarly susceptible to fictional death and, although Cambridge has given us Professor Glyn Daniel's Sir Richard Cherrington, there is no competition in the murder stakes. The modern writer who comes first to mind when one thinks of Oxford is Colin Dexter, who with his Inspector Morse has ensured that, in fiction, Oxford is the most murderous city in the UK. Dorothy L. Sayers, Oxford-educated, used the city and her imaginary women's college in *Gaudy Night*, and other detective novelists with whom we can walk these ancient and hallowed quads are Michael Innes, John C. Masterman and Margaret Yorke. Here, too, we have the power of contrast, a setting both beautiful and austere with which many readers will already be familiar, adding credibility to the plot while enabling them to contribute their own experience and visual images to that of the detective.

Setting in a more limited sense, particularly architecture and houses, is important to characterisation, since people react to their environment and are influenced by it. When an author describes a room in the victim's house, perhaps the one in which the body is found, the description can tell the perceptive reader a great deal about the victim's character and interests. Furniture, books, pictures, personal articles in cupboards and on shelves, all the sad detritus of the dead life tell their story. For this reason the place in which the body is found is particularly revealing and I regard the description of the finding of the body as one of the most important chapters of a detective novel. To find a murdered corpse is a horrible, sometimes life-changing experience for most normal people and the writing should be vivid and realistic enough to enable the reader to share the shock and horror, the revulsion and the pity. The emotions of that moment and the language used to convey them should, in my view, reflect

115

the person who makes the discovery. In *A Taste for Death* the description is particularly horror-invoking with the frequent reiteration of the word 'blood', because that is how the gentle and kindly spinster Miss Wharton experiences the moment of discovering the two bodies with their heads almost severed. In contrast, when Commander Adam Dalgliesh nearly stumbles over the body of a woman on a Suffolk beach his emotions are inevitably those of a professional detective. So although he is intrigued by his different emotional responses, between being called to a body knowing roughly what he will find and coming upon it unexpectedly at night on a lonely beach, nevertheless, almost instinctively, he is careful not to disturb the scene and notes all the details with the experienced eyes of an investigating officer. In Dorothy L. Sayers's first detective novel, *Whose Body?*, the corpse is found naked in the bath of a nervous and innocent architect, and the book begins with this image. The first question facing the police – and, of course, her detective Lord Peter Wimsey – is whether this was the corpse of Sir Reuben Levy, the missing Jewish financier. Whether the victim had or had not been circumcised would have answered the question at once, but this was a clue Miss Sayers was not permitted by her publishers to include in her novel and no doubt had she done so there would have been an outcry among the respectable readers of the Golden Age.

The detective story is neither irrational nor romantic, and its clues are rooted in the reality and minutiae of everyday life. This means that British writers who look to a foreign country for their setting need not only a sensitive response to the country's topography, speech and people, but a knowledge of its social structure including the criminal justice system. Writers who have achieved notable success include Michael Dibdin (1947–2007), whose stories featuring the professional detective Inspector Aurelio Zen are set in Italy, a country in which he had resided. H.R.F. Keating's Indian detective, Inspector Ganesh Vinayak Ghote of the Bombay Criminal Investigation Department, first appeared in *The Perfect Murder* in 1964. Ghote is attractively human, diffident and occasionally prone to error, but shrewd and intelligent, and it is remarkable how confident was Keating's touch in describing a country which, when he brought Ghote to life, he had never visited. A comparatively recent arrival is Alexander McCall Smith's Precious Ramotswe, the proprietor of the 'No. 1 Ladies' Detective Agency' in Botswana. Mma Ramotswe's heart is as ample as is her frame and although the most atrocious murders are unlikely to come her way, any injustice, large or small, engages her energies and compassion.

All these three characters, as well as their profession, have a private domestic life in which we can participate. The detective, whether professional or amateur, needs a domestic setting if the reader is to enter fully into his life, and most writers provide for their detective a known and familiar place in which he can be at home. The name Miss Jane Marple inevitably conjures up St Mary Mead, and although Ruth Rendell's Chief Inspector Wexford does occasionally travel outside England, we know that his natural place is Kingsmarkham in Sussex. Some detectives, of course, are more precisely housed. There can be very few aficionados of fictional murder who don't know that 221B Baker Street is the address of Sherlock Holmes, that Lord Peter Wimsey lives in an apartment at 110A Piccadilly,

Albert Campion in Bottle Street and Poirot in a modern London flat distinguished by the starkness and regularity of its contemporary furniture and, we may be sure, by the total absence of dust or disarray. If details of the apartments are not given, we can provide ourselves with a lively picture of these sanctums from the television series, indeed it is often television rather than the books themselves that furnishes us with our pictures of both the characters and the setting.

And their houses are more than a living space for the detective hero. They provide for us, the readers, reassuring safe houses of the mind from which we too can venture forth vicariously to encounter murder and danger before returning to domestic comfort and safety. Readers of Dorothy L. Sayers, travelling home to mortgaged Metroland or worried by the threat of unemployment and the storm clouds over Europe must have entered with relief into Lord Peter's flat with the fire burning, shedding its light on the bronze chrysanthemums, the comfortable chairs and the grand piano, while Bunter deferentially offers them a glass of expensive sherry or vintage wine and Lord Peter entertains them by playing Scarlatti. Sherlock Holmes's apartment, as described by Watson, perhaps offers a more dramatic and disturbing welcome, although we can rely on Mrs Hudson to put things to right. All Holmes's adventures start here and it is to this sanctum that he returns, so that it becomes a safe haven for the reader who can share this assurance of safety and home comfort before setting out with Holmes and Watson on yet one more perilous adventure. Michael Innes has admitted that his hero's natural setting was a great house and that Sir John Appleby found his way into those august dwellings largely because it was the kind of life he fancied. But for his creator the mansion or great country seat was really an extension of the sealed room, with the added advantage that it could define the territorial boundaries of the mystery more effectively and interestingly than could a cramped flat or semi-detached villa.

My own detective novels, with rare exceptions, have been inspired by the place rather than by a method of murder or a character; an example is *Devices and Desires*, which had its genesis while I was on a visit of exploration in East Anglia, standing on a deserted shingle beach. There were a few wooden boats drawn up on the beach, a couple of brown nets slung between poles and drying in the wind and, looking out over the sullen and dangerous North Sea, I could imagine myself standing in the same place hundreds of years ago with the taste of salt on my lips and the constant hiss and withdrawing rattle of the tide. Then, turning my eyes to the south, I saw the great outline of Sizewell nuclear power station and immediately I knew that I had found the setting for my next novel.

This moment of initial inspiration is always one of great excitement. I know that, however long the writing may take, I shall eventually have a novel. The idea takes possession of my mind and gradually over the months the book takes shape, the characters appear and become increasingly real to me, I know who will be murdered and where, when, how, why and by whom. I decide how my detective, Adam Dalgliesh, can logically be brought in to investigate outside the Metropolitan Police area. I began my research by visiting nuclear power stations in Suffolk and Dorset, speaking to the scientists and other staff and learning as much as I needed to know about nuclear power and the way a power station is run. As usual, all the people I consulted were unfailingly helpful. The novel which resulted from this research and the long months of writing began with that moment of solitude on an East Anglian beach.

One of the first decisions any novelist has to make, of equal importance to the choice of setting, is viewpoint. Through whose mind, eyes and ears should we, the readers, participate in the plot? Here the writer of detective stories has a particular problem arising from Monsignor Ronald Knox's insistence that the reader should not be allowed to follow the murderer's thoughts, a prohibition on which Dorothy L. Sayers so feelingly dwelt. But I wonder whether there might not be exceptions to Monsignor Knox's rule. Surely there must be some moments when the murderer's thoughts are not dominated by the enormity of what he has done and the risks of exposure. Could the writer not enter into his mind when he wakes in the small hours with memories of some traumatic event in his childhood which the writer can exploit in clue-making and use to give some idea of the killer's character? And there must be other brief moments in the day when something other than his own peril occupies his mind. But the difficulty remains.

The first-person narrative has the advantage of immediacy and of reader identification and sympathy with the one whose voice he hears. It can also be an aid to credibility, since the reader is more likely to suspend disbelief in the more improbable twists in the plot when hearing the explanation from the person most concerned. 'Looking back now I cannot really explain why I decided to put my wife's body in the refuse sack, carry it with some difficulty to the boot of the car and drive a hundred and fifty miles to drop it over Beachy Head. But I was desperate to get away from the house as quickly as possible and it seemed a good idea at the time.' I doubt whether this passage has ever been penned, but we have all read some uncomfortably like it. But the disadvantage of a first-person narrative is that the reader can only know what the narrator knows, seeing only through his eyes and experiencing only what he experiences and, in general, it is more appropriate to the fast-action thriller than to the detective story. One of the most effective uses of first-person narrative is by Raymond Chandler. In the brilliant opening to *The Big Sleep* the reader learns from a few short sentences where we are, what the day is like, the occupation of the hero, something about his personality, details of the clothes he is wearing, and finally why he is waiting at that particular door.

The story told by the Watson figure is less restricting because we can get his view of the detective's character and methods as well as the progress of the investigation, and was used with some success in the early days of the Golden Age. There is, however, the danger that if the character is portrayed as more than a functional necessity he will become too alive, too interesting and too important to the plot, competing as hero with the detective; if he is not vitally alive he becomes a superfluous if convenient mouthpiece for information which could be more subtly and interestingly conveyed.

Then there is the variation of the first-person narrative in which the story is told in the form of letters or in the actual voices of the characters, of which *The Moonstone* is a prime example. Dorothy L. Sayers was so admiring of Wilkie Collins's achievement that she decided to follow his example and write a novel more ambitious than her existing work and which would not feature Lord Peter Wimsey. In a letter to her scientific collaborator Eustace Barton MD, she wrote:

> In this story ... it is obvious that there must be a powerful love interest, and I am going to turn my mind to making this part of the book as modern and powerful as possible. The day of the two nice young people whose chaste affection is rewarded on the final page, has rather gone by.

Apart from the wish to do something new, she said she was looking forward to getting a rest from Lord Peter because 'his everlasting breeziness does become a bit of a tax at times'. The novel, *The Documents in the Case*, was loosely based on the tragic Thompson–Bywaters murder, where a dull and unloved husband is killed by the young lover of his wife, and the story is told variously through letters from a young man living in the same house as the married couple, the other participants in the story, the killer, and newspaper reports giving at length the evidence from the coroner's inquests. But Sayers knew that she hadn't succeeded in her ambition. The love affair is too tawdry and uninteresting to generate the passion necessary to provoke murder, and the novel is a depressing read. Sayers herself wrote:

> In my heart I know I have made a failure of it.... It has produced a mingled atmosphere of dullness and gloom which will, I fear, be fatal to the book ... I wish I could have done better with the brilliant plot.

It was an experiment she was not to repeat. No other crime novelist as far as I know has attempted to copy let alone emulate Wilkie Collins, but it would be interesting if someone were to try.

My own choice of viewpoint is partly authorial, a detached recorder of events, and partly to move into the minds of the different characters, seeing with their eyes, expressing their emotions, hearing their words. Most often the character will be Dalgliesh, Kate Miskin or a more junior member of the detective team, one of the suspects or a witness. This for me makes a novel more complex and interesting, and can also have a note of irony as this shifting viewpoint can show how differently we can all perceive the same event. I feel it is important, however, not to alter the viewpoint in any one chapter. The distinguished critic Percy Lubbock discussed the question of viewpoint in his 1921 book *The Craft of Fiction*. The novelist, he said, can either describe the characters from outside, as an impartial or partial observer, or can assume omniscience and describe them from within, or can place himself in the position of one of them and affect to be in the dark as to the motives of the rest. What he must not do, however, is to mix his methods and change from one point of view to another – as Dickens had done in *Bleak House* and Tolstoy in *War and Peace*. But there is no rule relating to the novel which a genius can't successfully circumvent – and I generally agree with E.M. Forster, who writes in his book *Aspects of the Novel*:

So next time you read a novel do look out for the 'point of view' – that is to say, the relation of the narrator to the story. Is he telling the story and describing the characters from the outside, or does he identify himself with one of the characters? Does he pretend that he knows and foresees everything? Or does he go in for being surprised? Does he shift his point of view – like Dickens in the first three chapters of *Bleak House?* And if he does, do you mind? I don't.

If we are talking of a genius, nor do I.

When I settled down in the mid-1950s to begin my first novel, it never occurred to me to make a start with anything other than a detective story. Mysteries were my favourite relaxation reading and I felt that if I could write one successfully it would stand a good chance of acceptance by a publisher. I had no wish to write an autobiographical first novel based on my experience of childhood trauma, the war or my husband's illness, although I have come to believe that most fiction is autobiographical and some autobiography partly fiction. I have always been fascinated by structure in the novel and detective fiction presented a number of technical problems, mainly how to construct a plot which was both credible and exciting with a setting which came alive for readers, and characters who were believable men and women faced with the trauma of a police investigation into murder. I therefore saw the detective story as an ideal apprenticeship for someone setting out with small hope of making a fortune but with ambitions to be regarded eventually as a good and serious novelist.

One of the first decisions was, of course, my choice of detective. If I started today it is likely that I would choose a woman, but this was not an option at the time when women were not active in the detective force. The main choice, therefore, was whether to have a male professional or an amateur of either sex, and as I was aiming at as much realism as possible, I chose the first option and Adam Dalgliesh, named after my English teacher at Cambridge High School, took root in my imagination.

I had learnt a lesson from Dorothy L. Sayers and Agatha Christie, both of whom started out with eccentric detectives with whom in time they became thoroughly disenchanted. So I decided to begin with a less egregiously bizarre character and ruthlessly killed off wife and newborn son in order to avoid involving myself in his emotional life, which I felt would be difficult successfully to incorporate into the structure of the classical detective story. I gave him the qualities I personally admire in either sex – intelligence, courage but not foolhardiness, sensitivity but not sentimentality, and reticence. I felt that this would provide me with a credible professional policeman capable of development should this first novel be the first of a series. A serial detective has, of course, particular advantages; an established character who does not have to be introduced afresh with each novel, a successful career in crime-solving which can add gravitas, an established family history and background and, above all, reader identification and loyalty. It is common for new hardback and paperback novels to carry the name of the detective on the jacket as well as that of the author and the title, so that prospective readers can be reassured that they will indeed encounter an old friend.

And what of the other characters, particularly the victim and the unfortunate suspects? They should certainly be more than stock figures provided out of necessity but in the

Golden Age were rarely in themselves of particular interest; nothing more was required of the victim than that he or she should be an undesirable, dangerous or unpleasant person whose death need cause no grief to anyone. It is certainly not easy to make the victim sympathetic, since he must necessarily have provoked murderous hatred for diverse reasons in a small group of people and usually, once dead, could be safely carried off to the mortuary where he was unlikely to receive the compliment of an autopsy. He has served his purpose and can be put out of mind. But if we do not care, or indeed to some extent empathise with the victim, it surely hardly matters to us whether he lives or dies. The victim is the catalyst at the heart of the novel and he dies because of who he is, what he is and where he is, and the destructive power he exercises, acknowledged or secret, over the life of at least one desperate enemy. His voice may be stilled for most of the novel, his testimony given in the voices of others, by the detritus he leaves in his rooms, his drawers and cupboards, and by the scalpels of the forensic pathologist, but for the reader, at least in thought, he must be powerfully alive. Murder is the unique crime, and its investigation tears down the privacy of both the living and the dead. It is this study of human beings under the stress of this self-revelatory probing which for a writer is one of the chief attractions of the genre.

The suspects should, I feel, be sufficient in number to provide the puzzle, and more than five is difficult if each is to be a credible living and breathing human being with motives that the reader will find convincing. And here again is the difficulty. In the Golden Age readers could accept that the victim was killed because he had damaging information

126

about the murderer's sexual immorality but today this will hardly suffice. People happily and lucratively confess their sexual adventures to the press with few if any detrimental consequences to career or reputation. But the fashion in public infamy changes; today the mere suggestion of paedophilia would be damaging probably beyond redemption. Money, particularly great wealth, is always a credible motive for murder, as is revenge and that deep-seated hatred which makes it almost impossible to tolerate the continued existence of an enemy. In one of my novels Dalgliesh remembers the words of a detective sergeant under whom he had served as a new recruit. 'All motives can be explained under the letter L: lust, lucre, loathing and love. They'll tell you the most dangerous is loathing but don't you believe it, boy; the most dangerous is love.' Certainly the desire to avenge someone deeply loved, to protect or save them, is always a credible motive and for such a murderer we may feel a measure of sympathy and self-identification. In the words of Ivy Compton-Burnett in a conversation with M. Jourdain in 1945:

> I never see why murder and perversion of justice are not normal subjects for a plot, or why they are particularly Elizabethan or Victorian, as some reviewers seem to think.... I believe it would go ill with many of us, if we were faced with a strong temptation, and I suspect that with some of us it does go ill.

In the detective story it frequently goes very ill indeed.

In speaking of my craft over the past decades, one of the commonest questions the audience asks is whether I

127

draw my characters from real life. I tended at first to say no, meaning that I have never taken people from life – members of the family, friends or colleagues – and after a few judicious alterations in appearance or character, put them in a book. But my answer was disingenuous. Of course I take my characters from real life; from where else can I take them? But the person I look to most is myself for experience endured or rejoiced in over nearly ninety years of living in this turbulent world. If I need to write about a character afflicted with such shyness that every new job, every encounter, becomes a torment, I am blessed not to suffer such misery. But I know from the embarrassments and uncertainties of adolescence what such shyness can feel like and it is my job to relive it and find the words to express it. And characters grow like plants in an author's mind during the months of writing, seeming to reveal more and more of themselves. As Anthony Trollope said in his *Autobiography*:

> They must be with him as he lies down to sleep, and as he wakes from his dreams. He must learn to hate them and to love them.... He must know of them whether they be cold-blooded or passionate, whether true or false, and how far true and how far false. The depth and the breadth, and the narrowness and the shallowness of each should be clear to him.

And however well I think I know my characters, they reveal themselves more clearly during the writing of the book, so that at the end, however carefully and intricately the work is plotted, I never get exactly the novel I planned. It feels, indeed, as if the characters and everything that happens to them exists in some limbo of the imagination, so that what I am doing is not inventing them but getting in touch with them and putting their story down in black and white, a process of revelation not of creation. But the process of creation remains mysterious. One writer who has attempted to explain it is E.M. Forster. The well-known passage may be a little high-flown, a little exaggerated in the importance Forster ascribes to the subconscious, but it comes with the authority of the author of *A Passage to India*, and I think most artists, whatever their medium, feel that it gets close to at least part of the truth.

> What about the creative state? In it a man is taken out of himself. He lets down as it were a bucket into his subconscious, and draws up something which is normally beyond his reach. He mixes this thing with his normal experiences, and out of the mixture he makes a work of art.... And when the process is over, when the picture or symphony or lyric or novel (or whatever it is) is complete, the artist, looking back on it, will wonder how on earth he did it. And indeed he did not do it on earth.

"This is criminal -- two wrong spellings and improper use of a semicolon."

7

Critics and Aficionados:
Why Some Don't Enjoy Them
and Why Others Do

In a perfect world there will be no need for detective stories:
but then there will be nothing to detect. Their disappearance at
this moment, however, will not bring the world any nearer to
perfection. The high-minded would say that the removal of this
form of relaxation would free the energies of the literate for the
contemplation of real mysteries and the overcoming of real evils.
I see no reason to count on that.

Erik Routley, 'The Case against the Detective Story'

Despite prognostications that the detective story, particularly in its classical form, is already outworn and doomed to die, it remains obstinately alive, and it is perhaps not surprising that during the decades since the Golden Age those critics not susceptible to its attractions have been vocal in their disparagement, complaining that the educated readers to whom detective fiction appeals – they include some illustrious names – should know better. Some of this aversion has been from readers who dislike detective fiction as others might dislike science fiction, romantic novels or stories in which the protagonist is a child. The field of fiction is rich and remarkably wide and we all have our favourite pastures.

One critic who was impervious to the charms of the genre was Edmund Wilson, who in 1945 published an influential essay entitled 'Who Cares Who Killed Roger Ackroyd?' As Mr Wilson had constantly been exposed to animated discussions on the merits of mystery writers, he enquired of aficionados what author they recommended him to try, and set out conscientiously to justify or modify his prejudice. His correspondents were almost unanimous in recommending Dorothy L. Sayers and placing her novel *The Nine Tailors* at the top of their reading list. After skipping what he described as 'conversations between conventional English village characters', 'boring information on campanology', and 'the awful whimsical patter of Lord Peter', he reached the conclusion that *The Nine Tailors* was one of the dullest books he had encountered in any field. No doubt, thus filleted, it was.

Mr Wilson and others of his ilk are certainly entitled to their preferences and no efforts on the part of their friends are likely to change their minds. And much criticism still relates primarily to the Golden Age: the old argument that the story dominates over any interest in characterisation or setting and is frequently unconvincing; that the basic morality of the genre is strongly right-wing, upholding the right of the privileged against the dispossessed, in which working-class characters are little better than caricatures; and that detective fiction, so far from showing compassion either to victim or murderer, glories in a crude form of communal vengeance. In general these criticisms are so inappropriate to the majority of detective stories being written today that there is little point in refuting them. But a more interesting criticism made during the thirties still echoes in the minds of twenty-first-century critics. Its chief proponent was an influential American critic, Professor Jacques Barzun, who enjoyed detective stories but only those which, like the books of Agatha Christie, confined themselves to the pure puzzle. For him and those who agreed with him, the conventional mystery which relied on logical deduction, and in which the characters solved the plots from observed facts, had an intellectual and literary integrity which was lost if writers attempted to wade through the murky pools of abnormal psychology or to probe the psychological basis of their characters' actions and personalities. In short, these critics feared that the detective story might be getting above itself.

Somewhat surprisingly, Dorothy L. Sayers, who in *Gaudy Night* made theme and characterisation dominant over the plot, went some way to justify this view in her essay 'Aristotle on Detective Fiction', published in 1946, taking the great philosopher as her authority.

> One may string together a series of characteristic speeches of the utmost finish as regards diction and thought, and yet fail to produce the true dramatic effect; but one will have much better success with a story which, however inferior in these respects, has a plot.... The first essential, the life and soul so to speak of the detective story, is the plot and the characters come second.

Very few detective novelists would hold this view today, or hold it so uncompromisingly. Their aim – and it is mine – is

133

to write a good novel with the virtues those words imply, a novel which is at the same time a credible and satisfying mystery. This means that there must be a creative and reconciling correlation between plot, characterisation, setting and theme, and so far from the plot being dominant, it should arise naturally from the characters and the place.

Another ethical criticism of the detective story is that it has at its heart an appalling crime and the suffering of innocent people, and uses them to provide popular entertainment. In Sayers's novel *Gaudy Night*, Miss Barton, one of the Shrewsbury College tutors, challenges Harriet Vane about the morality of the books she writes. Surely the sufferings of innocent suspects ought to be taken seriously? To this Harriet replies that she does indeed take them seriously in real life, as must everyone. But was Miss Barton saying that anyone who had tragic experience of sex, for example, should never write an artificial drawing-room comedy? Although there was no comic side to murder, there could be a purely intellectual side to the detection. I myself would argue that it is possible to deal with the intellectual side of the detection while portraying with compassion and realism the emotional trauma of all the characters touched by this ultimate crime, whether as suspect, innocent bystander or indeed the perpetrator. In an Agatha Christie novel the crime is solved, the murderer arrested or dead, and the village returned to its customary calm and order. This does not happen in real life. Murder is a contaminating crime and no life which comes into close touch with it remains unaltered. The detective story is the novel of reason and justice, but it can affirm only the fallible justice of human beings, and the truth it celebrates can never be the whole truth any more than it is in a court of law.

The rarely heard objection to the detective novel that it might provide a real-life murderer with an idea or even a pattern for his crime surely need not be taken seriously. It has – although I think seldom – been used as a defence in real life, but hardly a valid or successful one. Apart from the fact that fictional murder is usually both more complicated and ingenious than murder in real life, it hardly provides a reliable model since the murderer is always found out. But the suggestion that detective fiction might influence those tempted to murder does raise a more interesting philosophical and moral question. Does every novelist have a moral responsibility for the possible effect of what he writes, and if so, what is this morality from which his responsibility derives? Are we not implying that there is an immutable value system, an accepted view of the universe, of our place in it, and a recognised standard of morality to which all right-minded people conform? Even if this were true – and, in our increasingly fragmented society, manifestly it is not – is it the business of the creative artist in any medium to express or promote it? And does it matter? I know that there are events about which I would find it repugnant to write, for example the torture of a child. But how far any writer, even of popular fiction, has a duty to do more than the best of which he is capable within the law, is a question which is likely to concern more than detective novelists increasingly in our secular and morally confused age.

One of the criticisms still levelled at the detective story of the Golden Age is frequently voiced in the clever phrase 'snobbery with violence', although when one considers

Agatha Christie and her ilk, snobbery with a little local unpleasantness would be closer to the truth. The violence is necessarily there but it is so muted that it is sometimes difficult, reading an Agatha Christie, to remember exactly how the victim died. Parents might well complain if their adolescent son were continually reading Agatha Christie when it was time he turned to the books set for his next examination, but they would be extremely unlikely to complain that he was immured in nothing but horror and violent death. But the allegation of snobbery is reiterated, particularly with regard to the women writers of the 1930s, and what I think many people forget is that those writers were producing for an age in which social divisions were clearly understood and generally accepted since they seemed an immutable part of the natural order. And we have to remember that the detective novelists of the thirties had been bred to a standard of ethics and manners in public and private life which today might well be seen as elitist. Even so, Dorothy L. Sayers in her fiction can be seen as something of an intellectual snob, Ngaio Marsh as a social snob and Josephine Tey as a class snob in her characters' attitudes to their servants, and there are risible passages which are difficult to read without embarrassment, including the unfortunate tendency of Ngaio Marsh's suspects to say what a comfort it is to be interrogated by a gent. I wonder what they would have made of the Continental Op.

This acceptance of class distinction was not confined to novelists. I have a number of volumes of the successful plays of the thirties, and almost without exception dramatists were writing for the middle class, about the middle class and were themselves middle class. This was, of course, decades before, on 8 May 1956, the English Stage Company produced John Osborne's iconoclastic play *Look Back in Anger*. Servants do appear in the interwar plays, but usually to provide what is seen as the necessary comic relief. Popular literature, whether detective stories or not, accepted the same division. Today the gap is between those who have wealth and celebrity – whether achieved through natural talent or, more commonly, as artefacts of the media – and those who have not. It is ostentatious wealth that bestows distinction and privilege. Although this new division has its disagreeable aspect, perhaps it is a fairer system since everyone can hope, however unreasonably, to win the lottery and move into the charmed circle of unlimited consumption and media attention, whereas distinction by breeding is immutably fixed at birth and intellectual ability in all classes largely the result of inherited intelligence which in the more fortunate can be fostered by good education. Snobbery is always with us; it merely embodies different prejudices and is directed at different victims. But I would expect even the most assiduous class warrior to welcome a form of popular literature which confirms the universal truth that jealousy, hatred and revenge can find a place in every human heart. In detective fiction the successful middle-class character is more often than not the murderer, and some would say with much less excuse than have the unfortunate and deprived. In general, the butler didn't do it.

The resilience of detective fiction, and particularly the fact that so many distinguished and powerful people are apparently under its spell, has puzzled both its admirers and its detractors and spawned a number of notable critical studies which attempt to explain this puzzling phenomenon. In 'The Guilty Vicarage' W.H. Auden wrote that his reading of detective stories was an addiction, the symptoms being the intensity of his craving, the specificity of the story, which, for him, had to be set in rural England, and last, its immediacy. He forgot the story as soon as he had finished the book and had no wish to read it again. Should he begin a detective story and then discover it was one he had already read, he was unable to continue. In all this the distinguished poet differed from me and, I suspect, from many other lovers of the genre. I enjoy rereading my favourite mysteries although I know full well how the book will end, and although I can understand the attraction of a rural setting, I am frequently happy to venture with my favourite detectives onto unfamiliar territory.

Auden states that the most curious fact about the detective story is that it appeals precisely to people who are immune to other forms of what he describes as daydream literature. He suspects that the typical reader of detective stories is, like himself, a person who suffers from a sense of sin, by which he is not implying that mysteries are read solely by law-abiding citizens so that they may gratify vicariously the impulse to violence. The fantasy which the mystery provides is one of escape to a prelapsarian state of innocence and the driving force behind the daydream is the discomfort of an unrecognised guilt. Since a sense of guilt seems natural to humanity, Auden's theory is not unreasonable and some critics have suggested that it explains the otherwise curious fact that the detective story had its beginning and flourishes best in Protestant countries where the majority of people don't resort to confession to a priest in order to receive absolution. It would be interesting to test this theory, but I hardly feel that an approach to the Archbishop of Canterbury and the Cardinal Archbishop of Westminster suggesting that their priests should take an exit poll after Sunday morning services would be sympathetically received. But certainly a sense of guilt, however ungrounded, seems inseparable from our Judeo-Christian inheritance, and few people opening their door to two grave-faced detectives with a request that they should accompany them to the police station would do so without a qualm of unease, however certain they may be of their complete innocence.

Other critics, particularly it seems in the USA and Germany, have attempted to explain addiction to the genre in Freudian terms. Apparently we mystery fans are innocent in the eyes of the criminal law but are burdened with 'an unconscious hysteric-passive tension', stemming in men from the 'negative' Oedipus complex, in women from the 'positive' Oedipus, and can obtain from detective stories temporary and vicarious release of tension. I suppose we must be grateful that, despite the complications of our psyche, we are law-abiding citizens who do no harm to others.

For those of us uneducated in the recesses of abnormal psychology, the attractions of the detective story are more obvious. Firstly, there is, of course, the story.

> Yes – oh dear yes – the novel tells a story. That is the fundamental aspect without which it could not exist.... We are all like Scheherazade's husband in that we want to know what happens next. That is universal and that is why the backbone of a novel

has to be a story.... Qua story, it can have only one
merit: that of making the audience want to know
what happens next. And conversely it can only have
one fault: that of making the audience not want to
know what happens next. These are the only two
criticisms that can be made on the story that is a
story. It is both the lowest and simplest of literary
organisms. Yet it is the highest factor common to
all the very complicated organisms known as novels.
(E.M. Forster, *Aspects of the Novel*)

Certainly all the major novelists in the canon of English
literature have told stories, some exciting, some tragic, some
slight, some mysterious, but all of them have the virtue of
leaving us with a need to know what happens next as we
turn each page. For a time in the late twentieth century it
seemed that the story was losing its status and that psychological analysis, a complicated and occasionally inaccessible
style and an egotistic introspection were taking over from
action. Happily there now seems to be a return to the art
of storytelling. But this, of course, the detective novel has
never lost. We are presented with a mystery at the heart of
the novel and we know that by the end it will be solved.
Very few readers can put down a detective story until it is
solved, although some have fallen into the reprehensible
expedient of taking a quick look at the last chapter.

Part of the attraction of the story is this satisfaction in
solving the mystery. The importance of this differs with the
individual reader. Some follow the clues assiduously and
at the end feel the same small triumph that they do after
a successful game of chess. Others find more interest in

the characterisation, the setting, the writing or the theme. Certainly if the mystery were dominant no one would wish to reread old favourites and many of us find that, reading in bed, the comfort and reassurance of a beloved mystery is the pleasantest prelude to falling asleep. And without wading too deeply into the pools of psychological analysis, there can be no doubt that the detective story produces a reassuring relief from the tensions and responsibilities of daily life; it is particularly popular in times of unrest, anxiety and uncertainty, when society can be faced with problems which no money, political theories or good intentions seem able to solve or alleviate. And here in the detective story we have a problem at the heart of the novel, and one which is solved, not by luck or divine intervention, but by human ingenuity, human intelligence and human courage. It confirms our hope that, despite some evidence to the contrary, we live in a beneficent and moral universe in which problems can be solved by rational means and peace and order restored from communal or personal disruption and chaos. And if it is true, as the evidence suggests, that the detective story flourishes best in the most difficult of times, we may well be at the beginning of a new Golden Age.

"Did Esme Draycott really go to her lover that night? Is Selwyn Plunkett dead or alive and well in Peru? Was Melanie Frayle asleep or drugged? Who was the man in the green Lagonda? Stay with us for Part Two, after the break."

– 8 –

Today and a Glimpse
of Tomorrow

*The detective novel ... is aimed above all at the intelligence; and
this could constitute for it a title to nobility. It is in any case
perhaps one of the reasons for the favour it enjoys. A good detective
story possesses certain qualities of harmony, internal organisation
and balance, which respond to certain needs of the spirit, needs
which some modern literature, priding itself on being superior,
very often neglects.*

Régis Messac, Le 'detective novel' et l'influence de la pensée scientifique (1929)

The classical detective story is the most paradoxical of the popular literary forms. The story has at its heart the crime of murder, often in its most horrific and violent form, yet we read the novels primarily for entertainment, a comforting, even cosy relief from the anxieties problems and irritations of everyday life. Its prime concern – indeed its *raison d'être* – is the establishment of truth, yet it employs and glories in deceit: the murderer attempts to deceive the detective; the writer sets out to deceive the reader, to make him believe that the guilty are innocent, the innocent guilty; and the better the deception the more effective the book. The detective story is concerned with great absolutes – death, retribution, punishment – yet in its clue-making it employs as the instruments of that justice the trivial artefacts and incidents of everyday life. It affirms the primacy of established law and order, yet its attitude to the police and the agencies of that law has often been ambiguous, the brilliance of the amateur detective contrasted with dull official orthodoxy and unimaginative incompetence. The detective story deals with the most dramatic and tragic manifestations of man's nature and the ultimate disruption of murder, yet the form itself is orderly, controlled, formulaic, providing a secure structure within which the imaginations of writer and reader alike can confront the unthinkable.

This paradox, true of the books of the Golden Age, remains true today, although perhaps to a lesser extent. But the detective story has changed since, as a teenager, I saved my pocket-money to buy the new book by Dorothy L. Sayers or Margery Allingham. It could hardly be otherwise. That was over seventy years ago, decades which have seen the Second World War, the atomic bomb, major advances in science and technology which have outstripped our ability to control them, great movements of a world population which threatens our resources of food and water, international terrorism and a planet at risk of becoming uninhabitable. Beside these momentous changes, no human activity, even popular art in any medium, can remain unaffected.

The way in which the typescript is physically produced has also changed dramatically. My secretary, Joyce McLennan, has been typing my novels for thirty-three years and recently we have been reminiscing about those early days when she used a manual typewriter, worked at home because she had young children, and I dictated onto a tape which her husband collected on his way home from work. She reminds me that since I also was working, the tape was often concealed in a large china pig hidden by the side gate. We then advanced to an electric typewriter, and then to a word processor, which seemed the acme of scientific progress. I still like to write by hand, but now I dictate each chapter to Joyce, who puts it onto the computer, printing it out in sections for me to revise. Finally it is sent simultaneously to my publisher, agent and editor through cyberspace, a system which I can neither operate nor understand. Many of my friends – perhaps the majority – have for years produced their books directly on the computer, but no machine made by man is user-friendly to me.

Publishing methods have also changed. New technology means that books can now be produced very quickly to meet demand. Small independent booksellers are finding it more and more difficult to compete with Internet selling. The advent and increasing popularity of the e-book has brought a dramatic change. For those of us who love books – the smell of the paper, the design, the print and the type, the feel of the book as we take it down from the shelf – reading by machine seems an odd preference. But if we accept that what is important is the text, not the means by which it comes to the reader's eyes and brain, it is easier to understand the popularity of this new resource, particularly for a generation which has become accustomed to technology from childhood. But how far, if at all, these changes will actually affect the variety and type of fiction produced remains to be seen.

What is surprising is not that the detective story has altered but that it has survived, and that what we have seen since the interwar years has been a development, not a rejection, followed by renewal. Crime fiction today is more realistic in its treatment of murder, more aware of scientific advances in the detection of crime, more sensitive to the environment in which it is set, more sexually explicit and closer than it has ever been to mainstream fiction. The difference between the crime novel in all its variety and detective fiction has become increasingly fudged, but there still remains a clear division between the generality of crime novels and the conventional detective story, even at its most exciting, which continues to be concerned with each individual death and the solving of the mystery through patient intelligence rather than physical violence and prowess.

I find it interesting that the detective hero, originated by Conan Doyle, has survived and is still at the heart of the story, like a secular priest expert in the extraction of confession, whose final revelation of the truth confers a vicarious absolution on all but the guilty. But, not surprisingly, he has changed. Because of the growing importance of realism for writers and readers, in part arising from the comparative reality of television series, the professional detective has largely taken over from the amateur. What we have are realistic portrayals of human beings undertaking a difficult, sometimes dangerous, and often disagreeable job, beset with the anxieties common to humanity: professional jealousies, uncooperative colleagues, the burden of bureaucracy and difficulties with wives or children. An example of the successful professional detective at peace with his job is Ruth Rendell's Inspector Reginald Wexford, who, so far from being a disillusioned maverick, is a hard-working, conscientious, liberal-minded police officer, happily married to Dora, who provides for him that stable background which helps to buttress him against the worst traumas of his daily work.

And policing itself has changed dramatically. In the Golden Age, police forces were not yet integrated into the forty-two large forces of today, and major cities and their county were separately policed. This gave opportunities for productive rivalry as each strove to be the more efficient, but the separation was economically expensive and could cause difficulties in co-operation and communication. Chief constables, so far from coming up through the ranks, were usually retired colonels or brigadiers, experienced in leading men and promoting loyalty to a common purpose but occasionally over-authoritative, and representative of only one class. But they were able to know individual officers and were known by them, and both they and the policemen on the beat were familiar and reassuring figures to the much smaller and homogenous community they served. The job of policing our multicultural, overcrowded island and its stressed democracy is fundamentally different from the job in, for example, the twenties and thirties. I remember as an eight-year-old being told by my father that if ever I were alone and afraid or in difficulties I should find a policeman. Police officers are as ready to help a child in distress now as they were then, but I wonder how many parents in the more deprived inner-city areas would give that advice today. The crime novelist today needs to understand something of the ethos, ramifications and problems of this rapidly changing world, particularly if his detective is a police officer.

The Watson in the form of a sidekick, created to be less intelligent than the hero and to ask questions which

147

the average reader might wish to put, has long since bowed out and, on the whole, to general relief. But the detective, whether professional or amateur, does need some character in whom he can rationally confide if the reader is to be provided with enough information to be engaged in the solution. For a professional detective it is usually the detective-sergeant, whose background and personality provide a contrast to that of the hero and an ongoing relationship which is not always easy. The reader becomes involved in the sergeant's different domestic background and different view of the job itself. Notable examples are Colin Dexter's Morse and Lewis, Reginald Hill's Dalziel and Pascoe, Ruth Rendell's Wexford and Burden, and Ian Rankin's Rebus and Siobhan Clarke, where we have the added advantage of a woman's point of view. In the hands of such masters of the detective story they are subordinate to their boss in rank but not in importance. It is not surprising that Morse has been successfully replaced by Lewis, who has grown in authority since his promotion and now has a very different, more intellectual subordinate of his own, Sergeant Hathaway, to fulfil the function that was previously his.

A.A. Milne had a passion for detective stories, although he didn't persist in writing them, and is best known for *The Red House Mystery*, first published in 1922. In a reissue of the novel in 1926, he wrote an entertaining introduction in which he addressed the issue of the Watson.

Are we to have a Watson? We are. Death to the author who keeps his unravelling for the last chapter, making all the other chapters but prologue to a five-

minute drama. This is no way to write a story. Let us
know from chapter to chapter what the detective is
thinking. For this he must watsonize or soliloquize;
the one is merely a dialogue form of the other, and,
by that, more readable. A Watson, then, but not of
necessity a fool of a Watson. A little slow, let him be,
as so many of us are, but friendly, human, likeable...

'Friendly, human, likeable', an accurate description of the
detective-sergeant Watsons of today, and long may they
flourish.

Writers of the Golden Age, and indeed for some decades after, were little concerned with forensic or scientific
research. The present system of forensic science laborato-
ries was not yet in prospect and few of the victims were
subjected to an autopsy, or if they were, this unpleasant
procedure was seldom mentioned. Occasionally a post-
mortem was undertaken by the local general practitioner
who within hours was able to inform the detective from
exactly which poison the victim died, a feat which would
occupy a modern laboratory for some weeks.

The discovery of DNA is only one, but among the most
important, of the scientific and technological discoveries
which have revolutionised the investigation of crime.
These include advanced systems of communication, the
scientific analysis of trace elements, greater definition in the
analysis of blood, increasingly sophisticated cameras which
can identify bloodstains among multi-stained coloured
surfaces, laser techniques which can raise fingerprints from
skin and other surfaces which previously offered no hope
of a successful print, and medical advances which affect the

work of forensic pathologists. Modern writers of detective fiction need to be methodical in their research and the results integrated into the narrative, but not so intrusively that the reader is aware of the trouble taken and feels that he is being subjected to a brief lesson in forensic science. Some novelists manage so well without the inclusion of this scientific knowledge that the reader doesn't feel the lack of it. I can remember only one instance in which Morse mentions a forensic science laboratory but, reading the books or watching the televised adaptations, we never for a moment suppose that the Thames Valley Constabulary is bereft of this necessary resource.

I like to do my own research, as do most detective novelists, and am grateful for the help I have received over the years both from the Metropolitan Police and from the scientists at the Lambeth Laboratory. But there have been mistakes. These usually arise, not from facts about which I am ignorant, but from those which I fondly and mistakenly imagine I already know. In one of my early novels I described a motorcyclist, disguised by his oilskins and goggles, 'reversing noisily down the lane'. This led to a letter from a male reader complaining that, although I was usually meticulous in my choice of words, the sentence gave the impression that I thought that a two-stroke motorcycle could go backwards. So indeed I did. This mistake proved expensive, leading over the years to much correspondence, invariably from male readers, sometimes explaining in minute detail and occasionally with the aid of a diagram precisely why I was wrong. Salvation came some years ago in the form of a message on a postcard which said simply, 'That motorbike – it can if it's a Harley Davidson.'

The search for a new location and fresh ideas continues. Despite the reasonable view of some critics that the detective story can't exist until a society has developed an institutional system of law enforcement, a number of writers have with success looked to the past for inspiration. Private murder, as opposed to mass killing by the state, has been regarded as the unique crime in almost every society however primitive, an abomination to be avenged, if not by a legal system, by the family involving the further shedding of blood, by banishment or public dishonour. The classical detective story can work in any age provided murder is regarded as an act which necessitates the discovery of the perpetrator and the cleansing of society of its stain. Writers who have returned to Victorian England include Peter Lovesey, with Sergeant Cribb and Constable Thackeray, and Anne Perry, whose novels feature Police Inspector Thomas Pitt and his wife Charlotte, who assists him. Ellis Peters has written twenty novels which feature Brother Cadfael, a twelfth-century Benedictine monk, while Lindsey Davis goes back even further with her detective, Marcus Didius Falco, a private eye in ancient Rome. A notable comparative newcomer to the historical mystery is C.J. Sansom, who has become one of the most popular and accomplished crime writers. His novels are set in Tudor England, an age as dangerous as our own, particularly for those in the orbit of the formidable Henry VIII. His hero is a hunchback lawyer, Matthew Shardlake, sensitive, liberal, highly intelligent, whose life and the age of which he is part become so real that the sights, the voices, the very smell of Tudor England seem to rise from the page. The historical detective story is one of the most difficult to write well, requiring sensitive identification with the past, the ability to bring it vividly to life and meticulous research, but in expert hands it shows no sign of losing its popularity.

From the beginning, film and crime writing have enjoyed a sustaining and lucrative partnership in crime, but never more so than today. Some of the earliest films were taken from crime stories and any list of the most memorable and successful ever made will include crime movies. In general producers have opted for the fast-action thriller with its dominant testosterone-fuelled hero and its opportunities for spectacular action sequences, stunts and a far-ranging variety of locations which modern cameramen can exploit in pictures of breathtaking natural scenery or the cluttered danger and excitement of the great cities of the world. Alfred Hitchcock, who found his inspiration in murder and mayhem, explained in a television interview the problem of filming the classical detective story. He wanted his audience to be in thrall to suspense and horror; in a detective story they were more likely to be exercising their brains in deciding who would prove to be guilty. In the end this would be revealed, and in an anticlimax rather than a final shudder. The exceptions to this dominance of the thriller in films and television are, of course, the ubiquitous Holmes and Poirot. Holmes first appeared in 1903 in an extraordinarily short silent film, *Sherlock Holmes Baffled*, and later there was a series of his adventures in two-reelers made in Denmark from 1908 to 1911. Poirot first appeared in 1931, five years after *The Murder of Roger Ackroyd* was published. It was filmed in England, and thereafter every few years Agatha Christie's iconic character has appeared in film and television played by a variety of actors, one of the most famous films being *Murder on the Orient Express* in 1974, with its international all-star cast, a story which, despite having so many improbabilities as suspects, remains a masterpiece of its type.

The classical detective story appears on television chiefly as a serial which exploits the existing popularity in print of the detective, of which Colin Dexter's Inspector Morse is probably the best known. Films and television series which, while generally adhering to the classical form of the detective story, combine clues with action are the highly successful police procedurals. The police service has provided material for film and television for decades and there has been a remarkable transition from the avuncular goodnight salute of Dixon of Dock Green, both in the film *The Blue Lamp* and on television, through the greater realism of *Z-Cars*, *Softly-Softly*, *The Sweeney* to *Law and Order*. In *Prime Suspect*, written by Lynda La Plante, we are taken into the disturbing search for a psychopathic killer; the heroine, Jane Tennison, is at once an effective senior detective and a vulnerable woman coping with the cost to her emotional life of this dangerous and still predominantly masculine world. Undoubtedly the importance of film and television will increase now that DVDs enable the best to be viewed at home. But how far the demands of film and television will influence the writing of crime fiction, including the detective story, is less easy to assess.

The crime novel, including the detective story, is now international, the most distinguished both in English and foreign languages being best-sellers throughout the world, and undoubtedly the translation of detective stories into English will continue. A catalogue I picked up in a

153

Cambridge bookshop named 730 recent and forthcoming crime novels, many of which are detective stories, and what to me is new and interesting is the number of translations. The majority are from the Swedish, but France, Poland, Italy, Russia, Iceland and Japan are represented. I can't imagine a catalogue in my youth featuring so many crime books in such variety or with so many translations from writers worldwide. The Swedish writer Henning Mankell is likely to become increasingly popular since his detective Kurt Wallander has recently successfully appeared on British television, the hero played by Kenneth Branagh. The list confirms my impression that although private sleuths still appear and in great variety, there is a growing preference among writers for a professional detective. But are we in danger of reducing the fictional police officer to a stereotype – solitary, divorced, hard-drinking, psychologically flawed and disillusioned? Real-life senior detectives are not stereotypes. Would anyone, I wonder, create a fictional detective who enjoys his work, gets on well with his colleagues, is happily married, has a couple of attractive well-behaved children who cause him no trouble, reads the lesson in his parish church and spends his few free hours playing the cello in an amateur string quartet? I doubt whether readers would find him wholly credible, but he would certainly be an original.

Among foreign detective writers, Georges Simenon, one of the most highly regarded and influential of twentieth-century crime novelists, has been available in English for decades. We look to Simenon for a strong narrative, a setting which is brilliantly and sensitively evoked, a cast in which every character, however minor, is uniquely alive, psychological acuity and an empathy with the secret lives of apparently ordinary men and women in a style which combines economy of words with strength and elegance, and which has given him a literary reputation rare among crime novelists. Inevitably, despite the apparent simplicity of style, he is a novelist who loses much in translation, but he still exerts an influence over the modern detective story.

I was interested also in a number of Golden Age writers who are reappearing in print, published largely by small independent houses. These include such popular stalwarts as Gladys Mitchell, Nicholas Blake, H.C. Bailey and John Dickson Carr, master of the locked-room mystery. It is highly unlikely that these emotionally unthreatening and nostalgic detective stories would be written today except as ingenious and clever pastiche or as tributes to the Golden Age. How strongly the typical mysteries of the interwar years linger in memory; invariably set in large country houses in the depths of winter, cut off from the outside world by snowdrifts and fallen telegraph wires and with a most unpleasant house guest found in the library with an ornate dagger in the heart. How fortunate that the world's greatest detective should have run his coupé into a snowdrift and taken refuge in Mayhem Manor. But does the success of a pastiche or the reissue of old favourites mean that readers for whom the detective story is primarily entertainment will begin to turn from the gritty realities of today in search of remembered satisfactions? This seems to me unlikely. I see the detective story becoming more firmly rooted in the reality and the uncertainties of the twenty-first century, while still providing that central certainty that even the most intractable problems will in the end be subject to reason.

Whether we live in a more violent age than did, for example, the Victorians is a question for statisticians and sociologists, but we certainly feel more threatened by crime and disorder than at any other time I remember in my long life. This constant awareness of the dark undercurrents of society and of human personality is probably partly due to the modern media, when details of the most atrocious murders, of civil strife and violent protests, come daily into our living rooms from television screens and other forms of modern technology. Increasingly writers of crime novels and detective stories will reflect this tumultuous world in their work and deal with it with far greater realism than would have been possible in the Golden Age. The solving of the mystery is still at the heart of a detective story but today it is no longer isolated from contemporary society. We know that the police are not invariably more virtuous and honest than the society from which they are recruited, and that corruption can stalk the corridors of power and lie at the very heart of government and the criminal justice system.

Today there is undoubtedly an increased interest in detective fiction. New novels are being reviewed with respect, many of them by names unfamiliar to me. It is apparent that publishers and readers are continuing to look for well-written mysteries which afford the expected satisfaction of a credible plot but can legitimately be enjoyed as serious novels. A number of novelists have successfully moved between detective fiction, non-fiction and mainstream novels, Frances Fyfield, Ruth Rendell writing as Barbara Vine, Susan

Hill, Joan Smith, John Banville and Kate Atkinson being examples. Although I have mentioned the names of crime writers, alive and dead, to illustrate my text, I have neither the wish nor the competence to undertake the function of a reviewer. All lovers of detective fiction will have their favourites. But the variety and quality of detective fiction being produced today, both by established writers and by newcomers, will ensure that the future of the genre is in safe hands.

Our planet has always been a dangerous, violent and mysterious habitation for humankind and we all are adept at creating those pleasures and comforts, large and small, sometimes dangerous and destructive, which offer at least temporary relief from the inevitable tensions and anxieties of contemporary life. A love of detective fiction is certainly among the least harmful. We do not expect popular literature to be great literature, but fiction which provides excitement, mystery and humour also ministers to essential human needs. We can honour and celebrate the genius which produced *Middlemarch*, *War and Peace* and *Ulysses* without devaluing *Treasure Island*, *The Moonstone* and *The Inimitable Jeeves*. The detective story at its best can stand in such company and its popularity suggests that in the twenty-first century, as in the past, many of us will continue to turn for relief, entertainment and mild intellectual challenge to these unpretentious celebrations of reason and order in our increasingly complex and disorderly world.

Bibliography and Suggested Reading

Barnard, Robert. *A Talent to Deceive: An Appreciation of Agatha Christie*. Collins, London, 1980.

Booth, Martin. *The Doctor, the Detective and Arthur Conan Doyle*. Hodder & Stoughton, London, 1997.

Craig, Patricia, and Mary Cadogan. *The Lady Investigates: Women Detectives and Spies in Fiction*. Victor Gollancz, London, 1981.

Keating, H.R.F., ed. *Crime Writers: Reflection on Crime Fiction*. BBC, London, 1978.

Lewis, Margaret. *Ngaio Marsh: A Life*. Chatto & Windus, London 1991; The Hogarth Press, London, 1992.

Morgan, Janet. *Agatha Christie: A Biography*. Collins, London, 1984.

Most, Glenn W., and William W. Stowe, eds. *The Poetics of Murder: Detective Fiction and Literary Theory*. Harcourt Brace Jovanovich, San Diego, 1983.

Penzler, Otto, ed. *The Great Detectives*. Little, Brown, Boston and Toronto, 1978.

Reynolds, Barbara. *Dorothy L. Sayers: Her Life and Soul*. Hodder & Stoughton, London, 1993.

Reynolds, Barbara, ed. *The Letters of Dorothy L. Sayers 1899–1936: The Making of a Detective Novelist*. Hodder & Stoughton, London, 1995.

Stewart, R. F. *And Always a Detective: Chapters on the History of Detective Fiction*. David & Charles, Newton Abbot, 1980.

Symons, Julian. *Bloody Murder*. Faber & Faber, London, 1972; Viking, 1985; Warner Books, 1992.

Summerscale, Kate. *The Suspicions of Mr Whicher or The Murder at Road Hill House*. Bloomsbury, London, 2008.

Thompson, Laura. *Agatha Christie: An English Mystery*. Headline Review, London, 2007.

Thorogood, Julia. *Margery Allingham: A Biography*. William Heinemann, London, 1991. Now reissued as Julia Jones, *The Adventures of Margery Allingham*. Golden Duck Publishing, Chelmsford, 2009.

Watson, Colin. *Snobbery with Violence*. Eyre & Spottiswoode, London, 1971; Eyre Methuen, London, 1979, 1987.

Winks, Robin. *Detective Fiction*. Prentice-Hall, New Jersey, 1980.

Part of the proceeds from this paperback edition is being donated to the Bodleian Library

Bodleian Library
UNIVERSITY OF OXFORD

Founded in 1602 by Sir Thomas Bodley, who made it his mission to serve the 'Republic of Letters', the Bodleian Library is home to over 9 million volumes and a large number of manuscripts and rare books. These include four thirteenth-century Magna Cartae (one quarter of the world's surviving collection), the oldest surviving road map of Britain – The Gough Map – dating from c.1360, and Shakespeare's First Folio, which the Bodleian received in 1623. It is the oldest and largest university library in Britain and the second largest library in the UK. Today, it is a world-renowned destination for scholars across the globe and an essential resource for teaching and research.

The Bodleian Library also serves a broader public through a wide-ranging programme of cultural engagement and outreach. Already in the eighteenth century the Bodleian was providing Britain with the first publicly accessible picture gallery (in the upper floor of the Old Library). Today, over a million items have been digitized, providing unlimited access to researchers anywhere in the world. The Bodleian also provides wider access to its collections by hosting regular exhibitions of its treasures and through its robust publishing programme which brings the riches of the Library to readers worldwide.

The Bodleian is currently undergoing a period of substantial modernization and change, with an ambitious building and refurbishment programme to secure its heritage collections for future generations.

P.D. James has written this book for the Library.
What can you do?
Visit: www.campaign.ox.ac.uk/libraries

Praise for **MR FOX**

'A master of magic realism, Helen Oyeyemi confirms her place as a literary heavyweight with her latest mystical offering . . . The narrative oscillates between St John's everyday life and flirtatious storytelling with Mary, but these whimsical digressions are pertinent enough not to be confusing, and cleverly confirm that this is a man enslaved by his imagination . . . The language is intensely vibrant, and Oyeyemi's characters almost dance on their pages in celebration of the limitless powers of the mind. An outstanding addition to an impressive body of work, this is Oyeyemi's best, most beautiful novel yet.' **Independent on Sunday**

'The dialogue zips along and Oyeyemi reveals a twinkling sense of humour . . . Lovers of metafiction, magic realism and all things fabulist will find Oyeyemi's energetic imagination a delight.' **Independent**

'The fabulous Oyeyemi is playing with us, but it's delightful . . . Helen Oyeyemi handles her extraordinary narrative with wit, charm and an infectious enjoyment' **The Times**

'Funny, deep, shocking, wry, heart-warming and spine-chilling. She offers a phantasmagorical rendering of the deepest emotional truths, not least among which is a razor-sharp dissection of the topsy-turvy logic of misogyny that blames women for the violence inflicted on them. "She's not real, honey," St John assures Daphne about Mary. "She's only an idea. I made her up." Oyeyemi breathes life into ideas like nobody else.' **Guardian**

'Her fiction is sexy, funny and frankly, positively trippy. In a good way.' *GQ*

'Funny and fresh, piercingly astute . . . Oyeyemi's writing contains a kernel of truth and wit. *Mr Fox* is full of luminous moments' ***Daily Telegraph***

'This prodigiously talented writer's take on the Bluebeard myth is a piece of modern magical realism that is not just vibrantly imaginative but filled with wit and wisdom . . . Oyeyemi's remarkable gift for depicting multiple worlds populated with the living, ghosts, of the dead and creatures of the imagination makes *Mr Fox* her best book so far.'

Metro 4*

'Remarkably assured . . . So beautifully done . . . It leaves no doubt about the scale of Oyeyemi's talent' ***Daily Mail***

'Oyeyemi has a sharp wit and isn't afraid to use it. She punctuates the narrative with her protagonist's own gruesome fairy tales, blurring the line between what you suppose is fact and hope to be fiction.' ***Stylist***

'Outside Scotland, my favourite novel this year is Helen Oyeyemi's *Mr Fox*. What an amazing young writer she is – what range, ambition and composure. Ali Smith spotted her talent as a teenager, and she's rightly been championed by many senior writers, but with this fourth novel she hits new heights. I think she's the most interesting female novelist around, dealing with issues of gender in a subtle, powerful way. A lightness of touch but a real depth as well.'

***Herald* Books of the Year**

Mr Fox

Helen Oyeyemi is the author of *The Icarus Girl*,
The Opposite House, and *White is for Witching*, which
won a 2010 Somerset Maugham Award. Her story
'My Daughter the Racist' was shortlisted for the
2010 BBC National Short Story Award.

Also by Helen Oyeyemi

THE ICARUS GIRL

THE OPPOSITE HOUSE

WHITE IS FOR WITCHING

Helen Oyeyemi

MR FOX

PICADOR

First published 2011 in paperback by Picador

This edition published 2012 by Picador
an imprint of Pan Macmillan, a division of Macmillan Publishers Limited
Pan Macmillan, 20 New Wharf Road, London N1 9RR
Basingstoke and Oxford
Associated companies throughout the world
www.panmacmillan.com

ISBN 978-0-330-53469-7

1 3 5 7 9 8 6 4 2

A CIP catalogue record for this book is available from
the British Library.

Printed and bound by CPI Group (UK) Ltd, Croydon CR0 4YY

For my Mr Fox

(whoever you are.)

In the darkness they wondered if they could do it, and knew they had to try to do it.

MARY OLIVER

Mary Foxe came by the other day – the last person on earth I was expecting to see. I'd have tidied up if I'd known she was coming. I'd have combed my hair, I'd have shaved. At least I was wearing a suit; I strive for a sense of professionalism. I was sitting in my study, writing badly, just making words on the page, waiting for something good to come through, some sentence I could keep. It was taking longer that day than it usually did, but I didn't mind. The windows were open. I was sort of listening to something by Glazunov; there's a symphony of his you can't listen to with the windows closed, you just can't. Well I guess you could, but you'd get agitated and run at the walls. Maybe that's just me.

My wife was upstairs. Looking at magazines or painting or something, who knows what Daphne does. Hobbies. The symphony in my study was as loud as it could be, but that was nothing new, and she's never complained about all the noise. She doesn't complain about anything I do; she is physically unable to. That's because I fixed her early. I told her in heartfelt tones that one of the reasons I love her is because she never complains. So now of course she doesn't dare complain.

Anyway, I'd left the study door open and Mary slipped in. Without looking up, I smiled gently and murmured: 'Hello, honey . . .' I thought she was Daphne. I hadn't seen her in a

1

while, and Daphne was the only other person in the house, as far as I was aware. When she didn't answer, I looked up.

Mary Foxe approached my desk with her hand stuck out. She wanted to shake hands. Shake hands! My long-absent muse saunters in for a handshake – I threw my telephone at her. I snatched it off the desk and the socket spat out the wire that connected it to the wall and I hurled the thing. She dodged it neatly. The phone landed on the floor beside my wastepaper can and jangled for a few seconds. I guess it was a half-hearted throw.

'Your temper,' Mary said.

'What's it been – six, seven years?' I asked.

She drew up a chair from a corner of the room, picked up my globe and sat opposite me, spinning oceans around and around on her lap. I watched her and I couldn't think straight. It's the way she moves, the way she looks at you. I guess her English accent helps too.

'Seven years,' she agreed. Then she asked me how I'd been. Real casual, like she already knew how I'd answer.

'Same as always – in love with you, Mary,' I told her. I wished to hell I wouldn't keep telling her that. I don't think it's even true. But whenever she's around I feel as if I should give it a try. I mean, it would be interesting if she believed me.

'Really?' she asked.

'Really. You're the only girl for me.'

'The only girl for you,' she said, and laughed at the ceiling.

'Go ahead and laugh – hurt my feelings . . . what do you care,' I said mournfully, enjoying myself.

'Oh, your *feelings* . . . well. Let's go further in, Mr Fox.

Would you love me if I were your husband and you were my wife?'

'This is dumb.'

'Would you, though?'

'Well, yes, I could see that working out.'

'Would you love me if . . . we were both men?'

'Uh . . . I guess so.'

'If we were both women?'

'Sure.'

'If I were a witch?'

'You're enchanting enough as it is.'

'If you were my mother?'

'No more,' I said. 'I'm crazy about you, okay?'

'Oh, you don't love me,' Mary said. She undid the collar of her dress and bared her neck. 'You love that,' she said. She unbuttoned further and cupped her breasts. She pushed her skirt up past the knees, past the thighs, higher, and we both looked at her smoothness, her softness, her lace frills. 'You love that,' she said.

I nodded.

'This is all you love,' she said, pulling her own hair, slapping her own face. If it wasn't for the serenity in her eyes I would've thought she'd lost her mind. I stood up, to stop her, but the second I did, she stopped of her own accord.

'I don't want you like this. You have to change,' she said.

The symphony ended, and I went to the Victrola and started it up again.

'I have to change? You mean you want to hear me say I love you for your . . .' I allowed myself to smirk, 'soul?'

'It's nothing to do with that. You simply have to change. You're a villain.'

I waited a moment, to see if she was serious, and whether she had anything to add. She was, and she didn't. She stared at me – really came on with the frost, like she hated me. I whistled.

'A villain, you say. Is that so? I'm at church nearly every Sunday, Mary. I slip beggars change. I pay my taxes. And every Christmas I send a check to my mother's favorite charity. Where's the villainy in that? Nowhere, that's where.'

My study door was still open, and I began listening out for my wife. Mary rearranged her clothes so that she looked respectable. There was a brief but heavy silence, which Mary broke by saying: 'You kill women. You're a serial killer. Can you grasp that?'

Of all the—

I hadn't seen that one coming.

She walked up to my desk and picked up one of my notepads, read a few lines to herself. 'Can you tell me why it's necessary for Roberta to saw off a hand and a foot and bleed to death at the church altar?' She flipped through a couple more pages. 'Especially given that this other story ends with Louise falling to the ground riddled with bullets, the mountain rebels having mistaken her for her traitorous brother. And *must* Mrs McGuire hang herself from a door handle because she's so afraid of what Mr McGuire will do when he gets home and finds out that she's burnt dinner? From a door handle? Really, Mr Fox?'

I found myself grinning – the complete opposite of what I wanted my face to do. Scornful and stern, I told my face. Scornful and stern. Not sheepish . . .

'You have no sense of humor, Mary,' I said.

'You're right,' she said. 'I don't.'

4

I tried again: 'It's ridiculous to be so sensitive about the content of fiction. It's not real. I mean, come on. It's all just a lot of games.'

Mary twirled a strand of hair around her finger. 'Oh . . . how does it go . . . we dream, it is good we are dreaming. It would hurt us, were we awake. But since it is playing, kill us. And – we are playing – shriek . . .'

'Couldn't have said it better myself.'

'What would you do for me?' she asked.

I studied her and she seemed perfectly serious. She was making an offer.

'Slay a dragon. Ten dragons. Anything,' I said.

She smiled. 'I'm glad you're playing along. It's a good sign.'

'It is? Okay. By the way, what exactly is it we're talking about?'

'Just be flexible,' she said. I seemed to have accepted some challenge. Only I had no idea what it was.

'I'll keep that in mind. When do we start this thing?'

She drew closer. 'Presently. Scared?'

'Me? No.'

The crazy thing is, I actually did have the jitters, just a little. Suddenly her hand was on my neck. The gesture was tender, which, coming from her, worried me even more. My hand covered hers – I was trying, I think, to get free.

'Ready?' she said. 'Now—'

dr lustucru

Doctor Lustucru's wife was not particularly talkative. But he beheaded her anyway, thinking to himself that he could replace her head when he wished for her to speak.

How long had the Doc been crazy? I don't know. Quite some time, I guess. Don't worry. He was only a general practitioner.

The beheading was done as cleanly as possible, and briskly tidied up. Afterwards Lustucru set both head and body aside in a bare room that the couple had hoped to use as a nursery. Then he went about his daily business as usual.

The Doc's wife had been a good woman, so her body remained intact and she did not give off a smell of decay.

After a week or so old Lustucru got around to thinking that he missed his wife. No one to warm his slippers, etc. In the nursery he replaced his wife's head, but of course it wouldn't stay on just like that. He reached for a suture kit. No need. The body put its hands up and held the head on at the neck. The wife's eyes blinked and the wife's mouth spoke: 'Do you think there will be another war? After the widespread damage of the Great War it is very unlikely. Do you think there will be another war? After the widespread damage of the Great War it is very unlikely. Do you think . . .' And so on.

Disturbed by this, the doctor tried to remove his wife's head again. But the body was having none of it and hung on pretty grimly. What a mess. He was forced to leave her there, locked in the nursery, asking and answering the same question over and over again.

The next night she broke a window and escaped.

Lustucru then understood that he'd been bad to the woman. He lay awake long nights, dreading her return. What got him the most was the idea that her vengeance would be fast, that he would be suddenly dead without a moment in which to understand. With that in mind, he prepared no verbal defences of his behaviour. Eventually his dread reached a peak he could live on. In fact it came to sustain him and it cured him of his craziness, a problem that he had not even known he had. After several months there was no sign of his horror beyond a heartbeat that was slightly faster than normal. His whole life, old Lustucru readied himself to hear from his wife again, to answer to her. But he never did.

'Hey . . . what's going on here?' I asked. We'd changed positions. I was in a chair, sprawled across it, as if I'd fallen. I assumed we were still in my study – I couldn't say for sure because Mary's hands were pressed firmly over my eyelids.

'Mary?'

She didn't answer.

'What's going on?' I asked again.

'I'd rather you didn't look at me just now,' she said.

'Are you all right?'

'What do you think? After what you did, you – you great *oaf*.'

'Are you saying that that was us? Actually us? Me and you? The doctor and his lady wife?'

She was curt. 'Yes, yes. I just need a couple of minutes, if that isn't too much trouble.'

I whistled 'I Can't Get Started' until what she was saying sank in. That's my go-to tune, my haven during many a mindless hour. I experimented with the length of the notes, drawing a couple of bars out here, rushing over a couple of bars there, fast, slow, fast, fast, slow, slow, slow. The tremor in Mary's hands told me she was laughing silently. That was reassuring. I broke off halfway through the third rendition to ask if I could look at her yet.

'No, better not—'

8

She didn't need to tell me it was bad. Put it this way – she was close, right in front of me, but her voice was coming from another direction entirely, from my far left.

'Listen – how did we get – I mean, how did that happen? How did we do that? How is that even possible? For us to do that together?'

'It's all very technical,' she said, haughtily. 'You couldn't possibly understand.'

'Try me.'

'This isn't a good time, I'm afraid.'

I missed her hands when she took them away. 'Don't look – I mean it,' she warned. A moment passed, I heard a clicking sound, and she gave a ragged gasp. I kept my eyes closed.

'Mary – that's just the way the story went. I didn't know that was us. Maybe if you'd explained beforehand—'

'Oh, you knew. Of course you did.' Her voice was thin. 'But never mind. Serves me right for letting you go first. The next move is mine, and I assure you, you're not going to like it.'

be bold, be bold, but not too bold

February 17th, 1936

St John Fox
c/o Astor Press
490 West 58th Street
New York City

Dear Mr Fox,

I read <u>Dr Lustucru</u> with great interest. It really
wasn't bad. In fact I congratulate you on it. Whilst not
expecting a reply I feel compelled to ask why none of
your books contain a photograph of their author. Are
you particularly ugly, particularly shy, or is it simply
that you transcend physical existence?

Best regards,
Mary Foxe
85 East 65th Street, Apartment 11
New York City

June 2nd, 1936

Mary Foxe
85 East 65th Street, Apartment 11
New York City

Dear Mary (you will forgive my familiarity, as it is
potentially less presumptuous than calling you 'Miss'
when you may be a 'Mrs', or 'Mrs' when you may be a
'Miss'),

Thanks for your letter – such courtesies mean a lot to
me.

I'm replying to confirm that I'm astoundingly ugly.
I have been the sorrowful owner of several dogs, each
of whom I named Nestor, each of whom has found my
features exhausting and run away from home.

I have a hunch that you, however, are the complete
opposite. True? I invite you to enclose a photograph of
yourself by return.

Cordially,
S.J. Fox
c/o Astor Press
490 West 58th Street
New York City

July 2nd, 1936

St John Fox
c/o Astor Press
490 West 58th Street
New York City

Mr Fox,

Having reread my initial letter to you, I don't believe it
merited such an insulting reply. If you are so sensitive
about your looks perhaps you ought to refrain from
responding to enquiries about them. And if the short
piece in January 4th's <u>New York Times</u> is correct and
you have indeed recently obtained your third divorce,
isn't it extremely unlikely that dogs would be repelled
by you yet women continually attracted? They say
sarcasm is the lowest form of humour and I agree.

M.F.
85 East 65th Street, Apartment 11
New York City

July 6th, 1936

Mary Foxe
85 East 65th Street, Apartment 11
New York City

M.F.,

How delightfully easily insulted you are, how
unnervingly well-informed. You also appear to be
British ('humour').

As you can see, I have rushed a reply out to you, so
great is my anxiety that your opinion of me has been
lowered. Has it? Say it ain't so.

St John
c/o Astor Press
490 West 58th Street
New York City

PS – your failure to include a photograph with your last
letter has been noted.

July 11th, 1936

St John Fox
c/o Astor Press
490 West 58th Street
New York City

You seem bitter, Mr Fox. Are you having trouble with the next book?

M. Foxe
85 East 65th Street, Apartment 11
New York City

July 16th, 1936

'Mary Foxe'
85 East 65th Street, Apartment 11
New York City

Dear 'Mary Foxe',

Is this your true name? Have we met someplace; are we
acquainted? Have I wronged you in some way?

Be direct. Allow me to make amends,
St John Fox
c/o Astor Press
490 West 58th Street
New York City

July 22nd, 1936

St John Fox
c/o Astor Press
490 West 58th Street
New York City

Dear Mr Fox,

I found your questions asinine.

Yours sincerely,
Mary Foxe
85 East 65th Street, Apartment 11
New York City

July 28th, 1936

Mary Foxe
85 East 65th Street, Apartment 11
New York City

My dear Miss Foxe,

That's quite some vocabulary you've got there. But this
is not the day and age to waste paper, ink and stamps.
What is it that you want from me?

S.J.F.
177 West 77th Street, Apartment 25
New York City

August 2nd, 1936

St John Fox
177 West 77th Street, Apartment 25
New York City

I've written a few stories, and I'd like you to read them.

M.F.
85 East 65th Street, Apartment 11
New York City

August 6th, 1936

Mary Foxe
85 East 65th Street, Apartment 11
New York City

Why me?

S.J.F.
177 West 77th Street, Apartment 25
New York City

September 1st, 1936

St John Fox
177 West 77th Street, Apartment 25
New York City

Mr Fox,
I apologise for the brevity of my previous note, which
was due to a combination of factors: I was surprised by
the frankness of your letter and the fact that you had
included what appears to be your actual home address.
Also I had been having a difficult week but wanted to
reply promptly, so was forced to do so without niceties.
Why you? My answer is unoriginal: I-have-long-been-
an-admirer-of-your-work-and-have-found-it-a-great-
encouragement-whilst-in-the-midst-of-my-amateur-
scribbling-to-imagine-you-reading-what-I-have-written.
There, that's over with. In short, I ask for nothing but
your honest opinion of my stories. I'm aware that even
asking this is an imposition, one that I would certainly
resent if our situations were reversed, therefore I'll take
no offence at your ending this correspondence by dint of
silence and shall remain,

Your interested reader,
Mary Foxe
85 East 65th Street, Apartment 11
New York City

September 10th, 1936

Mary Foxe
85 East 65th Street, Apartment 11
New York City

Little Miss Foxe,

If you'd really been doing your homework you'd know
that I am the last person in the world to consult with
about your writing. It surprises me that you're able to
make reference to the January <u>New York Times</u> piece
about my third divorce without also recalling the
February piece that described me as 'a suffocating
presence across the breakfast table . . . harsh destroyer
of the feminine creative impulse'. Why don't you write
to the author of that piece? I'm sure she has some handy
hints for you.

Sincerely,
S.J. Fox
177 West 77th Street, Apartment 25
New York City

September 13th, 1936

St John Fox
177 West 77th Street, Apartment 25
New York City

Mr Fox,

You are suspicious of me. Don't be. You feel exposed
by recent scrutiny of your private life and you sense
that I am mocking you or preparing the way for some
kind of punchline, that I will send you some satirical
pages about a writer with thirty seven ex-wives, all of
whom hate him and blame him for their own failures.
I find it disappointing that you so transparently view
your every interaction as a narrative. It is cliché, if
you'll forgive my saying so.

I had a birthday in June and became twenty one
years old. No I am not pretty. Not at all pretty, I'm
afraid. Yes I am a Brit, in fact directly related to the
author of <u>Foxe's Book of Martyrs</u> (I am very proud – I
consider Foxe's Martyrs to be the sixteenth century's
best book). I grew up in a rectory, my father is a vicar,
as a child I suspected him of having written the Bible.
I am sole occupant of one medium sized bedroom in a
penthouse apartment not so very far from you; the place
is full of Objects I am afraid I shall accidentally break.
For almost a year now I have been tutor and general
companion – there is not really a name for my job – to a

fourteen year old girl who was asked not to return to school because the majority of her fellow pupils were frightened of her. On weekends the family usually leave town, and that is when I take the opportunity to type what I have written in my notebook. I am not sure what I mean by writing this to you, or how much, if at all, my listing these things will strike you as reassuring, or even interesting. I'm not what you think I am, that's all.

M. Foxe
85 East 65th Street, Apartment 11
New York City

October 17th, 1936

Mary Foxe
85 East 65th Street, Apartment 11
New York City

Dear M.,

Your letters have interested me more than any I've been
sent in a long while, and if you'd still like me to read
your pages I'd be glad to. You must give them to me in
person, though – I only read the work of people I am
personally acquainted with. And before you make a
smart remark, yes, I knew Shakespeare. I really am that
old.

I almost always pass an hour or two at the bar of the
Mercier hotel of a Sunday – not even eavesdropping –
everybody tries too hard to be shocking nowadays – just
drinking. It would be my pleasure if you could join me
there next Sunday. 7pm. No need to write back this
time, just show up, and let's see if we can pick each
other out. If you have your pages in full view I'll
consider you a spoilsport.

Warm regards,
S.J.
177 West 77th Street, Apartment 25
New York City

*

I received that letter on Wednesday morning and opened it at the breakfast table while Mitzi Cole licked grapefruit segments and Katherine Cole sat with her eyes closed, repeating 'split the lark split the lark split the lark split the lark' in what she thought was an English accent. After a few minutes, Mitzi joined in: 'split the lark split the lark split the lark split the lark' but gabbled, her words hastily jammed into the pauses Katherine took to breathe.

Katherine opened her ice-blue eyes to intone: 'And you'll find the music.'

Mitzi poked my wrist with her spoon. 'Anything of note?' she asked.

I shook my head. 'Just a letter from my father.' I hadn't exactly lied – beside my plate there was an envelope addressed in my father's handwriting, but unopened.

The Coles have a musical clock hung on a bracket in their living room; it is lantern-shaped with a circular opening for the clock face. It chimes the hour every hour from seven in the morning to ten at night, and it also plays a snatch of 'Für Elise'. It makes me laugh now to think that 'Für Elise' ever used to send a chill down my spine. Katherine has said several times that the clock offends her sensibilities, but Mr Cole likes it, so it stays. When the family interviewed me in London, the second or third thing Mr Cole told me after shaking my hand was that he had no culture, none at all. Mitzi, tiny, white-blonde and warmly rounded, like a soft diamond, had immediately interjected: 'God bless our Papa Bear; he doesn't need any culture.'

The clock chimed nine just as Katherine turned to her mother and said: 'You know, your elocution is really terrible.'

Mitzi smoothed Katherine's hair and said, 'Why, thank you, my sweet.'

Katherine replied: 'You had grapefruit juice on your hands and now it's in my hair.' She left the table immediately – with purpose more than petulance. Mitzi and I heard the bathroom taps go on and we looked at each other.

'I find it slightly ridiculous that Katy is my child,' Mitzi remarked, and resumed with her grapefruit. She was simultaneously reading the dictionary – (I saw she had just begun the letter 'K') and looking through a Bergdorf Goodman catalogue, choosing clothes for Katherine.

Katherine returned to the table damp-haired. Mitzi tapped a page of the catalogue with her pen and asked, 'Honey, what do you think of this little skirt suit here?'

'It's great, I'll take it,' Katherine said, without looking. Katherine is Mitzi miniaturised, brunette, and wiped entirely clean of conscience. I have the strong feeling that unless Katherine is closely watched she will one day do something terrible to another person, or perhaps even to a large group of people. The key is not to aggravate her, I think.

Mitzi placed a large tick on the catalogue page.

Let's see if we can pick each other out . . .

I looked at the walls as I ate my toast – everything was butter and marmalade. The blondest wood that Mitzi had been able to find, yellow countertops, yellow tablecloth, linoleum of the same colour but in such a shocking hue that I can never quite believe in it and constantly find myself walking or sitting with only my toes on the ground, never my full weight.

Katherine's white silk blouse was wet from her washing,

possibly ruined. I would take it to the dry-cleaner's before our morning walk. Her pine green skirt was cut so simply that I knew it cost the equivalent of at least three months of my wages.

'Better change your blouse, Katherine,' I said. If she heard me, she gave no sign. I took Mr Fox's letter (*If you'd still like me to read your pages I'd be glad to . . .* glad to, he'd be glad to . . .) and the letter from home, took them to my bedroom and tucked them in alongside the others, between the covers of my copy of Foxe's *Martyrs*, a book to which Katherine had shown an aversion, so I knew they'd be safe from her eyes.

Mitzi had switched on the wireless set; a band was swinging Gershwin, trombones loudest. I returned to the kitchen to clear the plates and cups.

'I've been reading some of your poems,' Katherine told her mother. Mitzi went wide-eyed with alarm and said: 'And?'

'They don't make any sense,' Katherine said. 'You know that? I have some questions.' She pulled a square of paper out of her skirt pocket and unfolded it. Mitzi looked to all four corners of the room for help. I turned quickly and ran water over the dishes.

'Oh it's blank,' Mitzi whispered, hoarse with relief. 'Honey, it's blank. What a dirty trick to play on your old ma.'

'April Fool's,' Katherine explained.

'It's October,' Mitzi told her.

Katherine didn't say anything for some time; she seemed to be brooding. No one else said anything either. The band on the radio heaved into another song and I began drying the dishes. I would give Mr Fox just three stories – I already knew which ones. The previous weekend I'd looked at the stories I'd typed, reading them over and over. If Mr Fox doesn't think you're any good, I asked myself, what will you do?

The dishcloth was yellow, too – as I dried each cup I checked my hands for jaundice. Katherine appeared at my side. She had changed into a grey dress. 'Come on, Mary,' she said, handing me my coat. 'Let's go for our walk.'

It had rained overnight, and in the trees it was still raining. Every branch along 65th Street shed leaves on us. The leaves were dark and their moisture made noise. There was a sense that at any time they might bite – they were like bats. The Mercier Hotel was down the block on our way to Central Park. Pigeons stumbled across the white portico that jutted over the doors, and I could distantly hear the bustle, see people moving behind the smoky glass.

We stopped at the dry-cleaner's with Katherine's blouse and a couple of Mr Cole's suits, then I told Katherine about the literature assignment I was setting her: read *The Woman in White* and *The Count of Monte Cristo*, then answer the question 'What is a villain?' I had two copies of each book in my satchel for when she settled down to read at the park. I meant to read along with her, to see if it was possible to catch her thinking. It wasn't the reading itself that would throw Katherine – she read everything. The problem was eliciting a response from her afterwards. If asked for a review she impersonally rehashed every detail of the story. 'Oh, everyone's got a view, haven't they . . . everyone's got something to say,' she'd tell me, when all I wanted to know was whether she'd liked the book or not.

As I'd expected, Katherine wasn't listening to what I was

telling her. She picked leaves off her black beret. 'Say, do you think Ma'll let me bob my hair like yours?'

We crossed at the light, hand in hand.

'Your hair suits you as it is.'

'But I want a bob. Ma says it's quaint because it's so out of style.'

I blushed hard. No point asking whether Mitzi had really said that.

Katherine looked sideways at me. 'Why *do* you bob your hair? Waiting on a flapper revival?'

'I bob my hair because I don't care about trends, only about what suits me, thank you very much for asking,' I said, severely.

Really I bob my hair because I've given up on it. It's so palely coloured that if I pull it back from my face I look bald. My mother used to kiss my cheeks and run her fingers through my hair. She'd hold locks of it up to the light and say: 'Look at that colour, spun gold. You'll be such a beautiful woman . . .'

I always understood that it was a story, like all her other ones, the fairy tales she told. I've taken no harm from its not coming true. I don't expect it to come true.

*

I spent Sunday morning typing fresh copies of the three stories I meant to give Mr Fox. Usually I make plenty of mistakes, and I waste quite a lot of paper that way. But this time mistakes were minimal – adrenalin lent me precision. I played 'Mama Loves Papa' over and over on Katherine's gramophone, which she'd placed in my room before leaving for Long Island with her parents. All three had left wearing starched tennis whites; they planned to take turns playing doubles on their tennis court, to help Mr Cole forget the hassle of his working week. I haven't been to the Long Island house, but I've seen photographs, and I hope the Coles never think to ask me along. Beside the tennis court they have a swimming pool and a topiary maze. Also a cook. What would I do in such a place? Die, I expect. Some Depression the Coles are having.

Mitzi occasionally asks me how I spend my weekends, and I tell her I volunteer at a soup kitchen on Times Square.

When I'd finished typing, I slid the pages into a black folder and put the folder in my satchel. My stomach sprang up my throat and I tried to be sick in the bathroom, but had no such luck. I lay on my bed with *The Count of Monte Cristo*, rereading his astounding escape from the Château d'If. Good for you, Count of Monte Cristo. Your escape is one in the eye for jailers everywhere. I've given up trying to position my bed in such a way that the sky can be seen from the bedroom window – there just isn't any sky in this part of Manhattan. On sunny days clouds are reflected in the plate glass halfway up the tallest buildings, but that's the best this place can do.

It's odd the way I keep to my bedroom even when the apartment is empty, more so when it is empty, actually. I can't explain it – it's not an attachment to the room itself, not anything to do with a sense of security or ownership. Not timidity, not disorientation. Maybe the Coles chose me for this very reason, they looked at me and thought, this girl is no threat to our home, to our cut crystal and heirloom silver, our framed landscapes and lace, oh, our lace. She's English but she's not hoity-toity. She knows her place, she sure does know her place. There's something ghostlike about this girl

... she will appear at certain times and in certain places and at other times she will recede into a disinterested dark. Mary 'Ghost' Foxe.

*

I would be at the bar before he arrived, I decided. To spy him before he spied me. I would sit close to the door with a glass of wine, drinking it slowly with my eyes half-closed. Then, at 7 p.m., I would look up and examine all those gathered around me. It would be like the ending of an Agatha Christie mystery, all possible culprits together in a locked room.

At 7:03 I would stride over to the man whose appearance was the least remarkable and say: 'Mind if I join you, Mr Fox,' without a question mark. We would talk for one hour, I would hand over the stories and be back by 8:10, 8:30 at the latest. The Coles would be home at 9.

I chose to make my entrance at 6:30. His inviting me for 7 made it unlikely he would arrive before 6:30 himself. Unless 7 represented the latter half of the 'hour or two' he passed at the bar, in which case he would be already seated, ice cubes melting into his whisky. None of the characters in any of his stories drink whisky, they drink everything under the sun but that, I've noticed, so whisky is probably a drink Mr Fox reserves for himself. He'd wait until ice and alcohol had merged completely before taking his first sip. Whilst waiting he'd . . . what? Did he really go to the bar of the Mercier hotel alone 'most Sundays', or did he have a drinking buddy named something like Sal, flat-headed sleepy-blinking Sal, a sports journalist whose lethargy concealed an encyclopaedic knowledge of every professional boxing statistic since the sport began? Good old Sal, uncomplicated company. Or perhaps Mr Fox liked to drink with admirers of his books, young newspapermen with rolled-up shirtsleeves, smartly dressed girls who typed rejection letters on behalf of various publishers and literary agencies. He probably liked actresses. He hadn't yet been married to or linked to an actress, only writers, but maybe a Broadway starlet was on the cards, an antidote to his run of bad luck. If I found Mr Fox sitting at the bar with a simpering actress, I wouldn't bother speaking to him, I'd leave immediately.

At ten minutes to six I walked into Katherine's room and opened her wardrobe, which was so tidy it looked empty. I took her green skirt off a hanger and put it on; it fitted well. Next I went into Mitzi's room. The clock chimed six and hammered out 'Für Elise'. I sat at the dressing table in Katherine's skirt and my own black brassiere (twenty minutes left – it would take me ten minutes to walk down to the Mercier) and used everything in sight. I powdered my face, rouged my cheeks, painted my eyelashes, combed my eyebrows. When I had finished, I washed my face clean, because the results were exactly as I had expected and I looked ghastly. With three minutes remaining I buttoned up Katherine's silk blouse, turned the gramophone off and left.

The lift attendant asked if I was going on a date. I ignored him. It's quite an experience, ignoring the speech of someone you're sharing a lift with. I suppose it should only be done when one has absolutely nothing to say. He tugged his cap and said: 'Well la-di-da and good evening to you too,' when I got out at the ground floor.

Inside, the Mercier was all brass and mahogany and polished rosewood. Red velvet, too, and perfume soaked so deep in tar that it smelt dirty; a nice sort of dirty. I took a cramped corner table that a couple had just vacated. They looked happy together, walked out with their coat collars turned up and their fingertips just touching. I put my wine glass down between their empty glasses and asked the waitress not to clear them away. From the bar's vast marble crest to the bank of tables and chairs that surrounded it, hardly anyone sat alone. There were a few more couples, but mainly mixed groups of five, six, seven, the women sipping at cocktails with prettily wrinkled noses, the men using their cigars and whisky tumblers to emphasise the points they were making.

At 6:40 someone said: 'Hi there.'

I looked up at a man with a beer glass in his hand. His hair was slicked across his head with each strand distinct, like the markings on a leaf. He grinned.

'All on your lonesome?'

'Are you Mr Fox?'

He winked and drew out the chair opposite me. 'Sure, I'm him. I've been looking at you, and—'

I dropped my satchel onto the chair before he could sit down. 'I'm waiting for someone.'

The man moved on without argument, took a seat at the bar, swivelled his stool to face my table and smiled at me whenever I looked his way. I couldn't help looking every now and again, for comparison's sake. I began to feel certain that the man at the bar was Mr Fox after all. His eyes were quite beady, there was too much white to them and they sat too close together, but his smile was pleasant, soothing despite them.

At 7:10 a waitress came over with another glass of wine for me. 'Gentleman at the bar's taken a shine to you. Sends this with his compliments. Says his name's Jack.'

I nodded and let her put the glass down before me. I didn't drink from it. It sat there, buying me time to wait here alone in this place. I looked into the wine and felt myself drowning in it. Mr Fox didn't come, he didn't come, he didn't.

It was 8:30 when I left the bar. The night was very stark, alternate streams of town cars and chequered taxi-cabs, blaring horns busily staking claims – here is the road and here is the sidewalk. But the road looked so much livelier, what if I tried the road?

I often think it would be such luxury to go mad, and not have to worry about anything. Others would have to worry for me, about me. There would be some sort of doctor there to tell me, *Don't worry, Mary, it's just that you are mad. Now be quiet, and take this pill.* And I would think, So that's all it is, and I would be so glad. But aloud I would say: 'What? I'm perfectly sane! *You're* mad . . .' Only mildly, though; just for show, really.

*

November 1st, 1936

St John Fox
177 West 77th Street, Apartment 25
New York City

Abominable Mr Fox,
Contemptible Mr Fox,
Nefarious Mr Fox,
Vile Mr Fox,
Loathsome Mr Fox,
Putrid Mr Fox,

I closed my thesaurus and pulled the letter out of the typewriter with such haste that it tore; half of it was left in the scroll above the type bar. When I touched the two halves together they didn't even fit any more.

Katherine was on my bed, reading a book I hadn't set her. She looked up when I crushed the letter to Mr Fox in my hand – that's Katherine for you, she'd hardly blinked while I was pounding the typewriter keys, but the moment I quietly made something smaller between my fingers, she was all interest.

I asked her what she was reading.

She shrugged. 'Some book.'

'So you've already finished reading the books I set you, have you?'

She turned a page. 'Not yet, I'm getting to it.'

'I shall tell your mother that you're not applying yourself.'

Katherine seemed intrigued. I had never threatened her before.

'You probably should. After all, it's my education that's at stake. Maybe I need a new teacher or something. You missing London?'

I laughed at her indifference, the way she'd spoken without even bothering to inject a nasty insinuating tone into her words.

'Katherine, I could die horribly here in this chair, and my blood could spray all over the room and cover the pages of that fascinating book you're reading, and I believe, I really do believe, that you'd just wipe the worst away and keep going.'

Katherine stretched her legs. 'That's a pretty gruesome thing to say, Mary.' She shook her head. 'Pretty gruesome.'

She left the room, and I picked up the book she'd been reading. On the cover was an illustration of a steamboat. I glanced at the back. Vampires in the Deep South.

Katherine returned with *The Woman in White* and settled in the chair before my typewriter. 'Happy now?' she asked. I said I was happy. I had gone from standing by my bed to lying on it. I had been quite tired the past few days; sleeping longer than usual, feeling the shock of waking throughout my body, as if I had been flung against a wall. Katherine started typing. I didn't open my eyes (when had I closed them?) but I said: 'Hands off my typewriter, Katherine.'

She didn't stop. I hadn't really expected her to. I like to hear the marching of typewriter keys, the shudder of the spacebar, the metallic 'ding' as the paper is scrolled up. Those sounds are encouraging, sounds made by someone who is interested in you and in what you're saying, someone who understands exactly what you're getting at. 'Hmm,' the typewriter says. And 'Mmmm. I-see-I-see-I-see.' And sometimes it chuckles . . .

When I woke up my bedroom door was closed.

'Katherine,' I called.

'What?' she called back. So she had not absconded. I relaxed somewhat. She would not have to be collected from a police station at a quarter to midnight, as she had on the Coles' London trip. Katherine had given Hester, her previous companion, the slip in Covent Garden in order to engage in a vigorous bout of shoplifting. Having deemed Hester unable to cope with Katherine, the Coles had sacked her, then advertised for an immediate replacement. They hadn't employed an English companion before and wanted someone well-spoken and unapproachable, as if these traits could cow their daughter.

I looked inside my typewriter. There's a city in there. Black and grey columns and no inhabitants.

'I've done all my algebra. And I'm on page two hundred and goddamn five of this book you're making me read,' Katherine announced.

'Don't say "goddamn",' I replied. 'Walkies now!'

She barked quite realistically.

*

One evening I encountered Mr Cole alone in the kitchen, bending over the toaster, using it to light his cigar. 'Couldn't find my matches,' he said, when he straightened up. I said, 'Ah,' and began going away again. My cup of tea could wait. But he reached out – not very far – he is built quite power-fully and I'm like a doll beside him – and grabbed my hand. He twirled me around the room, propped me up with my back against the counter, then took a puff on his cigar (he had not troubled himself to put it out the entire time). He leant so close to me that I could very clearly see the roots of hairs that had escaped his razor. I looked at his mouth because I thought he was going to kiss me and I hoped that if I paid attention he would not kiss me. That would have been my first kiss and it would have tasted of ash.

He didn't kiss me, but he put his hand on my breast. He continued to smoke whilst squeezing my breast through my brassiere and dress. I know I should have felt angry or vio-lated, and I did try to, but his expression was distracted, as if he was doodling on a pad whilst mulling over another thing. Mainly I felt very confused. He had been looking at my forehead, but as he squeezed for the third time, he looked into my eyes. And let go immediately. 'Places to go, people to see, Mary.' He walked backwards to the door, removing his cigar from his mouth for long enough to place a finger over his lips and wink. I wish there was someone I could have written to after that, someone I could have written to to explain how awful it was to have someone touch you, then look at you properly and change their mind.

Mr Cole was at home when Katherine and I returned from our walk, sitting in an armchair with Mitzi on his lap. Mitzi opened her arms to Katherine, inviting her to join the tableau. Katherine regarded her parents with frozen eyes and swerved around them, opting for the dining room, where a coloured maid in a white cap stood beside a stacked trolley, covering the table with trays full of vol-au-vents that no one would eat.

'How much time do I have to get away before the ladies descend?' Mr Cole asked. He seemed genuinely worried. Mitzi squeezed his neck and cooed that he was a grumpy bear, wasn't he, wasn't he.

Mitzi only hosted her women's club once a month, so it was tolerable. The wives of her husband's colleagues would gather at the Coles' apartment and fill it with cigarette smoke. Nothing was consumed but cocktails and crudités; everyone was trying to reduce. They'd go around in a circle, these women, each telling the others what she'd been reading, what she'd seen at the theatre or at the pictures, which art exhibition was most divine. Katherine and I would barricade ourselves into my room or hers, with a chair against the door in case Mitzi had too much to drink and was suddenly possessed with a desire to display her offspring. We sprawled in a nest of our own laps and legs, reading and crunching animal crackers. Katherine swore she wouldn't have anything to do with any goddamn women's club when she grew up. My only reply was: '*Don't* say "goddamn".' Sooner or later Katherine will be expected to contribute to her mother's gatherings, and having endured it once, the next time will be easier, and so on until this brief moment when Katherine and I are in perfect agreement is lost, and it'll be strange to both of us to remember that we ever understood each other. Katherine is completely different from me, and it's more than just the fact that her father's money will erode her until she is no longer abrasive to the rest of her social set, until she is able to mingle and marry amongst them quite contentedly. It's also that she's already very pretty. A little long in the nose, but on the whole, very pretty. After a while it will seem odd that she has these looks and makes no attempt to use them. Why doesn't she smile and bat her eyelashes, the way her mother must have practically from birth? I wanted to tell her. Don't look at people so strongly, Katherine Cole. Let your gaze swoon a little. Don't speak so firmly; falter. Lisp, even. Your failure to do these things made me mistake you for someone like me.

'Katherine is improving in English literature,' I told her parents, because I felt I should say something. Then I hurried to my room. Katherine joined me when the clock struck seven. And there we stayed, safe from the clinking of glasses and the lilting sound of civilised conversation. Katherine had been teaching herself how to read Tarot, and she told my fortune, laying down card after card, telling me what each one was supposed to predict. They were all bad cards. A heart spiked with sword blades, a lightning-struck tower, a demon holding a man and a woman on the same chain, a hooded figure walking away from cups that lay empty on the ground. She was taken aback; she reshuffled the cards. 'Let's start again,' she said.

'Let's not,' I said. 'That's cheating.' We put on shoes and coats and slid past the lounge and out of the front door. In the garden at the side of the building, we knelt by the pond and fed the koi carp. There had been more rain earlier in the evening, so we turned up plenty of their favourite food without much effort. The fish surged to the surface of the water and ate the earthworms live from our fingers. Lamps lit the rosebushes as bright as day and sirens sounded and resounded, their screams strangely pure, choral. I had been all over this city on my own, looked down from its heights, looked up from its swarming pavements – I'd spoken to no one, everyone passed me by at a clip. It occurred to me that I was unhappy. And it didn't feel so very terrible. No urgency, nothing. I could slip out of my life on a slow wave like this – it didn't matter. I don't have to be happy. All I have to do is hold on to something and wait.

*

Once Katherine was asleep I read and marked her illustrated history project on the Church of England. I had to give her a C because she spoilt an otherwise thoughtful piece by suddenly concluding that the Church of England was Anne Boleyn's 'fault'. A Church is not the 'fault' of anybody. Next, I set about preparing a lesson on stars, galaxies and planets, poring over fat books I had withdrawn from the public library on Katherine's ticket. There was so much information. I had to select things that would interest her, place them strategically alongside the things that were bound to bore her, the figures and units of measurement, in such a way as to disarm her objections to the important facts. I didn't finish until 1 a.m., and by then it was too late to reach for my typewriter and add to the other pages I had been accumulating. So I sat beside the typewriter in the dark, and I pretended that I was working at it, then I pretended that all the work was finished and I touched the keys that would make the page say

THE END THE END THE END

*

November 9th, 1936

Mary Foxe
85 East 65th Street, Apartment 11
New York City

Mary,

Many thanks for your letter of November 1st. Here is
what I propose: to have my secretary wait for you this
Saturday at 1pm, in order to collect the pages you want
me to look at, and to buy you a consolatory lunch if
you're hungry. Salmagundi, on Lexington and 61st, is a
personal favorite of mine – if you object to the time,
place, date, or all three, then please say so by return.
Otherwise, save your stationery.

Yours most chastened,
The abominable, contemptible, vile, *execrable*, etc.,
Mr Fox
177 West 77th Street, Apartment 25
New York City

*

I telephoned Katherine at the Long Island house. Mitzi answered, and I told her that this was an impromptu French oral examination, to keep Katherine's skills elastic.

'Bonjour,' Katherine said, when she came to the phone. She was slightly out of breath – all that tennis. 'Comment ça va?'

'Got a letter from Mr Fox,' I said.

She laughed, and I heard her clap her hands. 'What did he say? Did he sock it to you?'

She stopped laughing as she soaked up the realisation that I couldn't speak. I was in too much of a state.

Once I'd recovered I asked: 'Why did you send it, Katherine?'

'I just thought it would be fun.' As she spoke I pictured her standing before me, eyeing me with all the defiance of Lucifer. In a smaller, meeker, voice she said: 'Stop hating me . . . who is he, anyway?'

'Just a man,' I said. In my mind I was already reorganising the contents of the black folder. I'd kept working on the stories, and they were stronger now, and better; I was sure of it. It was just as well he hadn't met me at the Mercier.

*

On Saturday afternoon I stood paralysed on the pavement outside the restaurant, which had these smart black-and-silver revolving doors; every time someone stepped into them I knew I was meant to take the next empty space and push myself into the lobby. But when I finally did I found that I couldn't stop pushing at the door until I had spun back out into the street again. I tried to be firm with myself, but with each glimpse of the restaurant full of marble and women genteelly eating salad, I lost my nerve to join them and ran inside the doors like a rodent in a glass maze. On the corner a man in a suit was standing beside an apple cart. 'Apples,' he said. 'Getcha apples!' No one was buying, so he began juggling them. 'Look what I've sunk to,' he sang. 'God I hate these apples, I'd rather starve to death than eat these apples, tra la la.' He was a tenor. Finally he started telling the people passing that he had kids at home. Someone suggested he feed the apples to his kids. He caught my eye. 'You're my witness. When you're out of work people think they can talk to you anyhow!' I nodded and went back in for another bout with the revolving doors. By now people trying to enter the restaurant from the street were asking me if I was crazy or what; the fifth time I saw the maître d' frowning menacingly, and the sixth time a woman came to meet me out on the street. She seized my arm as if I was a naughty child about to scamper off somewhere. 'That's enough of that,' she said. 'You'll tire yourself out.'

I coughed out an 'Ouch, do you mind?' and hoped the apple-seller wasn't looking. The woman's grip was surprisingly strong. She wore a brown skirt-suit and a tiny brown hat tipped coquettishly over one eye.

'Let go of me,' I said.

When she didn't, I pleaded: 'I'm meeting someone.'

'Who?' she asked.

'I don't see how that's any of your business—'

She shook me a little. 'Mr Fox's secretary,' I said. 'I'm meeting Mr Fox's secretary.'

'Then it's just as well, isn't it, that I'm her.'

She released me at last, and we stood nose to nose. I glared, and she just looked back, with an air of melancholy.

'You'd better prove it,' I said. For some reason, I'd thought the secretary would be a man.

'You're . . . Mary Foxe?' she said, looking me over.

'I'm Mary Foxe,' I said.

The woman produced an envelope from her handbag, pulled my letter out of it and showed me.

Abominable Mr Fox,

I read, then winced, and returned it to her, apologising. She said: 'Don't apologise, I think it's funny.' But she didn't laugh, or even smile.

'What's your name?' I asked.

'Doesn't matter,' she said.

I handed her the black folder full of stories and I asked her what Mr Fox was like.

The secretary blinked slowly, thinking. 'He's kind of quiet,' she said.

She wandered away with the folder sticking out of her handbag, leaving me alone on the sidewalk. I watched her, thinking she might suddenly remember something and turn around. Once I was sure that she'd gone I hailed a cab.

*

A week went by; he didn't write to me. He had my folder and he didn't write to me. Then three more silent weeks, six, eight. My fingernails crept down into their beds, my eyes grew glassy, I brushed my hair with my back to the mirror. I had no interest in looking at myself; it was the sensation of teeth against my scalp that subdued me.

It was all I could do not to write to him again.

'You should go get your stories back,' Katherine said, when I briefly explained the situation to her. 'He's probably going to steal them or something.'

'How would you know they're good enough for him to want to steal them?'

'Oh, I know,' Katherine said, sagely. 'I read 'em. All of them. I especially like the one about the disappearing zoo. That's the best one.'

I grabbed her before she could escape and, unexpectedly, found myself hugging her. I liked the fluffy weight of her head against my chest. She was just as surprised as I was. I neutralised it by calling her a bloody nosey parker.

'Maybe that goddamn secretary stole the stories,' Katherine suggested.

'I told you not to say that word.'

'Which? Secretary? Stories? Maybe . . . ?'

Maybe, maybe, maybe.

One morning Mitzi said I ought to take a break. That was alarming. I stopped buttering my toast and said: 'Why? I'm fine. Thanks all the same, Mrs Cole, but the weekends are enough for me.' I made a swift analysis of my behaviour of the past two weeks or so. I had not said or done anything particularly strange; I had behaved more or less as I always did.

Mitzi rose from her seat and cupped my face in her flower-scented hands. I was so nervous I could have bitten her. 'Honey, no one's saying you're not doing a good job. You're doing a wonderful job. Isn't she, Katy?'

Katherine said yes and stuck her tongue out at me.

'It's just that you can't give your weekends to a soup kitchen and your weekdays to this little fiend of mine and just go on and on without stopping. What if you burned out or something? Honey – I'm telling you, I'd never forgive myself.' She had a new bracelet on, stacked with emeralds brighter than her eyes. I hate rich people.

'Your face is all pinched,' Katherine told me helpfully.

So that morning, instead of taking Katherine to the Metropolitan Museum of Art, I went to get my stories back.

177 West 77th Street was easy to find. It was a posh apartment block, much like the Coles', but smaller. More exclusive, I suppose. I entered the building behind a grocery delivery boy who pulled a small township of brown-paper bags along on a trolley behind him. The building directory indicated that Mr Fox, at number 25, was on the fourth floor. As I waited by the lift I caught sight of myself in the polished steel doors. I was grinning. On the fourth floor I approached number 25 casually, as if I might not stop, as if I might well walk past it and continue on down the red-carpeted corridor. But I did stop at 25. And I rang the doorbell, and I knocked, hard.

The secretary answered the door. She wasn't wearing any lipstick or powder, and she'd yanked her hair up into a knot on the top of her head. She had a pencil behind each ear and one in her hand. She looked very, very young.

'What can I do for you?' she asked. She didn't appear to recognise me.

'My name's Mary Foxe,' I said.

'Mary Foxe,' she said, as if repeating the name would help jog her memory.

'I corresponded with Mr Fox about some stories of mine – he said he'd read them, but I suppose he's too busy – I've come to take them off his hands.'

She hesitated. Oh God. She'd thrown my stories away. Or there was a mountain of manuscripts somewhere behind her, and she'd never find mine.

'I met you outside Salmagundi on 61st and Lexington a

couple of months ago,' I said. 'There was a bit of a fuss with some revolving doors.'

Her eyes lit up at last. 'Oh, right,' she said. 'Right.'

She looked over her shoulder, though no one had spoken. 'Be right back.'

She closed the door before I could peer into the flat. It seemed strange to me that Mr Fox's secretary should be at his flat – I mean, secretaries belong in offices.

Ten minutes later she opened the door again and handed me my folder. I looked through it quickly – all the stories appeared to be there. The pages were well thumbed, and some parts were underlined.

'He – er – he read them?'

Suddenly I felt as if I could knock this woman down and charge into his study, pull up a chair, and settle down to talk. As if she knew what I was thinking, she took a firmer stance in the doorway. She twirled her pencil between her slim fingers. 'Yes. He did.'

I didn't like the look in her eyes. My throat went dry. 'And?'

She shook her head. 'You don't really want to write . . . what you want is love. Go find yourself a beau. You're so young, Miss Foxe. Go have a little fun.'

'Did Mr Fox say that? Or is this coming from you?'

She looked down.

'It's coming from me,' she told the floor.

'I want to talk to Mr Fox,' I said.

I stepped towards the secretary and she held her pencil out at eye level, in an unmistakably threatening gesture. The point was very sharp.

'What did Mr Fox say?' I said. 'Just tell me that, and I'll go.'

She didn't answer, and I said: 'Are you Mr Fox?'

She laughed. 'No.'

'You are, aren't you? You're Mr Fox –' I caught sight of a bare passageway, a telephone on a stand, the receiver off the hook – I heard no dial tone – 'you're him.'

She frowned. 'I'm not.'

'What did he say, then?'

'Wait.'

The door closed again. When it opened, the secretary was holding a lit taper. The flame cast her eyes into shadow.

'He said . . .' She paused, and sighed. 'He said I should do this.'

She touched the taper to the black folder, and it caught fire. She blew the taper out before the flame struck her fingers. But I didn't let the folder go. The leather cover burned with a harsh sound like someone trying to hold back a cry between their teeth. Still I held the folder. I felt the skin on my fingers shrink. I watched words turn amber and float away.

I liked these stories. Katherine liked them. I'd worked hard on them.

There was so much smoke in my eyes.

But I held on.

Mary Foxe had known that it was more than a matter of snapping her fingers and having Mr Fox change his ways – she'd known it would be difficult, but this was beyond all her expectations. She'd been asleep for days, in a four-poster bed in a dark blue room. There wasn't a part of her body that didn't ache. Her brain ached most of all. She'd felt terrible burning his stories, which she'd actually thought were rather good. She couldn't have let Mr Fox get away with beheading her, though. That was exactly the kind of behaviour she had set out to discourage. She was aware of a large clock ticking outside the bedroom door, but it didn't wake her up. Mary was busy having a very long dream.

In her dream, she was a spinster. Fastidious, polite, and thirty-eight years old. Her features were plain and unremarkable – they had always been plain and unremarkable. She had been a dutiful daughter when her parents were alive, and now Dream-Mary lived in the attic of the house her parents had left her. The remainder of the house she had hoped to let to a family – but no family liked the idea of living there with her up in the attic like that. So Mary let the house below to a solicitor named Pizarsky. He was out all day – that was good. He was punctual with his rent – also good. In the evenings, however, he hosted parties that were exclusively attended by attractive young ladies who giggled for hours on end. That was tiresome.

Mary and Mr Pizarsky kept their exchanges as brief as possible:

'Morning, Miss F.'

'Good morning, Mr Pizarsky.'

'Here's the rent, Miss F.'

'Thank you, Mr Pizarsky.'

'Off home for Christmas now, Miss F.'

'Merry Christmas, Mr Pizarsky.'

On Valentine's Day, Dream-Mary bought herself a single red rose, then immediately ran back into the shop, confused and embarrassed, to return it.

Most days Dream-Mary stayed at her desk until sunset, working in the special quiet of the otherwise empty house, the settling of floorboards and the ticking of clocks. She wrote romance novels under the pen name Wendy Darling. Hers were gloriously improbable tales, stuffed with happy coincidences, eternal devotion and the unwavering recognition of inner beauty. They were in great demand, Mary's novels. They were read-them-once-and-throw-them-away sort of books, really. And Mary had seen people doing just that, throwing her novels away, or very deliberately leaving them behind on park benches and bus seats once they had finished. She tried not to let it get her down. She didn't like to brood. She kept a framed photograph of her parents on her desk, to remind herself of their story, which amazed her. They had fallen in love and kept it up far into old age; that was all. Her father was the hero in every story she wrote, and her mother was the heroine. They had been gone five years, but she brought them together again and again, thirty-five lines of cream-coloured foolscap folio at a time. And they never tired of finding each other, even when she was reduced, in the final chapters, to typing with just one finger, her little finger, jabbing out words until her hand curled up and could do no more. She completed a novel every other month and took August and December off.

It was Dream-Mary's custom to read the local newspaper as she ate her evening meal in the dining corner of her attic. She read it thoroughly, without omitting a single paragraph or page. It was much more difficult to be alarmed by the events of a day that was almost over. After that she would go for a walk, to keep fit. And upon her return to her attic she would say a few phrases aloud, experimenting with a friendly tone of voice. She didn't often socialise, but it was important to keep her hand in. She rehearsed small talk about the weather, and about children and the cost of living. From Mr Pizarsky's party below, a gramophone puffed jazz up at her like smoke rings until she stopped trying. She put on her nightgown, did her stretching exercises, applied cold cream to her face and went to bed. Her days were pleasant and her mood was even.

One evening Mary went for her after-dinner walk as usual. She went through town, passing the tidy shop fronts, their signs beautifully lettered in glossy paint and print, striding over the mushy bank of sawdust outside the butcher's. The entire neighbourhood was at home; wireless sets buzzed gently at her as she passed. Each house stood in its own square of garden, each garden with its own picket fence and its own garden gate. Not a curtain twitched. Mary climbed Murder Hill. It was a funny old hill. It started off as easily as walking on flat ground, and continued to seem flat, even after she had begun to feel short of breath. She looked down at all the chimney tops and picked lavender.

When she returned from her walk she found the house suspiciously quiet.

There was no rustling or giggling, no chiming of glassware to be heard anywhere in the house, she noticed. No party this evening. Mr Pizarsky appeared, carrying a cake; it prickled with lit candles, at first glance there appeared to be hundreds of them. 'Happy birthday, Miss Foxe,' he said, smiling warily.

He was right. It was her birthday. Dream-Mary thought she might be sick. 'Mr Pizarsky,' she said. 'You shouldn't have.' It was meant to sound light-hearted, but it didn't.

He looked crestfallen. 'You don't like cake.'

'No, I do. How did you know it was my birthday?'

In the kitchen, Mr Pizarsky carefully dropped his burden onto the table. He stared at the candle flames. They both did. It seemed rude to look at each other just then.

'I gave my room a good spring cleaning last week,' he said. 'I found a birthday card. Dated.'

So he slept in her old room. She hadn't known that, hadn't checked to see whether or not he'd been keeping the lower half of the house in order, whether he had changed any aspect of the furnishing. The hallway and main stairs were tidy enough, and as long as the house didn't fall down she didn't care. In the last few weeks of her mother's illness they'd spent whole afternoons in that room. Afterwards she'd moved out of that part of the house in a hurry. And she hadn't gone back for anything since, had waited in the parlour while prospective tenants looked the property over. She must have left a great many things in there.

'I've taken a liberty, haven't I?' Mr Pizarsky gestured towards the birthday cake. 'Even as I bought it, I wasn't sure. You like to have secret birthdays? You English . . . I am forever offending you.'

'No, no—' Mary searched for her manners and caught hold of them again. 'It's a lovely surprise.'

She pretended to make a wish and blew out the candles – only thirty of them, she counted. Such flattery. She found two small plates and put a slice of the cake on each, then remained standing, holding her slice away from her. He stood too – he couldn't very well sit down and eat while she stood there, not eating. As they exchanged remarks she was aware of treating him shabbily.

'I hope you didn't cancel a gathering on my account, Mr Pizarsky.'

'No, I've been abandoned tonight.'

Mr Pizarsky was unkempt for a man of the law – his hair wanted combing, and the elbows of his jacket could have done with a thorough darning.

'I'm sure they'll come back,' Mary soothed.

'I hope she will. That is to say – to tell you the truth, Miss Foxe, there is only one of them I particularly care for. The others are just her friends.'

She hadn't taken a proper look at any of the girls that crowded the downstairs rooms most evenings; they all looked exactly the same to her.

'Well – best of luck, Mr Pizarsky. Is your name Russian?'

'I'm a Pole, Miss F . . . though I have met Russians who bear the name. Have you ever been to my country?'

'Poland? No – no. I haven't been anywhere. Brighton.

The Lake District and the Cotswolds, a few times. London sometimes.'

'A pity. Mine is a lovely country, in parts – simple and honest and strong. The landscapes, the buildings, the mead.'

'Oh – I must go there one day.'

He smiled sadly, with his mouth closed.

'One day. Not now. The rioting. And more to come.'

'Really . . . ?'

Her question was feeble, but he considered it with a quizzical twist of his mouth.

'Why, yes, of course! "Really", you say. You don't think riots are so bad. Are you thinking of them as you do the weather here? A nuisance, but it's not so difficult to get on with things despite them?' He described the three riots he had witnessed first-hand, in three different cities. He made the anger of the poor and put upon sound like a storm on the ground; it scorched buildings when it woke, its first touch killed. 'That is why I am here,' he finished. 'Otherwise, pork pies and jellied eels be damned; give me my country.'

Mary suspected her father would have especially liked this man.

'Are you – forgive me, I know nothing about solicitors – but is it quite usual to find solicitors like you, Mr Pizarsky?'

She had delighted him. 'Let me see . . . perhaps not. I was a poet.'

'Oh a poet . . . but what's that?' Wishy-washy, that was how she found most poetry – it just missed the point over and over again.

'What's that,' he agreed, laughing. 'What's that . . .'

He took her plate from her hand. 'And now I will release

you, even though you are unfair and have told me nothing in exchange.'

She assured him that there was nothing to tell.

'Perhaps you could sing a song, then,' he suggested. 'Or turn a cartwheel – or – you could laugh, yes, laugh wonderfully, just as you are doing at the moment.'

She left him with the cake and went up to her attic. She put on her nightgown, did her stretching exercises, applied cold cream to her face and arranged herself on her bed with a stack of pillows supporting her head and neck. She looked up through her attic windows, up into the cloudy night. So Mr Pizarsky had been a poet? That was how he'd said it: 'I was a poet.' As if the poet had died. He was in hiding, perhaps. He might have written something that someone powerful hadn't liked . . .

. . . there she lay, casting him as a character in one of her own romances. He didn't cut anything like a dashing figure. And he'd need to be four inches taller before he could even make an appearance in her prose. *No more nonsense. At the count of three I shall go straight to sleep*, she informed herself. *One. Two. Thr –*

Mary Foxe woke up, feeling refreshed. And a little regretful. What if she were to abandon the task at hand? Mr Fox was a hard nut to crack. It was good that he didn't know how Mary tried to take care of him, alphabetising his reference books and checking and correcting his spelling and grammar while he lay asleep with his wife in his arms. If he knew how Mary loved him he would turn it against her somehow; he would play with it. Because that was what Mr Fox did – he played. And there was something appealing about this Mr Pizarsky . . . perhaps she could find him, or someone like him, out in the world. She imagined their courtship – quiet, restrained, but full of tenderness. She would learn more about Poland and he would learn more about England and they would clear up many funny little misunderstandings. They would pore over maps together – *I was born here, I went to school here . . .* They'd go to the seaside, and sit on the pier under umbrellas, in the rain. He would take her to the pictures and bring her violet creams. He would declare himself without words, bring her a daisy and retire with haste. And just thinking of how much he desired her but dared not presume, she would swoon over the tiny flower, dragging its petals across her lips and the backs of her hands, then shyly, languorously, along her inner thighs . . . and in time, and by being a good woman, and a patient woman, she would have won a good and patient man.

Mary turned onto her side. The pillow she was lying on was covered in spidery words; tiny, but legible. She rubbed her nose against one of the words and smudged it. The words were carefully spaced so that the pale green of the pillowcase haloed them. 'What . . .' Whole paragraphs. And they were numbered. 7, 8, 9. She turned again. Her head was surrounded with more writing. There was yet more under her hands, long lines of words meandered all along the duvet, some running horizontal, some diagonal, some fitting into each other like puzzles. And numbered, all numbered. Laughing in an appalled sort of way, Mary Foxe pulled the pillow out from under her head and read:

1. *I may not be here when you wake up. If I am not here, read on.*

2. *Mary Mary, quite contrary. I'm the easy option. You won't want me.*

3. *I have bought you more pillowcases and another duvet cover, in case you cannot stand what I have done to these ones. I took them off the bed before I wrote on them, so there's no need to worry about the ink bleeding into the pillows, etc.*

4. *My English is probably better than yours. I deliberately muddle my grammar when I speak. It puts people at ease. They become friendly when I get things wrong – they speak slowly, use shorter words, to help me. I hate it, but it's the best way to get on. You have never done this with me. Thank you.*

5. *I often sing Christmas carols in June, and I don't think it's bad luck. Do you?*

6. *It was on April 2nd last year that I discovered you had a dimple in your right cheek. You smiled at me for some reason (why? I had done nothing to deserve it. Please explain, if you remember April 2nd.) On the calendar in my office I made a note: 'M.F. revealed dimple today.' What do you think of sentimental men? I'm sure you hate them. And you'd be right to.*

Mary sat bolt upright. Was Mr Pizarsky a dream, or not? She studied her surroundings. She had no idea where she was. There was a vaseful of foxgloves on her bedside table, their petals the pale, shocking blue of the veins in a wrist. She moved on to the next pillow.

7. *I learnt English when I went to war. People think I'm lying when I say that, but that's how it was. We were in Galicia, Poles in Russian uniforms, trying to court independence; we only managed to occupy a slice of the place while the Germans and the*

*Austrians made off with the rest. We were fighting
so very hard and achieving so very little aside from
staying alive. BUT THAT'S EVERYTHING, my
father wrote to me, when I told him that in a letter. I
studied to take my mind off things. At dead of night
in the mess hut – Pride and Prejudice, an English to
Polish dictionary, and a candle. I could have burnt
the place down. But I had to do it. I needed words,
lots of words to think about while I was going about
the rest of the day. And I didn't want anything
affected. I wanted nothing to do with those Romance
languages. I wanted clipped words, full of common
sense. Thoughts to wear beneath my thoughts. Allow,
express, oath, vow, dismay, matter, splash, mollify.
I liked those words. I liked saying them. I still do.*

8. *I helped to load cannons. People are not good at
war. Can I really say that, when all I know is that
I and those around me were not good at war? Don't
say our hearts weren't in it – they were. But we got
sick, some of us unto death. Spanish flu and the rot
of trench foot, and there were such smells, they made
us sick to our stomachs. A few of our men dropped
cannonballs and broke their legs. That sort of thing.
And then there was my cousin Karol. The first time
he successfully shot a man, he didn't see a way to
stop shooting; he knew he had to do more, and with
greater speed than the first kill. He couldn't aim
steadily at anyone else so he turned his rifle on
himself – and missed, and missed, each time he did
it was as if he was playing some sort of horrible trick*

on himself, the worst kind of bluff. He told me all about it. 'Calm down, Karol,' I told him. 'You must keep your head.'

9. *Wake up, Mary.*

10. *I had a great uncle; he was rich and we shared a Christian name. He liked me. I made him laugh, without even trying. I said naive things that I really believed in. Things about life, and money. He almost killed himself laughing at me. He liked to slap me on the back and tell me I looked like a peasant. When he died he left me a lot of money. I liked him then. Before that, I must say I had often daydreamed about punching him in the throat. His neck was very fat. He owned factories, and I used to think that people like him were the source of all that was evil in the land.*

11. *Wake up, wake up . . .*

12. *When I was in Galicia I tried not to think of my fiancée. I didn't write to her much, and in her own way she reproached me for that. She had every right to, so I won't dwell on the maddening, indirect ways in which she reproached me. Anyhow I lost her. When I came back she looked through me and seemed displeased – I might have been the ghost of Banquo for all the pleasure she took in my company. She's happy now – she married my cousin, a good boy, who is tender with her (yes, Karol – I believe I mentioned him in point 8).*

Round and round. Blissfully, Mary rolled in the words, propped her head up on some and her heels on others. She liked this man.

13. *When I saw you for the first time, I thought you had
a secret life. You had your hair up out of the way
and you were wearing your reading spectacles and
your dress was buttoned up all the way to your chin.
Still, I noticed – if you will excuse my noticing –
the fullness of your lips, and the way they parted
every now and then as if responding to changes in
the breeze. And fleetingly, so fleetingly that it's
possible you weren't aware you were doing it, you
moved your hand from your cheek to your neck to
the centre of your chest; you held your own waist
and smoothed your skirt over your hips. Yes, you
looked as if you had a secret, or you were a secret
in yourself. I had seen better lodgings further out –
better lodgings for a bachelor, that is. A set of rooms
I would have had all to myself, and I could have
cycled to work and back. But I rented this house
because of the lady who lived in the attic. To see if
I could catch her out.*

14. *I took a lot of my inheritance money and I told
everyone that I would be a lawyer. And I came here
to study. When I got here I was restless and nothing
interested me. At the end of every evening I got very
drunk and vowed to give up my studies, and every
morning I was back at the books. I am just trying
to show you that my nature is not a consistent one.
Sometimes I do what I say I'm going to do, but more
often I don't. It's a failing. The least of my failings,
and the only one I feel up to admitting at the
moment. The rest will emerge if you choose to see
it. I don't know if I'm the kind of man that is*

acceptable to you; I have heard that your father was a priest.

15. *Shall I tell you how many times I came up these steps while you were typing? Vowing that today would be the day that I asked you to the pictures. And I'd buy you a pound of violet creams, two pounds of them, whatever you wanted. But then I'd hear you at your typewriter, and I'd go away again. I decided that since I could not approach you, I would make you jealous. I asked my sister Elizaveta if it would work, and she said no. She also said you sounded too old for me. My mother and sisters are all very concerned about who I will marry. I am an only son.*

16. *This Mr Fox. Is he better looking than me?*

Cold blew onto Mary Foxe's blood, as if she had no skin at all.

17. *My hand is getting tired. That must be why I slipped up just now.*

18. *You're slipping yourself, Mary. Good thing you woke up before our little picnic on Murder Hill. A blue-eyed poet with some stories, a good line in wry humility and some English as a second language bullshit . . . is that all it takes to turn you fickle these days? Never mind . . . we'll pretend it didn't happen. A hundred years hence (or a hundred washes, whichever comes first) these words will be gone . . .*

The game was still on.

fitcher's bird

Miss Foxe referred to herself as a florist, but really she was a florist's assistant. She swept plant debris off the shop floor, and she wrapped flowers for the customers and did everything else that the shop owner, Mrs Nash, didn't feel like doing. Miss Foxe wasn't allowed to cut and arrange the flowers used in the window display; nor was she allowed to advise people on the perfect floral gift. Miss Foxe knew much more about flowers than Mrs Nash, but all she could do was listen while Mrs Nash told the anxious relatives of spring-time invalids to send pink azaleas. Evidently Mrs Nash was not aware that in the language of flowers azaleas meant 'take care of yourself for me'. A touching thought, but by giving a sick person a bunch of azaleas you were telling them that they were on their own. Mrs Nash's agenda was simply to shift stock. In summer Mrs Nash prescribed marigolds left, right and centre – for birthdays, apologies, and romantic overtures – even though those flowers were better as especial comfort to the heartsick. But Miss Foxe kept all that to herself, for fear of losing her job. As it was, Mrs Nash snapped at her and called her slow and asked her if she was an idiot nineteen times a day. Miss Foxe liked to be near the flowers, especially in winter, when it was easy to forget that there had ever been such a thing as a flower.

Flowers, and thoughts of flowers, were Miss Foxe's main occupation. She didn't especially care for motion pictures; she found them too noisy. She would have liked to have had friends to lend books to, and borrow pie dishes from. But it was difficult for Miss Foxe to reach that stage with anyone. She spoke so quietly that people couldn't understand what she was saying and quickly lost patience. When she paid for things in shops, the change was invariably placed on the counter instead of in her hand. Miss Foxe occasionally wondered whether she had spent her life approaching invisibility, and had finally arrived at it. She encouraged herself to see her very small presence in the world as a good thing, a power, something that a hero might possess.

Miss Foxe's other passion was fairy tales. She loved the transformations in them. Everybody was in disguise, or on their way to becoming something else. And all was overcome by order in the end. Love could not prevail if the order of the tale didn't wish it, and neither could hatred, nor grief, nor cunning. If you were the first of three siblings, then you were going to make a big mistake, and that was that. If you were the third sibling, you couldn't fail. *Here is the truth about everything*, Miss Foxe would think, after a night with Madame D'Aulnoy, or Madame de Villeneuve.

Flowers and fairy tales were all very well, but they began to take their toll on her. Independently and in unison they made insinuations, the flowers and the fairy tales. When Mrs Nash was being especially nasty, Miss Foxe imagined herself surrounded by leafy branches that changed as her tears dripped onto them – glossy green tips shrank and smoothed into skin, the branches gripped her firmly, like arms . . .

One morning Miss Foxe gave in. It was high time she

found herself a companion. But how, and where? She knew what kind of man she wanted; someone passionate, someone who would understand her. But she didn't meet people. Every man who came into the flower shop was invariably attached, or had someone else in mind.

Miss Foxe went to bars, and was overlooked with a thoroughness that chilled her marrow. She had chosen seedy bars on purpose, bars where (she had heard Mrs Nash say) the men were voracious and anything went. And it was true. Even cross-eyed girls who laughed like hyenas were bought drinks. Anything went but Miss Foxe. She wasn't bad-looking – it was just that it took a great deal of effort to be able to actually see her, especially in noisy, crowded places.

Miss Foxe tried libraries, but talking wasn't allowed.

Miss Foxe tried bookshops, but was frightened off every time she saw the titles of the books the interesting-looking men happened to be holding. Such weighty and joyless words: *Fear and Trembling*, *Anatomy of Melancholy*, *The Nicomachean Ethics* and the like.

One afternoon Mrs Nash barked at her. 'You've been late back from lunch five days running now. Explain yourself. And don't fob me off with any more lies, or you'll be out of work.'

Miss Foxe explained that she had been trying different things.

'What does that mean? Spit it out.'

'I've been looking in the bookshops for a gentleman friend,' poor Miss Foxe stammered.

Mrs Nash threw her head back and laughed for ten minutes without stopping. Then she said: 'You'd better advertise.'

And that is what Miss Foxe did. In a national newspaper, no less.

Fairytale princess seeks fairytale prince. Sarcastic and or/ironic replies will be ignored; I am in earnest, and you had better be too.

If the advertisement sounded as if Miss Foxe was fed up, that's because she was.

As a result of her advertisement, Miss Foxe received seventeen moderately interesting propositions, fifteen pages of lunatic verse (from fifteen different lunatics), twelve sarcastic and/or ironic replies (six of each) and a single foxglove wrapped in clear cellophane. The foxglove was accompanied by a card that read: *Fitcher*. The name was printed above an address not too far from where Miss Foxe lived.

Miss Foxe held the flower and walked all around her bedroom in quick circles. Her steps sped up so that she was almost running. She felt her heart beating in her fingertips. She knew the foxglove's meaning in the language of flowers – beauty and danger, poison and antidote. The digitalis made the heart contract. If your heart was too slow, then it worked to make you well. If your heart was sound, the digitalis killed. This Fitcher, whoever he was, understood the beautiful risk of the fairy tale. She wrote to Fitcher at once, and three days later he met her at a coffee shop after work.

Fitcher bemused Miss Foxe. He looked at her. He looked at her eyes, her ears, her teeth, her neck, her breasts. And he was a quiet man, but not in the way that she was quiet. His quiet was of the measured kind, entered into to conceal his thoughts. He stepped noiselessly upon the floor. She dreaded that at first.

'Is Fitcher your only name?' she asked him.

He answered: 'I have no other.'

They spoke of fairy tales, and found their tastes were exactly matched. Encouraged, she met him again, and again. At their fourth meeting, as they walked between glass cases at the British Museum, Fitcher threaded Miss Foxe's fingers through his own. She froze. She did not find it easy to be touched by Fitcher; she found that her hand was warming his, and that though his hand was strong, it moved gently with hers.

At their sixth meeting, Fitcher brought Miss Foxe a nightingale in a gold-painted cage. He set the cage down on the shop counter and draped a black cloth over it. And the bird sang out its hope, the silly little romantic calling out for a mate, not caring if this nightfall was a trick.

Mrs Nash approved of Fitcher. 'A proper Romeo, that one,' she said.

'He doesn't talk much, though,' Miss Foxe confided. 'It worries me.'

'It's better that way,' Mrs Nash returned. 'Pay attention to what he does, not what he says – that's the rule.'

And to this she added various other adages, such as 'It's in his kiss', etc.

By their seventh meeting, Miss Foxe had grown so sure of Fitcher that she felt ready for the next step. She invited him to her flat, where she cooked him dinner and they drank wine by candlelight. Fitcher seemed appreciative, but as usual, said little. At last they were sitting on the sofa, together. She fed him bites of lemon tart. Fitcher looked as if he was enjoying both the food and the attention. Once that was over with, Miss Foxe reached behind the sofa and produced an antique sword that had been in her family for many years. It was half her height, and heavy, but shiny and sharp, as she had recently had it oiled and sharpened. She laid the sword across their laps.

'Take this sword,' Miss Foxe said, solemnly, 'and cut off my head!'

Fitcher and Miss Foxe both fell to thinking of their favourite fairy tale, The White Cat, and the enchanted princess, pleading with her love to strike the blow that would release her from her animal form.

'Are you sure?' Fitcher asked. From Miss Foxe's bedroom, the nightingale sang in its cage.

Miss Foxe sighed. 'Don't you believe . . . ?'

'Oh I do,' said Fitcher. 'I do.' And without further argument he unsheathed the sword and cleaved Miss Foxe's head from her neck. He knew what was supposed to happen. He knew that this awkward, whispering creature before him should now transform into a princess – dazzlingly beautiful, free, and made wise by her hardship.

That is not what happened.

I walked into my study – I don't know where from. Where *had* I just come from? What had I been doing? My step, at least, was sprightly – maybe I'd just come from a book launch, or an award ceremony, or a meeting with an effusive film executive. I searched my pockets for clues, but my pockets were empty. Well. Wherever I had been, Mary Foxe had been there too. Was I certain about that, or was I guessing? I whipped open the study door and regarded the hallway with a measure of suspicion. Everything was in order. I turned back to my study and registered the condition it was in – books and crumpled paper and broken records were scattered around me as if they had rained from the sky. The windows stood wide open, and a cold wind flowed in and made the torn pages of my books whisper. One of my shelves had fallen, or been pushed, down, and I had to walk across the back of it to get to my desk, which was soaked in ink. Thorough. The rampage had been thorough. I whistled, and then I closed the windows. The sound must have alerted Daphne, because she came and knocked on the door. Which wasn't closed, so why knock . . .

'Come in,' I said. I picked up half of a coffee mug and half of a phonograph record and idly held them together. A domestic chimera. Daphne came in with her arms full of books, and her eyes blazing like two poisoned moons.

'How'd you like the mess, St John?' It would've been better if she'd screamed. The question was in monotone, and was accompanied by a hardback German edition of my first book, *Stinging the Bees*. More followed – books and flat statements, all aimed at my head – I was stunned and defended myself as best I could with my arms, but there was nowhere to hide. Daphne said she hadn't finished yet. She said she ought to burn the house down, and she just might do it, while I was sleeping. She said I was a dead man walking. She said she was going to Reno. She said she should never, never have married a tarnished individual like me. Finally, at the top of her voice she said: 'WHO IS SHE? THIS WOMAN YOU'RE HUMILIATING ME WITH.'

She ran out of books and stood there, crying, her hands fluttering over her face. I'd fallen into a crouch to weather the storm, and I waited a second before I straightened up. My ear was bleeding a little, and when she saw that, she sobbed even harder. We looked at the crack she'd made in one of the windows – the Japanese edition of *The Butcher's Boots* is no slim tome.

'Who is she?'

'Who is who?'

Daphne turned on her heel and made for the door.

'Where are you going?'

'To Reno. You'd better not contest the papers, either.'

I crossed the room and caught her hand, which seemed like the coldest and most fragile little thing in the world just then. I held her hand, patted it. She looked away and just let me hold it, as if it was of no use to her any more. My wife was pretty, I noticed. Sort of elfin, but vulnerable-looking with it. All these wispy curls surrounding a heart-shaped face.

'Don't go to Reno,' I said. She looked at me out of the corner of her eye.

'That's it? That's your best shot at making me stay? "Don't go to Reno"?'

'I hadn't finished, D. I also wanted to tell you that you're paranoid. I don't even know what you're talking about. All I've been doing is trying to win us some bread.' I raised her hand and kissed her wrist – she likes that. 'Give me a week or two and then we'll go someplace nice, just you and me.'

She was melting; she made a face. 'Of course just you and me . . . who else would go with us, dummy?'

Quite clearly she had no solid evidence. It was interesting to know that I'd married someone who could cause this much destruction on a hunch. It made me like her more.

'D . . .' I pulled her into my arms. She buried her face in my sweater and reached up with her handkerchief, pressing it against my ear. 'Greta says I shouldn't listen to a word you say. You're a liar.'

I took custody of the handkerchief; it was awkward, her holding it, and she was applying more pressure than was necessary. 'Greta lies more than me.'

'How would you know that?'

'I don't, but I've got to defend myself.'

'You're the liar. If you hadn't been up to anything you'd be furious that I wrecked your study. You'd have thrown a hot iron at my head or something.'

'Is there a hot iron to hand?'

She sniffled. 'Yes. I was pressing my divorce dress.'

Daphne had bought a divorce dress with my money. Even more interesting. I'd had her down as a starry-eyed idealist who didn't notice my flaws. I'd have to keep an eye on her.

'Your heart is – *jerking*,' she mumbled.

'Oh, so you can hear that?' I said into her hair. 'It's saying: Da – phne, Da – phne. How embarrassing. Don't tell anyone you heard.'

'She keeps calling,' Daphne said. 'And hanging up. While you've been God knows where—'

'Who keeps calling and hanging up?'

'That girl you've got on the side. Don't deny it, St John, I just know.'

'You just know.'

'Yes.' She looked up at me, so piercingly that my first instinct was to look away – but that would have been a mistake. 'But I don't want to leave you. Not really. So just drop her, and we'll forget about it.'

'Daphne. There is no girl on the side.'

'Say whatever you want, just drop her. Please.'

'I can't,' I said. 'She's in my head.'

I saw her expression and I talked fast. 'What I mean is, she's not real, honey. She's only an idea. I made her up.'

'What?'

'I know this sounds unlikely, but you've got to believe me. If you don't, I've got nothing else to tell you.'

'Keep talking, St John.'

'Not a lot to tell. Her name's Mary. You'd like her, I think. She's kind of direct. No-nonsense. I made her up during the war. She started off as nothing but a stern British accent saying things like, "Chin up, Fox," and, "Where's your pluck?" Just a precaution for the times I came dangerously close to feeling sorry for myself. Don't look like that, D, I don't need a doctor. Anyhow – you see now, don't you, that she couldn't possibly call the house? That's just people getting wrong numbers, or one of your brothers phoning you up to ask for money and then losing his nerve.'

'Less of the stuff about my brothers. Back to Miss A Hundred Per Cent Imaginary, Miss Only An Idea. Do you take her out to the movies?'

I couldn't tell if she was kidding. 'Absolutely not,' I said, vehemently.

'Do you tell her secrets?'

'It isn't like that.'

'Is she pretty?'

'Uh . . .'

Daphne gave me a knowing look.

'Prettier than me?'

'D . . .'

'You say "it isn't like that", so tell me what it's like. I'm just trying to figure out whether you're crazy or not.'

'I'm not crazy. At all times I remain fully aware of her status as an idea.'

'So she's kind of like a character in one of your stories?'

'Kind of.' I resisted the urge to pat her on the head and tell her not to worry about it.

'So nothing I should worry about?'

'No, ma'am. Absolutely not.'

Daphne kissed my cheek and backed away. 'Okay, honey. Sorry about the mess.'

I nodded and waved a hand, as if it was nothing. I was proud of myself. In the old days I would have lost my cool. But other things were happening now; I needed to focus on those and I didn't seem to have anything left over for rage. There's also the fact that all the men in her family, and a few of the women, are basically thugs.

'I think I'll go see a movie with Greta now.'

'Have fun.'

She closed the door very quietly behind her. Pinching my ear through Daphne's handkerchief, I crossed the fallen bookshelf again and sat down at my desk, watching ink drip onto the carpet. Mary Foxe was trying to ruin my life. By rights I should be on the edge of some sort of nervous breakdown. But I was happy.

'Impressive conflict management,' Mary remarked, from beneath my desk. Her arms were tucked around her knees, and her chin was resting on them.

'Well, hello there.' I held out a hand to her and she came out from under the desk. She settled on my lap with her arms around my neck. Nice. Carefully, I span the chair around, for a garden view, and we watched the rain falling on the old cedar tree.

'Would you mind terribly if you die next time?' she asked.

'Yes, I'd mind. To be honest, I don't like the sound of that at all. Why do you ask?'

'I just want to see . . .'

'No.'

'No?'

'*No.*'

'But, Mr Fox,' she said. 'It's all just a lot of games . . .'

like this

. . . they will say: 'The one
you love,
is not a woman for you,
Why do you love her? I think
you could find one more beautiful,
more serious, more deep,
more other . . .'

Neruda

There was a Yoruba woman and there was an Englishman, and . . .

That might sound like the beginning of a joke, but those
two were seriously in love.

They tried their best with each other, but it just wasn't
any good. I don't know if you know what a Yoruba woman
can be like sometimes. Any house they lived in together
burnt down. They fought; their weapons were cakes of soap,
suitcases, fists and hardback encyclopaedias. There were
injuries.

The man liked to make things. He took a chisel to
stone with kindness and enquiry, as if finding out what else
the stone would like to be. But his woman kept him from

76

working – that's why they were poor. They wondered why things were like that between them when other people loved each other less and had peace. There were days when she'd open her eyes and be him for six hours in a row; she knew all his secrets and nothing he had done seemed wrong to her, she knew how it was, how things had been, she was there. There were days when he touched the tip of her nose and it was enough, a miracle of plenty.

But who finds happiness interesting?

One day the woman stamped her foot and wished her man dead. So he died. (And now you know what a Yoruba woman can be like sometimes.)

She had a devil of a time getting him back after that one. Books and candles and all the tears she could cry, and yet more – she had to borrow some from friends, and some from trees at dawn. Finally she had to give up all the children she might ever have had. In the dead of night they were scraped under the knife of a witch with a steady hand and a smile . . .

It was the most expensive thing she had ever done. Once the woman was barren, her man returned. He wasn't grateful. He was tired; it hadn't been easy coming back. He said, Let's have no more of this. She nodded slowly, saying, I don't dare go on. She was still weak, and though he was only a little stronger he carried her to the car and sat beside her in there; he spread a map across their knees and told her to choose a place where he could leave her. She would not choose. Paris, then, he said. He remembered a visit he had made there long before he met her. He remembered how the river had charmed him, how it had seemed to talk to the sun and to the city it flowed through, bringing news from the sea rolling in under the bridges. He remembered lion heads carved above great, heavy doors, and how in their old age the heads had yawned instead of roaring. He thought that she would like it there, and that she would not be lonely.

He showed her the route that they would take, and they agreed that at any point before Paris she could say 'stop' and leave him then. She hadn't packed any of her belongings. She wore a brown dress, flat brown shoes and a shabby coat of the same colour. The coat belonged to the man, and he had put a little money in an inside pocket. The woman's hands spent the entire journey folded on her lap, safe and still. Sometimes she looked out of the car window at the things that passed them by. Sometimes she looked at him. They didn't really talk. At one point he coughed and said, 'Excuse me.'

When they got to Dunkirk she didn't feel able to say stop, nor could she say it at Lille, or Amiens. She wasn't particularly worried about where she would go or what she would do. Those things didn't seem important. Silently, he changed his mind again and again, but at every turn he remembered how she had told him to die.

At Paris, on a tiny street that ran alongside a vast, busy one, he let her out of the car, and she was like a moth in her drab dress as she leaned in and told him that she had never meant him harm.

He mumbled that he hoped she would be well.

He drove away and the buildings around her drew closer together. With her eyes she climbed their sepia stonework, the curls and flourishes. There was a ring on her finger; he had given it to her in exchange for their thousandth kiss, and she turned it around and around, trying to find a way out of her skin. I have loved a fool who counted kisses, she thought. The sky passed above like glass. She sat down on the pavement and watched people walking around. There was a cafe directly opposite her. Couples went in holding hands and the dust on the windows hid what they did next, where they sat, what they had to drink. A woman came out of the cafe alone. She was dressed entirely in navy blue. In one perfectly manicured hand she held twelve fountain pens. In the other she held a white cup. She took a seat on the pavement, too.

'Drink this,' said the woman in blue.

'What is it?' asked the woman in brown.

Blue became brisk: 'It'll buck you up. Hurry.'

Listlessly, obediently, Brown drained the little white cup in one gulp. Bitter espresso, that's all it was.

'Now. Take these.' Blue handed Brown the fountain pens. 'You have to go soon. You've got a lot to catch up on.'

Brown did not feel particularly bucked up. If anything, she felt duller. 'Go where? Catch up on what?'

'Writing,' Blue replied. 'You write things. I was never any good at it, but you will be. That's where you'll live and work.' And she pointed at the front door of a house a few steps away. The door was painted bright blue, so you couldn't miss it.

'Er . . . what?'

Blue laughed; her laughter was delightful. 'Oh . . . you'll see.'

'Who are you?'

'That man who just dropped you off and drove away . . . I'm the one who was meant for him,' Blue said, calmly. 'There was a terrible mistake a few decades ago; there are many cases like ours, and they're only just being sorted out. From now on, I'm in charge. I'll take care of everything. All you have to do is go through that door and into your proper place in life. And you will forget him. You will forget today, you will forget everything.'

Brown was astonished, and said nothing.

'Doesn't that please you?' Blue asked.

'No it doesn't,' said Brown. 'I don't want to forget about him. I don't want my proper place in life. I don't want to go in at that door. I don't want—'

'Your heart is broken, poor little fool,' Blue interrupted. 'You have no idea what you want.'

'It isn't broken,' Brown said, stubbornly.

Blue spread her hands: 'Well . . . what do you propose doing instead?'

All around them people were speaking a language Brown didn't understand; it was like silence with sharp edges in it. Sound broke against her eardrums. It didn't hurt, but it wasn't pleasant. Brown looked at Blue carefully. Their skin was more or less the same shade of brown, but after that there were only differences. Blue was much better-looking than Brown was; smaller and tidier-looking, too. There was a sweetness to the corners of Blue's mouth, and her manner was warm. She would be good to him. Speaking as quickly as she could, Brown told Blue about the man she was meant for; just small details off the top of her head, the things that years boil down to. Blue produced a small book and pencil, nodded, listened, and made notes.

Then Brown went through her new front door with her hands full of fountain pens.

She didn't look back, so she didn't see Blue throw the

notebook away. She didn't see the car, returning to the spot where it had left her, inching along as her lover stuck his head out of the window, looking for her. Blue walked over to him, and as the man spoke, Blue tilted her head and listened with an expression of great sympathy . . .

*

Brown walked into her home under a row of crystal chandeliers, their octopus arms outstretched, their hearts layered with old gold. The high ceiling was painted with a map that looked both old and new – it was faded, the paint cracked, but the fade was bright. The map showed that the world had edges you could fall off, into blank white. *Here . . . be . . . dragons.*

Upstairs, on a desk by a window, there lay a fountain pen that looked identical to the ones she held. Brown picked up the fountain pen and shook it. The cartridge sounded empty. She wished she'd bought new cartridges instead of new pens; it would have been far more economical. Beside the desk was a wastepaper basket full of crumpled paper. There were more fountain pens in there, too. She didn't really want to sit down at this desk, it seemed to be a place of nerves and wretchedness. But there was a fresh pad of paper open, and the chair was drawn out, so she sat down. She laid the new pens down one by one. She looked at them, twiddled her thumbs, picked a pen up, put it down, examined the notepad. She was clearly supposed to write something, but not a single idea made itself available to her. Was it meant to be a letter? Or a report? The fact that it was to be hand-written suggested a personal aspect. Her writing was to be addressed to someone in particular. Brown pushed a pen with her fingertip and it rolled against another pen, and all the pens fell off the table. How was she supposed to do this if she didn't know who she was doing it for? It was ridiculous.

After about twenty minutes, she heard scrabbling at the door and leapt to her feet.

But whoever it was, they weren't coming into the room, they were just pushing a piece of paper under the door.

It read:

Write the stories.

'Stories?' Brown howled. 'What stories?'

She ran through the rooms of her house, looking for the person who had ordered stories. She ran downstairs and watched the street. It could have been anyone. Anyone. How could someone have slipped in and slipped out again without her knowing? Perhaps they'd followed her in . . .

Brown returned to the desk and picked the pens up off the floor. She wrote down the words: *Once upon a time*, and then she stopped. She looked about her. There was something missing. There was something wrong. She found a mirror and turned around in front of it with her arms held out in front of her. She was all there, all in one piece. Then what? What had she lost?

Brown wrote down a list of things that had been stolen from her, things she had lost, both replaceable and irreplaceable. Umbrellas, gloves. Expensive tubes of mascara. Cheques. Earrings; one out of virtually every pair she had ever owned until she had had to leave off wearing earrings altogether. Several jackets, left at cafes and parties. A diary, once – a year's thinking. What else . . . a television and a cat, from the time she had lived by herself and left her front door unlocked one day. The thief had left a ransom note for the cat; she'd considered responding to it, but hadn't.

Another piece of paper came in under the door: *WRITE THE STORIES*.

This time Brown didn't bother searching for the person who wanted stories. She would not be toyed with, and she would not obey. Instead she went out into the city, to look for what she had lost. There was no guarantee that she would recognise it even if she found it, but trying felt better than sitting at that strange and awful desk. Everything seemed like a clue. The glances of strangers, the first letter of every street sign she passed – she tacked them together and created the name of a street that was impossible to reach. She didn't give up. She went looking every day.

And every day there was a note or two. *Write the stories*. And sometimes there was money, so that she could eat.

People began to call her Madame la Folle. One day she passed a man who stood playing his guitar on a corner of the Boulevard St-Germain, his back to the churchyard railings, and she realised he was singing about her – Madame la Folle with your money falling out of your pockets, trampling your own bread underfoot, leaving a trail of letters you meant to post . . . what else have you lost?

The list in her notepad grew and grew. As she read it she turned a ring round and round her finger. It was made of cheap brass, and it was slightly misshapen, as if unable to withstand the heat of her body. She could not recall exactly how she had come by the ring, or when she had first put it on. She pulled the ring off her finger and felt pain, which surprised her. She looked up at the map on the ceiling, inspecting continents through the brass circle she held in her hand. Seen through the ring, the borders of each country throbbed and blurred.

'Where are you?' she murmured. 'Where are you?' She wanted the question removed from her with forceps at white heat, leaving a clean cavity behind. Then, perhaps, she would be able to perform her task. She was beginning to feel that she owed it to whoever was keeping her alive.

There were moments in which Brown forgot her search. She came across a flock of red balloons once, tied to railings, and since no one was watching she popped them, one by one, with her sharp fingernails. And she enjoyed avoiding light. It made her feel triumphant. She made night-time trips to Sacré-Cœur, darting around the glare of the floodlights that the boats flung out as they passed along the river bank. When she reached the basilica she crept down its steps and jumped high where the bottom step sat directly on the hill. She jumped as high as she could and she closed her eyes and made believe that she had fallen into the city's arms. Madame la Folle.

*

Blue's man kept her waiting while he tried to get Brown back. He put up posters with photographs of Brown all around Paris, asking if anyone had seen her. But the wind blew the posters away into the Seine, or he saw people take the posters down and make off with them – a different person each time, and he would give chase, shouting out for an explanation. But no one explained, and no one helped him. He knew it was all coincidence – he told himself it was coincidence, because it was horrifying to think that, having made a decision, he was now being actively prevented from changing it. Blue was by his side at all times, and she was devoted and affectionate. Instead of asking annoying questions while he was working, she attended to her own affairs. Brown began to seem like a strange dream he had had. She would never come back, and it was perverse to chase her like this. Blue . . . Blue was no trouble at all. So he turned to her.

It didn't work. He kept it up for a couple of years, saying: 'Yes, I'm very lucky,' to anyone who complimented him on his improved circumstances. But it didn't feel like luck. It felt arranged. Blue was a stranger, and she never became a friend. One evening the man stood by the fireplace in their living room, looking at a photograph in a magazine. It accompanied an article about Blue and himself, a profile of them as an artisan couple. The man tried to read the article as if he were someone else, someone who didn't know them. The couple in the photograph complemented each other beautifully; her glossy head on his shoulder, his arm tucked around her with his cuff drawn up over his fingers, so he held her through the linen of his sleeve. That was how precious she was to him – she couldn't be touched with a naked hand. He built doll's houses and she peopled them with dolls. Film stars and sports stars bought them for their children. The couple in the photograph hoped for children of their own soon. Quoting a poet, the artisan man said that their love was a lifelong love, a love for all the lives they might ever have had. He read that again. Had he really said that? He repeated the words aloud. Then he threw the magazine onto the fire and didn't stay to watch it burn.

Blue was in her studio making eyes for her dolls, letting a single drop of dye fall from a pipette into each glass ball, watching it until it soaked through. She didn't greet him – she was lost in detail. He picked up a brown eye and was impressed, as always. The dye floated in the centre of the sphere, surrounded by clarity.

He handed the doll's eye back to his wife, a woman his friends gazed at with awe and admiration, a woman whose flaws were far outbalanced by her virtues, and he told her: 'Leave me.'

She looked up. 'I beg your pardon?'

'Go,' he said. 'Leave me. Please.'

'For how long?'

He turned away, so as not to have to look at her shock, so as not to have to watch her patience take form. He knew that he was bringing ruin upon himself.

'You're talking nonsense,' she said, to his back. 'We work well together. We have a life together.'

'I know,' he said. 'But if you don't leave, I will.'

'Is this about . . . her?' She didn't ask angrily. She sounded . . . curious, wistful. 'Still? After all this time?'

'No,' he lied.

'I don't understand you. Her love was bad. You told me so yourself.'

When he turned to face her he saw that she had picked up her pipette and returned to work. Drop after immaculate drop.

'Whatever you're feeling now, it will fade. I'm not leaving. And neither are you,' she said.

'I see,' he said. And he nodded. He went to his own studio, where he fell into a stupor he couldn't wake up from.

*

Brown thought she might be grieving for someone who had died. She walked around Père Lachaise, looking for a name that meant something to her alone. The cemetery watchmen pitied her. When she hid in the cemetery just before closing time, the watchmen all looked the other way. She was harmless. And perhaps the additional hours would help her find the right tomb at last. She passed the first few hours of the night surrounded by tall green fragrance. Lavender buds tickled her arms and back as she went up and down the tree-lined paths, looking at names carved in stone. Her hands were tucked into her sleeves in case of stinging nettles, so her torchlight kept faltering. Dormice shook the lavender with their paws and tails, caught Brown's reflection in the dark shine of their eyes and ran away with it. White-flowered shrubs thickened around her and so did sleep; it directed her limbs. Lie down now, sleep said, sweetly. Lie down. These are the secret hours of the day, the time that owls and bats take to themselves, the stars change places now; let them. You lie down.

She stopped walking when she saw the name Étienne Geoffroy for the fourth time. The cemetery was smaller than she had thought it was. Or there were parts of it that couldn't be brought to light, not by her torch, not even by the moon. She came to a path that divided into two, and she shone her torch to the left, then to the right—

She saw a man. He was standing on the other side of the path, half-hidden by a sapling. For a fraction of a second, less than that, she saw him. He darted out of sight; the rattling of branches deafened her. Her throat froze. Move, she told herself. You must move. *But if I take the wrong path – if I go deeper in –*

She listened for some sign, tried to find out where he was, but there was so much calling amongst the tombstones, croaking and chattering and echoes. *I must move. I must move*. After the first step the rest were easy, the way was sure, left, right, left right, and she fell down and cut her hands on stones because she heard him calling her. 'Madame la Folle! Madame la Folle? A word in your ear, if you please. Just a moment of your time . . .' She had lost her torch. A loud cracking sound nearby – him? Where was he? Everywhere. His voice was behind her, ahead of her, above, below. She rolled into a ball against the exposed roots of a tree for a moment. Then she raised herself up onto her knees and crawled, slowly, slowly, so slowly, *Cover me, leaves, cover me, earth, don't let him find me.*

Hands plunged through the leaves, seized her wrists and dragged her up. She screamed then. She screamed and screamed, first at the sky, which was whirling like water, then she was screaming into a hand clapped over her mouth. She looked into eyes too wide to be sane. He released her once she was quiet. A man with a shock of white hair and a face painted like a harlequin's, dead white with black diamonds around his eyes. His features were very hard. Skeletal.

'Why won't you just write the stories?' he said. 'You've been asked nicely.'

Fear pressed her tongue against her gums.

'Fear not, Madame,' the man told her. 'I am Reynardine. And I can get you whatever your heart desires.' He sat down upon a tombstone and patted the space beside him. What could she do? She joined him.

'The stories are for you?'

He shook his head. 'One moment.' He cleared his throat and his gaze grew shadowy, as if something dark had spilt into him. When he next spoke, it was with an accent that was familiar to her, but in a voice that was not. It was deep – more a vibration that came through the ground than a voice.

'Who is it?' she whispered.

'Can you see us?' And for a moment she saw and felt them all, crowding her. Faces she recognised from family photo albums, some she had never seen before, old ones leaning on walking sticks. They were all familiar. They all knew her, and she knew them. Then they relented and faded away.

'We're here,' they said, through Reynardine's lips.

'What do you want?'

'You are Yoruba.'

'Am I?'

'So you think your accent fools us . . .'

'But I can't even speak Yoruba!'

'That doesn't fool us either.'

'All right,' she said. 'I know. But look – I'm in Paris at the moment.'

'Don't interrupt,' they said. 'You might want to get away from us. You might feel that we crowd too close, that we want too much. But we like you. We think you're spirited. And we're trying to listen.'

'To what?'

'To what you won't tell us. We want your stories.'

'I don't have any. I don't know what to write.'

'Tell the stories. Tell them to us. We want to know all the ways you're still like us, and all the ways you've changed. Talk to us. We're from a different place and time . . .'

'I'm not lying to you,' she said, shaking her head. 'I really can't do it.'

'You can and you must,' they snapped. 'Those stories

belong to us. It doesn't matter what language they're in, or what they're about; they belong to us. And we gave them to you without looking at them first. So now it's time to see what we've done.'

After a long moment, the harlequin returned to himself and began speaking reasonably. They weren't asking for very much, were they? he asked. Just a few words on paper, anything she liked, anything that came to mind, nothing that anyone else need ever read. It didn't even have to be good.

He honestly expected her to believe that she could make a bad offering and her ancestors wouldn't mind.

'What's your part in this?' Brown demanded.

'Favours are a useful currency,' said Reynardine.

'You're working for them because favours are a useful currency?'

Reynardine yawned clownishly, and rubbed his eyes. Black paint came away on his knuckles. 'I work for myself,' he muttered. 'I'm freelance.'

Brown looked down at her hands. She had never been good at anything. There had never been any work that she'd been able to make her own. She raised a hand to the moonlight and the brass ring winked at her.

'I want what I lost,' she said.

'You should do this just because they asked you to. You came from these people. You owe them everything,' Reynardine pointed out.

Politely, she disagreed. She was vastly outnumbered, she knew that, but that didn't mean she would budge. There's a reason the Yoruba were famed as warriors.

Reynardine was amused.

'Do this and I'll restore what you lost,' he said.

Brown was suspicious. 'How? Why?'

Reynardine stood, and looked down at her. His gaze was very wild indeed; it seemed to have no focus. She came very close to flinching.

'How?' she asked again. 'Why?'

Reynardine made some answer, but it was muffled because he was walking into the ground; the earth covered his head.

*

Brown worked for days. She didn't know how many days – afterwards she would only ever be able to recall that time as a pause between two breaths she took. In between she ran through the twelve fountain pens. More appeared. She ran through blocks of paper, and more was provided. Occasionally she would feel a hand, a hand that was not her own, passing over her hair, as if blessing her. The words didn't come easily. She put large spaces between some of them for fear they would attack each other.

She'd thought she didn't have any stories, but in fact she had too many.

She put down things she didn't know she knew. She wrote about a girl who babysat herself while both her parents worked and worked for not enough pay. The girl didn't answer the door or the telephone because no one was meant to know she babysat herself, and besides, it might be the Home Office, and then they'd all be deported. So that she would not be scared, she pretended she was a spy and wrote secret spy notes on pink paper. She posted the spy notes out of the living-room window; she sent them spinning down onto the heads of passers-by, who picked them up and didn't understand them. They'd look up, but the girl had disappeared from the window – no one was supposed to know she was there.

Brown wrote about another girl who lived in a city that men were forbidden to enter. This girl knew nothing but the city and the stern stretch of coast that surrounded it, and she thought that men were just a funny story, and she didn't expect that she was missing much.

She wrote about an Okitipupa village boy who was nobody's boy, and earned money for himself by taking care of other children. She wrote about the afternoon nobody's boy returned to the village in despair, having mislaid four of his ten charges and roped the remaining six boys to his waist with a long piece of scarlet rope and a great many strong knots. He had spent two hours looking for those four boys, and was just on his way to the first of the boys' parents to confess what had happened when, in a moment like a nightmare, the missing boys jumped up from the shallow pits they'd been lying in, boy after boy shaking the earth with unearthly cries.

There was more, much more, and she put it all down, though she didn't see what good it could do. She put it all down for the ones who had said, Tell us. *Here are your stories, then. Have them back.*

Reynardine came then, and he smiled at her, and he took all her stories away.

What did Reynardine leave behind?

A man she knew.

He slumped against the wall of her room, with his legs stuck out in front of him. His eyes were open, but when she spoke to him, he didn't look at her. He didn't breathe. His heart didn't beat. His lips were blue. Brown lay down with him, and she tried to give him breath, and she asked him if he was dead.

'I don't know,' Reynardine answered, from the doorway. 'Probably.'

And Brown turned to him and cried out: 'Reynardine! Reynardine! What have you brought me?'

Reynardine tutted. 'I brought you what you lost.'

'But he's still lost! You tricked me.'

'Listen,' said Reynardine. 'Have you considered joining him?'

Brown sat listening, thinking. She held her man's hand, and she didn't feel able to let go just then.

'I dare you,' Reynardine said, 'to be lost together.'

She wasn't as worried as she could have been. She had recently been visited by people long deceased. They had seemed well enough, and had even been so bold as to make demands of her. She accepted the dare.

Reynardine snapped his fingers, and she stopped living.

*

Stiffly entwined in each other's arms, the two lovers were moved to Père Lachaise – *sans* coffins, and at dead of night. Reynardine took care of that. He was owed favours and he made the arrangements. It's said that Reynardine is monstrously cruel, but sometimes, to a woman who takes him at his word, he can show kindness.

The first moment in the tomb was the most forbidding. The silence, the stillness, the dark.

Then they realised: they were together, and there was no one else. She felt his lips tremble against her forehead. After that he became courageous and brought his arms down around her. He kissed her closed eyelids and he kissed her mouth and he kissed handfuls of her hair and he kissed her elbows. She placed her brass ring on the palm of his hand and closed his fingers around it. He opened his hand and the ring was gone. It had not fallen, unless it had fallen through him, and if so, it had left no mark. No more counting kisses.

Reynardine had thrown a candle and a box of matches in with them. They didn't need the candle . . . in the darkness they learnt to waltz. Then they lit the candle anyway – why not? And they let its flame warm their stone house for a little while as they danced on behind their locked door.

Mary Foxe saved my life once. She has a vested interest, of course – if I go, she goes. But she didn't do it as if she had a vested interest. She did it as if she cared. It was nine, maybe ten years ago. Before Daphne. I was working late at night, trying to get something down about a boy at war; he'd signed up to be a hero and had all sorts of ideas about standing aloof from both his equals and his superiors. I couldn't yet tell whether this kid's stupid ideas were going to get him killed, or whether he was simply going to be slapped down and made useful in some minor way. It was not a story about me – in France I learnt to do exactly what I was told. I'm talking about the Marne – frontal assaults; don't blink, don't think, just do. I looked around my study and everything was just too damn cosy. The anodyne calm. The gentle, sputtering dance of the fire, and the books that towered all around me, their spines turned out. I couldn't write down the echo of an exploded shell. I couldn't smear the smell of the trench across the page. I couldn't do this thing so that anyone could see what I meant. The things that had happened – things I laughed at when they crossed my mind – you can't hold onto them too long, unless you want to go crazy. The dead don't trouble me – dead is dead. It's the ones who took impact and lived. Joe Persano: shrapnel put his left eye out, and he refuses to wear an eye patch; a glass eye rolls slightly in the crumpled hole left for it. Tom Franklin has no hands. Ivor Ross's right trouser leg is empty and half his mouth is puckered up for a sour, perpetual kiss. And here I am, whole. It got so I had a pistol to my head, there in my cosy study, and I wasn't at all sure that I'd taken it out of my desk drawer myself. I must have been holding it, but there was no feeling in my fingers; the gun seemed to be floating, held up by Joe's ill will, Tom's, and Ivor's. The gun's nozzle pushed at my skin, as if trying to find the correct part of my skull to nestle against. Death like the insect, menacing the tree . . .

'Shhh,' said Mary Foxe. She reached over my shoulder, prised my fingers loose one by one, and took the gun. Then she stuck a pipe in my mouth. I watched tobacco trickle into the bowl. I watched her hand, tamping the tobacco down. Tap, tap, tap, and the pipe moved between my clenched teeth. Tap and pour, tap and pour. She lit a match, and I watched the flame circle the bowl once, twice, three times, before it took and a mist rose.

'I know you think you're going mad,' she said. 'But you're not. Don't be perverse. Celebrate.'

She poured some scotch from the decanter on my windowsill and pushed the glass towards me. Between that and the pipe my sense of perspective began to return. I opened the desk drawer and the gun was in there, looking innocent, as if it hadn't had an outing this evening, or ever.

Mary sat down and set the decanter at her feet. 'Say something, you,' she said, warningly.

'Mary,' I said. 'I seem to have a memory – false, I hope – of you being my wife at some point.'

Mary stirred in her seat. 'Oh yes?'

'Yes. My loving wife. I did all I could for you. But you weren't happy. You said I didn't listen to you and that I treated you like a child. You moved out of the nice house I was working overtime to pay for, the house I bought because you said you liked it. I waited a week – everyone told me to give it time, that you'd come to your senses. I was always home on time, and never ran around on you. On weekends I drove you all over town like I was your chauffeur, took you to see the friends you wanted to see. I took you to the opera on your birthday, for crying out loud. I hadn't put a foot wrong. But you didn't come back. Your friends had lent you money and you'd moved into some tiny one-room apartment. I found that out by visiting a friend of mine who was married to a friend of yours. He said he didn't want to get involved because his wife would raise hell for him if she ever found out he'd told me. So I turned on the water-works. It shocked him so much he told me where you were and said he hoped I got you and my manhood back . . .'

I stopped for a while, because it was strange. The more I said, the clearer the memory became. I didn't think I was going to be able to say any more – I just wanted to watch the thing play out in my head. Mary poured me some more scotch. That helped.

'I went round at dusk. I was drunk as drunk – that was my preparation for the possibility that there might be another guy there with you. I knocked on your door – I knocked with my head and my elbows, like I was trying to dance with the door. Amazingly, you opened the door, with this resigned look on your face that said you'd been expecting me. I said: Honey, and something else, something like Honey, look at me, can't you see how it is? Come home. And you looked kind of sorry for me. But I saw that you had a chain on the door, and you kept it on even when you saw that I was just a wreck, and begging. When I saw that you had that chain

on, I knew I was going to hurt you. I was going to get in there
and hurt you. It was kind of like caging up an animal –
something – the bars, the boundaries hard and cold like
that – it just makes the animal as mad as hell, even if it was
just a fluffy little lapdog before. It becomes another thing
altogether. I stood up straight and I lowered my voice and,
I don't know how, because I was out of my skull drunk
and could barely move my tongue, I began to talk to you as
if I was sober and possessed of reason. I spoke warmly
and with understanding and had some soothing response
to every objection you made to letting me in. You let me in,
and I almost fell in through the door, but I told myself keep
it together, keep it together, you still love her. There was
no one else there, you were all alone. I was so glad. I was so
glad. I tried to hold you, to get a kiss from you. And you said:
"St John, you're hurting me." I only wanted to kiss you – how
could that be hurting you? But you kept saying that I should
"stop it". I'd slapped you a few times by then. Trying to make
you quiet.'

She dimpled at me. 'Go on,' she said.

'Well . . . things went on like that between you and me . . .'

'Went on like what, exactly?'

'I kept hitting you, I guess. I picked up a chair and I
backed you up against a wall and started slamming it on
either side of your head, just to scare you, at first. "Shhh," I
said. "Shhh." You got too scared, or not scared enough. You
kept putting your hands up to protect your face – I just
grabbed your arm and punched you until you were on the
floor. I stomped on your hands.'

Mary nodded, as if going over a mental checklist.

'I kicked you in the head.'

She nodded again.

'Then you must have worked out that I kept going for you because you kept moving. So you kept still. I walked away and watched you from across the room, to see what you'd do if I gave you room. You didn't do anything, just lay there. I walked towards you again and you held your breath. I stayed close to you and you didn't exhale; you tried to die.'

'Go on,' Mary said, wanly. She wasn't smiling any more.

'I crouched down and I talked to you. Just some things in your ear. No idea what I was saying, nonsense probably. I was just talking to calm you down. While I was talking I slit your throat. Messily, because I couldn't walk in a straight line, let alone guide my hand from ear to ear without stopping. It was a real mess. A real mess.'

Mary didn't shudder, or look shocked. She looked polite, if anything. Somewhere between polite and bored.

'It couldn't have happened. I'd have got the chair for that.' I wasn't really talking to her – more thinking aloud.

'Yes. You would have. But too late for me. What made you do it?'

'What made me—'

'Yes. Why did you do it?'

'You're asking me why, in my false memory of our marriage, I killed you?'

'I'm trying to help you think.'

I made a few brief guesses – I was in a killing mood, I was afraid of time, I was fooled by some inexplicable assurance that I was merely dreaming out my revenge, making myself safe for the daylight hours. Love fit in somewhere, I wasn't sure how – disbelief that it had gone away, trying to force its return, trying to create an emergency that would scare love out of hiding.

'You did it because of love? Because you loved me too much?' she asked, jovially. Her merriment was giving me the creeps. The whole conversation was giving me the creeps – talking like this about something that hadn't really happened. I shouldn't have started it. She'd seemed so interested, though, and that was rare. Maybe she was trying to be nice in her own way.

Mary pulled the stopper out of the scotch decanter and took a long swallow. 'Okay, never mind about love,' she said, wiping her mouth. 'You hated me. Because I wouldn't come back and I was making you hate yourself, making you think there was something wrong with you.'

'No . . . I already told you. It was because of the chain on the door.'

'Mr Fox.' Mary toyed with the cut-glass stopper. 'Is this a joke?'

'You found it funny?'

'That you just recounted one of your stories to me as if it was something that you really did?'

'Hm,' I said. 'You're right. I'll write it down.'

'You already did,' she said, her forehead creased.

I waited blankly while she searched my stack of note-books and picked up number six. She licked her finger and opened it up near the end. There, in my handwriting, was the tale I had just told her. As soon as I saw it I remembered writing it, and I was flooded with relief. Thank God it wasn't me. Thank God I wasn't capable of doing such a thing. It was cold, but I was sweating. When I put the book down I saw that I'd left moist ovals on the paper.

'*Now* I'm worried,' Mary said.

the training at madame de silentio's

Madame de Silentio takes in delinquent ruffians between the ages of sixteen and eighteen and turns them into world-class husbands by the time they are twenty-one. You're admitted to Madame de Silentio's Academy if you answer at least 85% of her entrance exam correctly, and you graduate with a certificate that is respected in every strata of polite society. No one can ever remember any of the questions that were on Madame de Silentio's entrance exam. I know I can't – I tried my best to fail the exam. I preferred not to be educated, fearing it wouldn't suit me. Of course, I know better now. I won't lie, it took me half a year, but I now realise how lucky I am to have this opportunity to become a man of true worth, to have the man I will be intercept the boy that I was.

What is her secret, you may ask. How did Madame de Silentio attain her ranking amongst the great educators of the modern world? It's simple. Madame de Silentio knows what's best for young people. She knows what's appropriate. She refrains from cluttering our minds with information we don't need to know. Here at Madame de Silentio's our textbooks get straight to the point – European history is boiled down to a paragraph, with two sentences each for the histories of Africa, Asia and the Americas. Australasia doesn't count. Young men at Madame de Silentio's Academy learn practical skills that set us in good stead for lives as the husbands of wealthy and educated women. Here is a sample of the things we are taught:

Strong Handshakes, Silence, Rudimentary Car Mechanics, How to Mow the Lawn, Explosive Displays of Authority, Sport and Nutrition Against Impotence.

It says in the prospectus that Madame de Silentio's students eat, sleep and breathe good husbandry. That's true. We're taught to ask ourselves a certain question when we wake up in the morning and just before we fall asleep: *How can I make Her happy?* 'Her' being the terrible, wonderful goddess that we must simultaneously honour, obey and rule (she'd like us to rule her sometimes, we're told) – the future wife. In our Words of Love class we learn all the poems of Pablo Neruda by heart, and also Ira Gershwin and Dorothy Fields lyrics. Love Letters, a compulsory extracurricular course of study, involves a close reading of the letters of Héloïse and Abelard. Our Decisive Thinking examinations are conversations conducted before the entire class, and your grade depends not on the answer you give, but on the tenacity with which you cling to your choice. You earn a grade A by demonstrating, without a hint of nervousness or irritation, that you are impervious to any external logic. You earn an A+ if you manage this whilst affecting a mild and pleasant demeanour.

We sleep eight to a dormitory, and our dormitory bedsteads are iron, with shapes from the end of days twisted into the headboards – lions lying alongside lambs, children caressing serpents. Some of the boys sit up in these dormitory beds and scream in the night, but then the matron comes with a cup of warm milk and puts a few drops of her special bittersweet medicine in it, and the screaming boy drinks deep and the trouble goes away, far away. Madame de Silentio understands that becoming a man of true worth is a difficult process. And we understand that once we're in the academy we've got to stay here for as long as it takes – there's no recourse to parents or guardians, as they've signed their rights to us away in their contract with Madame de Silentio, and it's our own stupid fault for having been so unmanageable. Eighteen is the age at which any student is free to leave the Academy, but by then we've become used to the place. This is no philanthropic institution, mind you – the families of heiresses pay Madame de Silentio considerable sums of money, sums that we students can only guess at and whisper about, to ensure that they get the perfect husband for their precious Elaine, to ensure that their wayward Katherine is settled with the right life-partner. The Academy is in many ways a business, but there's nothing wrong with that. Madame de Silentio has found her niche, and the way of the world is such that if she did not demand recompense for her efforts she would receive none. So, good for Madame de Silentio.

Having recently been made Head Prefect, it's my duty to write a new chapter of the handbook that each new pupil is given on their first day, that awful first day when you just think you're not going to be able to stand it. The handbook provides some company. I take this responsibility very seriously, just as seriously as I take keeping the juniors in order and being a good ambassador for the Academy when we have to leave the grounds to round up the runaways. I've consulted the annals of school history, and I found mention of an act of disobedience committed by two moderately promising students – it happened twenty-five years ago, and the consequences were quite grave. I conducted interviews with Madame de Silentio herself, and with those teachers who remembered what had happened, and I've pieced together a narrative that I'd like to try out on you. I think it makes an invaluable cautionary tale for any new boy who is thinking of defying our headmistress.

*

Charles Wolfe and Charlie Wulf met in their second year of studies at Madame de Silentio's, when they were assigned neighbouring beds in the same dormitory. Charlie, at seventeen, was Charles's elder by a year. By all accounts the boys took notice of the fact that they essentially had the same name. In diaries, and in correspondence intercepted by staff, each boy declared that there must be meaning in the similarity between their names. They felt they were brothers. Interesting, because they were very different.

Photographs reveal Charlie Wulf to have been a bit of a pretty boy. Eyes like great big puddles, Byronic waves of hair, the spare frame of a long-time drug addict – before joining the student body he had been forcibly and abruptly weaned off opium in our soundproof music room, which was placed off-limits for three weeks. It seems favouritism brought Charlie to the Academy. I refer to the letter written to Madame de Silentio a full year before he was admitted, in which his mother and father, taking turns to write a word each, explain that in the silence of the heart every parent chooses a favourite. In Mr and Mrs Wulf's case they chose the same one, much to the jealousy and rage of their other nine children. Siblings always detect these things, but without proof there's not a lot they can do. Charlie seemed to have been born an escapist; at the age of seven, having complained of a boredom that made him 'feel sick in his tummy', he broke into his father's liquor cabinet and drank himself into a state of catalepsy. By the age of fifteen he was seeking oblivion in opium dens, and since his wealthy parents made him a separate allowance twice the size of that allotted to each of his siblings, Charlie was able to buy almost as much oblivion as he desired, running through a month's allowance in less than a week and beatifically starving until the time came for the next instalment. The letter from Mr and Mrs Wulf also lists certain diseases Charlie had contracted and been treated for, ending with a deadly scare that was the last straw. He'd been sent to rehabilitation clinics and boot camps and each time he had escaped with the aid of his captors. Mr and Mrs Wulf believed Madame de Silentio's Academy was the only institution without a trace of indulgence at its heart, and therefore the Academy was the only place that could clean their son up. They would give custody of their son over to Madame Silentio if it would save his life. *Charlie's life shall be saved*, Madame de Silentio assured them. *Better than that – his life shall be made useful.* Charlie Wulf was weak of character, consistently receiving D grades or lower for his Decisive Thinking. He was also a cheat when it came to exams, and a plagiarist when it came to essays – he was punished for the latter two faults twenty-seven times in his first year alone. These faults aside, he was well liked for his easy manner and the way he successfully avoided snitching on others, even when it was easier, perhaps even advantageous, to do so.

Charles Wolfe was fair-haired, and secretive. His features were crooked and unattractive. Much less is known about him, much more conjectured. Charles's father was a government official in India; his household included several guards and a poison taster, all of whom were present at every meal. Major Wolfe's very brief letter to Madame de Silentio, referring to Charles simply as 'the boy', indicates disgust at Charles's habit of stealing things. *'Blue things – always blue things – the boy seems to reckon there isn't enough blue in the world. See what you can do with him.'* Mr Curie, one of our science teachers, recalls seeing Charles Wolfe leaning against the Academy railings during recreation, drinking Coca-Cola through a blue straw, with such a tough look in his eyes that no one dared mock the dainty way he took his refreshment. Mrs Engels, one of our English literature teachers, recounts her suspicion, unsupported by any documentation, that it had taken Charles Wolfe much longer than normal to learn how to speak. He seemed to have learnt to read long before he learnt to speak. Mrs Engels says that she sometimes remarked on the unusual way Charles Wolfe formulated his sentences, and when she did he fell silent and seemed ashamed. Charles Wolfe held grudges. He wrote in his diary that he would like to kill Mrs Engels. It seems Charles Wolfe was capable of hating with a single-mindedness that sometimes took him into trances. *Subdue this*, he wrote several times in his diary. *Subdue this.* Charles Wolfe took every prize and passed every test and exam with distinction. He was going to make a first-rate husband. The teachers weren't sure about him, though. They kept an eye on him. There had been incidents in the first year – there had been no evidence that the incidents were connected to him. But still. We won't blame them for their vigilance.

The grounds of the Academy are extensive. One asset we

used to boast, but are now denied access to, is the lake. A thirty-year-old prospectus shows a group of prefects boating on the lake as a treat, but the lake has a dark and forbidding aspect, and the prefects don't seem to be having much fun. The boys were allowed to boat occasionally, but they were forbidden to swim. And Charles and Charlie seem to have been magnetised by the lake. *The water is very green and has a sweet taste*, both boys wrote in their diaries, at different times. Exactly the same phrase at different times. Charles Wolfe goes on to conjecture that it's a vial of the lake water that the matron carries around with her and uses when someone needs medicine in their warm milk. He notes that after a few mouthfuls of the lake water you 'feel fine. Like a king.' He also notes that Charlie Wulf guzzled the lake water in a manner that worried him slightly. If you're wondering about the diaries, Madame de Silentio insists that we keep them, and that we write full accounts of our thoughts and our days. Then she spends all Sunday reading them. It's a tricky business, writing the diaries. Madame de Silentio doesn't want to be acknowledged in our diaries, so we have to write them as if we don't know anyone's going to read them. It's like prayer, somehow. She never comments or acts on what she reads in our diaries, no matter what's in there – that makes it even more like prayer.

In his diary, Charlie, a weak swimmer, records the afternoon he leant too far into that sweet green taste and fell: '*Into the shock of the water. My mouth opened and the lake rushed into me, a strong, cold, never-ending arm rammed down my throat. I didn't know you could fall like that inside a body of water, that when you fall it's as hard and helpless a thing as falling through air.*' Charles Wolfe dived and retrieved his pathetic friend, and they both saw something incredible. I say incredible even though during my interview with her Madame de Silentio shrugged and spoke of it as something quite commonplace. In swimming to shore, the boys stirred the water with open eyes, and beneath them they saw a bed of silt and rock with a shape pressed into it. Each stroke was firm and clear, even the gap between the emaciated thighs. It was a man down there. A man trapped at the bottom of the lake, wrapped round and round with a great, rusty, padlocked chain. His face seemed very white and stiff to them at first, then they realised that a mask had been forced over it – a commedia dell'arte mask, with its thick ivory grimace. Under the weight of all that water, the man was alive, and he saw them seeing him, and he struggled, and struggled. 'Yes, I had a prisoner out there,' Madame de Silentio says. 'Thought it was the safest place, but no. Reynardine was his name. No use dwelling on all that, though. Won't do a blind bit of good.'

The next seven days of each boy's diary hold the dutifully scrawled lines: 'Nothing today', the bare minimum required to meet Madame de Silentio's demand that we record something every day. Matron Seacole, who has since retired, very kindly responded to my written enquiry with the recollection that Charlie Wulf kept the dormitory up three nights in a row with the shouting and kicking he did in his sleep, and had to be dosed a total of ten times. Charles Wolfe was wakeful, but didn't fuss and said he was fine. The boys wrote notes to each other, in a code that I have been unsuccessful in cracking. I can draw no firm conclusions as to what was happening inside the heads of these boys during the seven days of what they described as 'nothing'. Charlie's schoolwork slipped badly. Charles's schoolwork remained at an excellent standard.

On the eighth day, both boys meticulously recorded a 'conversation with a prisoner' in their diaries. They had learnt the prisoner's name, and they had learnt that he had been a prisoner a long time, longer than he could remember. They had learnt that Madame de Silentio had imprisoned this man, and that the man wished to be freed. And they wished to free him.

Madame de Silentio, Charles wrote in red ink, beneath that day's diary entry. *Why did you do this to Reynardine?*

Madame de Silentio stuck to her policy of not responding to diary entries.

The teachers suggested keeping a close watch on the boys, but Madame de Silentio insisted that they were intelligent boys undergoing a thought experiment, that they were not seriously planning to do anything.

The teachers kept the boys under close observation anyway.

Charles and Charlie didn't return to the lake for quite some time. If it were not for the fact that they knew the man's name was Reynardine, I would say the 'conversation with a prisoner' recorded in their diaries is a fabrication, and an artless one at that. It looks fake to me; the tone of the exchange is almost unbearably stilted. But then the entire situation is unusual. And if the conversation was indeed a fabrication, it's difficult to establish where else they could have got the name Reynardine from.

The boys must have developed some system of passing notes that made them feel safe – perhaps they found a hiding place: either way, they stopped corresponding in code. Flurries of extant notes are filled with guesses at the relationship between Reynardine and Madame de Silentio and, oddly, a semi-serious argument about Reynardine's face beneath his mask. *He must be like a freak – a fish*, Charles wrote to Charlie. *He can breathe down there. He can speak.* Charles writes to Charlie of having swum down with a diving light between his teeth and spoken face to face with the prisoner, of having held the padlock that bound him in both hands, of testing the mechanism inside with a fingernail while Reynardine breathed bubbles in his ear. This in the darkness of 3 a.m., while the rest of the school – including the heavily dosed Charlie Wulf – snored . . . I can't imagine.

I reckon he looks like you or me, Charlie responded. *The question is, which?*

What do you mean by that? Charles wrote back to him, in very precise, very black lettering, the handwriting of hostility.

Thinking that the boys had been reduced to mere squabbling over aesthetics, the teachers relaxed. That was their mistake, because when the staff relaxed, the boys struck, bribing three first-years to report a sighting of rats in a first-floor broom cupboard and locking Madame de Silentio and Miss Fortescue, the deputy head teacher, into the broom cupboard when those two worthy ladies went marching in to investigate. After that Charlie stood guard outside Madame de Silentio's office. Within, it was the work of a few minutes for Charles, the experienced thief of small items, to unobtrusively comb Madame de Silentio's belongings and pocket two keys. He knew his padlocks, but was too pressed for time to exercise proper Decisive Thinking – all he could be sure of was that one or the other of these keys would free Reynardine.

When imagining such relationships – prisoner and gaoler

– you'd imagine that the gaoler is always aware of the where-
abouts of the key that gives her her power. You – or I, let's
say I – imagine her stroking the key and gloating over it,
taking it out nightly and admiring it. Not so. Madame de
Silentio says she'd just tossed the key into a drawer somewhere and hadn't looked for it for years. She didn't miss it.
Her office was in the order she'd left it in, and the baffling
time spent in the broom cupboard was brief enough to be
passed off as minor mischief on the part of the first-years, all
of whom she punished with a severity disproportionate to the
crime. 'Can't be slapdash with these things. Got to let them
know it's not on.'

And so Reynardine was freed. That simply, that easily,
because Madame de Silentio was unable to believe that she
could be disobeyed, Reynardine was freed by a boy who conspicuously asked for a dose and let the milk run out of his
mouth and soak his pillow once the matron had walked down
to the other end of the dormitory.

Reynardine rose up amongst the loose chains, his legs
twitching, as he had forgotten how to walk. Neither of the
boys record this; that's just how I think those first few seconds of freedom were. He told Charles he would be gone by
morning. He flexed his hands in a way that worried Charles,
but gave a gurgling laugh and said: 'You have nothing to fear
from me, boy.'

He told me he won't forget what we did for him, Wolfe
wrote to Wulf.

By the middle of the next day, Madame de Silentio knew
that Reynardine had been released. This wasn't due to any
psychic connection; it was due to the local news. 'The thing
about Reynardine,' Madame de Silentio explains, 'is that he

is a woman-killer. He doesn't do it joyously – oh no, he does it with dolour and scowling. Women upset him. He said to me once that he hates their Ways, that from the moment he encounters one of them he's forced to play a Role, and he won't stand for it. Paranoid nonsense.' The night he was released he passed through Greenwich, killing and killing. Forty women gone between 2:30 and 4 a.m., and he went quickly on throughout the country, doing more. Worse, in the days that followed, other killers, killers of children and aged parents and love rivals and husbands, they, too, swelled the murder rate, as if inspired. A bad week in time, an awful week of red shivers, the streets empty of civilians and full of police.

Madame de Silentio called the boys into her office and took the key back from Charles. Useless now, but still, it was hers. The boys didn't know what they'd done, they didn't connect this red week with Reynardine, until Madame de Silentio explained it to them.

For the rest of their time at the Academy they were in hell, without her even laying a finger on them or saying another reproving word to them. The two boys went around together, always together, without speaking to each other, their hair limp, their eyes bulging, their faces the faces of drowned men. Each day brought news of Reynardine's work in the world. *He didn't look like what he was*, Charlie Wulf wrote in his diary. That was his last entry before all the leavers' diaries were handed in. Charles Wolfe didn't mention the lake incident again.

Upon their graduation, Madame de Silentio sold Charles to a beautiful woman named Helene. She had blue eyes, which it thrilled him to look into. He believed that the petty thievery of his childhood had simply been impatience for the day when he would have two blue eyes like these to adore. But Helene was haunted by her past self. She'd been a fat child, even her ankles had been fat. In a letter to Madame de Silentio, Charles wrote that Helene had a serious fit of the hysterics when she saw him making supper for her – he was frying fish fingers in oil. She was unable to accept a hot meal as a gesture of love; she was convinced Charles was trying to make her fat again. He was able to soothe her – our training covers all emergencies, but he wished he hadn't had to draw upon it. Helene didn't like introducing Charles to her friends, either, because she found him ugly. She left him at home, or if she entertained at home she left him skulking around in the kitchen. As a test, Charles went missing for two weeks, roaming London, sleeping under newspapers on park benches. When he came home, Helene spoke of a party she'd recently been to, running rapidly through a list of anecdotes connected to names he didn't know, and she looked irritated when he asked her to slow down and explain who was who. 'I already told you,' she said. She hadn't noticed that he'd been gone. She'd probably come home from her parties and chattered away to thin air, believing that he was hidden in it somewhere, listening attentively. She hadn't been worried at all during his fourteen-day absence, hadn't looked for him.

'How can I be a better husband?' he asked her, humbly.

Helene gave Charles Wolfe a mask to wear. A white mask. Not flat white; rather a colour suggestive of earth, brilliant but faintly fibrous, as it is beneath the skin of a pear. The mask's expression was neither happy nor sad. Its lips ran in a straight, geometric line, a humanly impossible one.

It was a heavy mask; it changed the way Charles held his head, and, by extension, it changed the way he moved. As long as Charles wore the mask, Helene allowed him to escort her to dinners out, friends' weddings, etc. Helene's friends tried to act as if her masked husband didn't bother them, but he bothered them tremendously. I suppose it's hard to find a face friendly if you see it every day and it never smiles at you.

Charlie Wulf . . . Charlie Wulf was sold to a plain-looking woman. Plain, but wholesome and good-hearted. Laurel. She turned her back on the frivolous pursuits of her class and trained as a nursery-school teacher. She wore long skirts and always found a kind word and a hug for even the most tiresome of the children that played at her feet. Charlie had absorbed more training than anyone had credited him with, and he had no trouble speaking Words of Love to his wife. Laurel didn't like to hear them. It was all too insincere. She worried about how they looked as a couple – on the street, in their home. She turned all the household mirrors to the wall. She heard people making fun of her, even though Charlie assured her that she was imagining things. She became jealous if he appeared to take too much of an interest in conversation with her female friends. Laurel wrote Charlie tear-stained letters, turned him out of the house again and again, arrived unannounced at his hotel room in the early hours of the morning, just to check that he was alone. She couldn't believe in him.

At his wits' end, he asked her what he could do to help her believe.

And Laurel gave Charlie a mask to wear . . .

Reynardine might have come to the rescue (that would

have been unfortunate for Mrs Wolfe and Mrs Wulf). But favours aren't always returned. Charles and Charlie don't seem to have communicated at all after graduating. Not a word, not even an attempt at a word. They no longer had need of each other.

Or—

I realise I'm reading very finely between the lines here, but maybe those two had fallen in love, and wanted to spare each other the anxiety of speaking with subtext, each wondering what the other wanted. A boy of weak character and his strong-minded friend; neither would have been likely to declare themselves first. It's not impossible, is it, that what I'm saying could be true? It's the abruptness more than anything. In the first place they seem to have chosen each other to confide in, out of all the boys in the academy, when actually it would have been safer to do as most of us do and confide only in our diaries. For many months these two found something to say to each other every day. Then they married, and nothing. There are feelings of some kind in this matter, even if I don't know what they are. The lake deeper than either of them had supposed, Charles kicking for shore with Charlie in his arms, the seconds without light or breath before both heads rose up and claimed them . . .

I'm surprising myself. I'm not a romantic.

At any rate I've derived some interest from finding out about my father's time at the school. Before this I had been looking for answers. I'd wondered about the cloud that seems to hang over my name when it's called in the register, and I'd wondered why the murder rate is so high nowadays, and I'd wondered about the mask, and about the difficulty my father had in looking at me and speaking to me. My mother didn't speak to me either – she was always busy, she sat on committees and things. Only after years of schooling do I talk as others do. Even now Mrs Engels sometimes looks more thoughtful than usual when I volunteer an answer in class. And I wondered, of course, why I was sent here when I hadn't done anything wrong. It must have just been Decisive Thinking.

Mr and Mrs Fox were hosting a dinner party. Downstairs, a motherly looking woman with fat grey pin curls laid the table and checked on the various items being cooked in the kitchen. Upstairs, the Foxes were engaged in a dispute. Mrs Fox had left her dressing-room blinds up, and Mary Foxe stood on a block of air and observed the scene with interest. Mrs Fox had a lot of nice things, and she was careless with them – perfume bottles with plush atomisers peeped out of embroidered pillowcases. Silk stockings tangled themselves around ivory combs shaped like castles. A gleaming sable fur rippled in the light. Mrs Fox seemed to be using it to protect the carpet from her pots of face cream. The lady herself sat at her dressing table, her hair swept up into a chignon, her eyes downturned. She spoke, then her husband spoke, then she spoke again, with stubborn emphasis, and all the while she toyed with a brooch, a pink and white gold fox, complete with filigreed brush tail. Its eyes were two garnets.

Mrs Fox pinned the brooch to the collar of her dress, stood and made for the door, which Mr Fox promptly closed and leant against with his hands in his pockets.

Mrs Fox said something sarcastic. Her husband looked into her eyes and said nothing. Mrs Fox laughed nervously until the gaze ended. Then Mr Fox saw Mary. He grimaced slightly, and winked. Mary grimaced and winked back.

'What do you care whether I wear it or not? No one will notice.'

'You know what our friends are, D. Everyone will notice. So shut up and put it on.'

'What did you say to me, St John Fox?'

'Shut up and put it on.'

'You can't tell me to—'

'Shut up and put it on. Or I'll 'phone round and cancel.'

'Appearances,' Mrs Fox said. 'Got to keep up those appearances, haven't we?'

'What do you want, a slap?' He made his offer in a tone of flat pragmatism, like an expert barterer at market; it was as if he was saying: *Let's face it, you'll be lucky to get a slap.*

'Ha ha!' Mrs Fox's voice rang out scornfully. 'Go ahead!'

He took a step towards her and she ducked behind a standing mirror. He moved it aside and scooped her up in his arms. Within moments Mr Fox was pacing around the room with his lady wife over his shoulder, kicking ineffectually.

'I can't wear it,' Mrs Fox said, breathlessly. 'I told you.'

'Yes, you said it gives you a rash.' Mr Fox exchanged disbelieving glances with Mary.

'It's true.'

'Why now? You've had it a while.'

'I don't know. Maybe because you don't love me.'

'That's a ridiculous thing to say,' Mr Fox said, in a voice that was both hearty and hollow.

'What's ridiculous is you bullying me like this. Put me down, please. I'll wear the stupid ring – I'll wear it, I said, even if it makes my finger swell up to the size of my head. Then you'll be sorry.'

Having been set on her feet again, Mrs Fox caught sight

of her disarranged hair and wailed. Mr Fox went downstairs and, as he spent a few minutes charmingly obstructing the caterer's efforts to finalise preparations, Mary watched Mrs Fox pick up her wedding ring and slip it onto her finger. Mary watched Mrs Fox rub at her ring finger as she redid her chignon, pushing the gold band first above, and then below her knuckle, until at last she yanked it off and crossed over to the sink in the next room, where she plunged her hand under a running tap, so relieved by the cold in the water that she fell to her knees and splashed her face and her dress. Mary would have liked to speak to the woman, to try and offer her some kind of assurance that she would be happy at a later date. The urge to do so became overwhelming, so she left. Mr Fox was out in the garden, smoking his pipe. He murmured a pleasantry, which Mary ignored.

'Mr Fox. You're not going to change, are you?'

'I don't think I will, no.' His tone was light, but measured.

'For example – you're working on something at the moment, aren't you?'

'Of course.'

'Tell me what it is.'

He looked at her, considering. 'You really want to know?'

'I really want to know.'

'Well. It's about a man who works hard as an accountant all day and likes to go out driving late at night, to . . . to relieve his stress. And one night he's driving so fast he doesn't see a woman who's trying to hitchhike from the side of the lane, and he knocks her down. But he keeps going because he's afraid he killed her and would be arrested and go to gaol and all sorts of unpleasantness like that. The next night he stays at home. But the night after that he goes driving again and, well, he more or less deliberately knocks someone down. Over six months he makes a real career of it, knocking down pedestrians; mainly hookers . . . it really relieves his tensions—'

'Stop,' Mary said, brusquely.

'But I haven't even told you the best part yet.'

'You'll always refuse to see – or refuse to admit – that what you're doing is building a world—'

He smiled slightly, and she amended her words: 'What you're doing is building a horrible kind of logic. People read what you write and they say, "Yes, he is talking about things that really happen," and they keep reading, and it makes sense to them. You're explaining things that can't be defended, and the explanations themselves are mad, just bizarre – but you offer them with such confidence. It was because she kept the chain on the door, it was because he needed to let off steam after a hard day's scraping and bowing at work, it was because she was irritating and stupid, it was because she lied to him, made a fool of him, it was because she had to die, she just had to, it makes dramatic sense, it was because "nothing is more poetic than the death of a beautiful woman", it was because of this, it was because of that. It's obscene to make such things reasonable.'

He shrugged. 'These are our circumstances. I'm just trying to make sense of them,' he said.

Mary was silent.

'Everyone dies.' He smiled, crookedly. 'I doubt it's ever a pleasant experience. So does it really matter how it happens?'

'Yes!' She put a hand on his arm, trying to pass her shock through his skin. '*Yes.*'

'I'm sorry I've been wasting your time,' Mr Fox said, softly. The darkness in the garden absorbed the blue-black mane of his hair and made it look as if the sides of his face and the top of his head had been chiselled away.

He asked her: 'Do you want to stop playing?'

Mary began to answer him, but the guests arrived, in pairs. Three couples in all, and each brought wine, even though their hosts had plenty waiting. A blonde woman called Greta was very huffy with Mr Fox, refused to surrender her cheek for a greeting kiss but somehow made a joke of it. Her husband, a sleek blond man with a strong jaw, touched Mrs Fox's arm as he kissed her hello. The blond man's accent had the slightest hint of the foreign to it, and everyone called him by his surname: Pizarsky. Even his wife called him that. Pizarsky . . . Mary recognised the name. Her eyes widened.

Pizarsky looked at Mrs Fox often throughout the evening, and each time he looked it was for a moment longer than was casual. His gaze was hesitant. Almost meek.

Nobody seemed to notice this but Mary, who saw it all from her place outside the window, her heels grinding into the flowerbed. Should Mr Fox fear this Pizarsky, as a rival? The man was so quiet that it was impossible to tell. The other husbands vied endlessly for the most outrageous comment of the evening, planned a forthcoming fishing trip in great detail and addressed Mrs Fox with elaborate compliments on the food. Mrs Fox, pale-faced, accepted their tributes without a single guilty blush. She displayed her wedding ring for five minutes or so, then kept her hand beneath the tabletop. She and the other women spoke of ascending and descending skirt hems, and how difficult it was to hit upon the right length. Their eyes danced with the satisfaction of secret-society members talking in code. They interrupted each other. 'Do you remember . . .' they said. 'Do you remember when . . .'

After dinner, the six of them moved to the withdrawing room. Mr Fox had a dab of sauce at the corner of his mouth – Mrs Fox removed it with a swift, affectionate gesture and the corner of a very white napkin. Mr Fox kissed Mrs Fox's hand. When the teasing started up he mildly remarked that he thought a man might kiss his wife in his own drawing room on a Sunday evening if he felt like it. The others laughed hysterically. They'd started out sipping genteelly from glasses, but as they got drunker the drinking grew more lavish, and was done straight from bottles. They played charades, very badly, and were unable to establish who had won.

To Mary it looked like a great deal of fun.

what happens next

There was a death on the plane back to London. It was the woman beside me. I didn't know it could happen like that. I mean I knew, but I didn't believe it.

We pushed our seats back at the same time, our eyes met, and we laughed. We'd both ordered vegetarian meals. 'I hate this food,' she said. 'But I like getting it before everyone else.' Her name was Yelena. She was from the Ukraine, she told me, and I reminded her of her younger daughter. She was fifty-something, I think. Late fifties. Her fuzzy brown hair, her round, shiny eyes. She reminded me of a duckling, a greying duckling. I'd only just met her, but I liked her. I don't know. We talked about New York. She'd been visiting her eldest daughter, a journalist for a fashion magazine. 'You don't know how far she's come,' she said. What else . . . she showed me a group photo of her eldest daughter, her son-in-law, and her grandson. They looked happy and wealthy, suntanned in winter. I told her that I'd just been visiting my mother. 'Good daughter,' she praised. I shook my head: 'Only child.' She asked me what my mother does and I said she's a yoga teacher. I almost always lie about my mother. This woman, Yelena, started watching a sitcom and giggling, so I put on my noise-cancelling headphones and drank three-quarters of a bottle of cough syrup. I like it because it wears off faster than sleeping pills. I licked my lips. My stomach felt full; it seemed to sigh. When I looked out of the window sleep came down over it, steadily building black, softening my neck so that my head lolled, gathering me up in its vapour so that I drifted above the cramped angle of my seat. At some point my neighbour began to drum a fist upon my arm, then she began to groan and gripped my wrist; I shrank away and turned my face deeper into the flight cushion. I was dreaming.

I dimly recall hearing a beeping sound, and another noise, like a toy rattle being shaken. But they might have been in the dream. I love sleeping. Waking is more and more hateful the older I get. I say this as if I've lived too long. I'm twenty-two.

I woke as they were taking her away. Everyone was talking – everyone, in every seat. I felt their voices through my back and in my hair. There was still daylight in the cabin, but the overhead lights were on. Two male flight attendants carried Yelena away down the aisle, wrapped in blankets. And a balding man with a stethoscope walked behind them. I kept my head very still and just took my time to look and listen, without saying anything. Yelena's arm kept trailing; her palm touched the floor, and the attendant who had the upper half of her kept catching her arm, but couldn't keep it aloft. Not to worry, said the flight attendants, and the man with the stethoscope said something similar with every step. They were taking her through to first class, which was almost empty, something Yelena and I had complained to each other about at the beginning of the flight. Someone asked if Yelena was dead. The flight attendant said something about her having been 'taken ill'. But you've covered her face, someone else said. A beige silk scarf had been laid in a floppy triangle over Yelena's eyes, mouth and nose. Someone behind me started praying, in Latin, and rattling beads. People kept looking at me, and at the empty seat beside me. There was Yelena's handbag, beneath the seat in front of us. Her tray, with the remains of her meal on it, had been hastily pushed on top of my own tray. Her seat was still warm. The sitcom was still running on the little screen. I kept listening to what was being said: I heard the words 'cardiac arrest'. I should look after Yelena's handbag. When would they come back for it? Should I take it up to the front . . .

The stares from the other passengers grew fixed, and I realised that my lips were moving, so I stopped moving them. Someone asked me if I was all right. Yes, I think so, thank you. Someone else asked me if I was all right. Yes, I think so, thank you. She seemed fine. Maybe she wasn't well but didn't want to say so . . .

I shouldn't have drunk so much of that cough syrup. A quarter of a bottle would have been sufficient. Half at the most.

The people around me kept asking if I was all right. Their voices were very kind, filled with concern, as if it was I who needed their concern. I couldn't see exactly who was talking to me – it all seemed to be coming from every direction at once. My nose ran. Tears fell; they stung, like hail. Sorry, I said. Sorry. Eventually someone came and took me away, and I scooped up all my things and Yelena's and followed behind the air hostess, dropping books and bottles and passports. Leave them, leave them, Miss Foxe, the air hostess said. I'll bring your things along for you in a minute. I had a moment of bewilderment – *who is Miss Foxe?* – then I just let everything go and went to First Class, which is where they wanted me to sit so that I could tremble out of sight of my former cabin mates, so that I wouldn't distress them, so that I wouldn't complain later about how I'd been treated after the incident. Yelena was six seats away from me. There was an empty row in front of her and an empty row behind her. They'd arranged her in the seat as if she was sleeping – her face was still covered, but it looked better now that she was upright; it looked as if covering her face was something she did just to help her sleep. Her hands were folded on her lap. I know it sounds strange, but I calmed down a bit once I could see her. She looked lonely, but I didn't want to join her. The air hostess put Yelena's handbag beside her and brought me some gin. I huddled up under a blanket, dipped my thumb into the glass and sucked it. Yes, it was like that . . .

I closed my eyes and tried to do some stupid breathing exercises.

'Only two hours until landing,' a man's voice said. It seemed he had addressed the words to me, so I opened my eyes. He was sitting to my right, his whole body turned toward me, his chin on his fist as he studied me. I hadn't heard or felt him draw near. He was older than me, but I couldn't guess how much older. He was good-looking. Enough to make me feel uncomfortable. Tall and dark, etc. There was room between his eyes for a third eye of the same size – I've read that that's one of the standards of classical beauty. He was wearing a black suit, but it looked as if he'd slept in it for a week straight – wrinkles within wrinkles. 'I'm glad to hear it,' I replied.

'That woman over there is dead,' he remarked.

'I know. I – I was sat next to her.'

'What happened?'

'I think she had some sort of massive heart attack.'

He said, 'I see,' and spent a second or two thinking about it. 'Did you know her?'

'No.'

'Your eyes are just like a cat's,' he told me. His voice was husky. There was gravel in it, and waves. I blushed. It was the way he looked into my eyes, unfalteringly into my eyes as he spoke to me and heard my replies. As close and as direct as the look exchanged when standing face to face after a kiss, or at the peak of a bad fight. Worse than that, actually. Closer than that.

He lifted a lock of hair away from my face. 'Why is this part white?'

'I was struck by lightning when I was little.' A lie I tell everyone. It made him smile. I liked that he didn't believe me. I liked that he didn't question the story, but let it stand. We talked a bit more. His name was St John Fox. (St John . . . I thought that had died out as a first name centuries ago. Posh. He was definitely posh.) We made a half-hearted fuss about having almost identical surnames, wondered about being distant cousins. He'd just presented a paper at a psychiatry conference in Manhattan. I made a joke about him being Dr Fox and he said, seriously, that he preferred 'Mr'. I asked him what the subject of his paper was, but he said it wasn't particularly interesting. Which meant he thought I was stupid. I wished I hadn't told him that I model. To make up for it I told him about my psychology degree, and he said, 'I've got one of those too.' We talked until the plane landed, and then I broke off and stood up when the economy-class passengers started filing through the cabin, whispering and staring. I didn't want them to see me lounging around in First, chatting with a handsome doctor. I waited around to see what would be done about Yelena – the aeroplane staff told me they had to get everyone off the plane first. St John waited with me, though I hadn't asked him to. I spoke to the doctor and a representative from the airline; I answered their questions and told them all I could think of. We waited until they asked us to leave. That made me think they were going to do something bad. Stick Yelena on a trolley with some luggage, something like that. There was no wheelchair waiting. This worried me.

St John stepped off the plane. I didn't follow. He stopped and looked behind him, with an expression of mild surprise. 'It'll be all right, Mary. Let them sort this out. She's gone. We should go, too.'

We talked all the way through passport control and baggage reclaim. He wasn't wearing a wedding ring, but that didn't mean anything either way. I have married friends who don't wear rings. My parents were married and didn't wear rings. I finally got him to tell me about his paper. He was interested in fugue states. A fugue state is the result of an afflicted consciousness, he said. A person in a fugue state is somewhere between waking and dreaming, with the mere appearance of functioning normally. An already fragile man might suffer strain from some extraordinary life event at nine o clock one night, then wake up at seven o'clock the next morning and just walk away from his home, his family, his life. He might take a bus or a long train ride, or a flight, and once he is elsewhere he becomes someone else. He'll take a new name and forget his old one. His handwriting might change, the way he speaks and behaves changes subtly but significantly. He has no memory of his old life – until, abruptly, the fugue wears off, and what's left is a frightened, exhausted human being, miles and miles from home and unable to recall what he's seen and said and done since the evening of his dreadful shock.

'You said it wasn't an interesting subject.'

'Most of these cases are historical. It's been argued that fugue states are a nineteenth-century malaise, convenient for central European men looking for work in other countries, a disguise for individual attempts at economic migration, that sort of thing.'

'But you don't think so.'

'No.' His eyes were very bright; they'd been like that since he'd begun talking about his subject. He looked like someone in love. Well, in love the way people were in old movies.

'Are you working with fugue-state patients right now?'

'If I was, I wouldn't be allowed to discuss it.' He wheeled my suitcase up to the taxi rank. He only had a light-looking hold-all himself. 'My car's parked down there. I'd offer you a lift, but . . .'

'But?'

'But you shouldn't drive off with strange men you only just met on the plane.'

'Of course.'

(I would have gone with him.)

'It was nice to meet you, St John. Thanks—' I had no idea what I was thanking him for. He was gazing at me again, with that overwhelming concentration. I seemed to interest him very much – as an artefact, almost.

He drew a business card from his wallet, a pen from the top

pocket of his jacket and rested the card on top of my hard case. 'Look – you've had a bit of a shock today. And I have some concerns,' he said, writing a phone number on the back. 'It's because your eyes are like a cat's, you know, and you were struck by lightning. If you don't phone I'll assume the worst.'

'Bold,' I said, accepting the card.

He touched my wrist. Lightly, and with just one finger, but I shivered. It wasn't that his hand was especially cold. I think it was the subtlety. If I hadn't been looking, I wouldn't have even noticed what he'd done. *He took my pulse*, I thought. *Stole it.*

'Too bold?'

He walked away from me, backwards.

I didn't know how to answer. I think I just shrugged awkwardly and turned away.

*

I don't do anything I don't want to do. Not even for curiosity's sake.

For example: there's the time I went to Berlin to see a man I liked, a stage magician I'd done a shoot with to promote something or other. The visit went badly. I'd turned up at his door as a surprise, and he didn't like surprises. If I'd thought about it I would have realised that – a magician must control his props and the space in which he orchestrates his tricks – it looks like play, but the magician's mind must be as strict as an iron brace. We went for a walk and he told me that I didn't make much sense to him outside of the photographs. He seemed to be trying to tell me that I was a creature of chaos. I said: 'Okay, I'll go home today.'

The magician said: 'Thank you for understanding.' He turned homewards and I stood still.

'Aren't you coming?'

'No, I'm going home.'

'But your things—'

'Throw them away. I'll get new things. There are so many, all around.'

'You're angry.'

'I'm not. I swear I'm not.' I really wasn't angry. I did want him to go away, though, and quickly, so that I could begin to forget about him. So I smiled, and hugged him, to show that I wasn't angry. He left, calling after me that I should phone him if I changed my mind about picking up my things. I kept walking. Under a bridge in Prenzlauer Berg I came across a man playing a violin; he was wearing a top hat and dinner jacket and his notes were apple-crisp. Because he was playing so well I looked at him. At first I thought my sight was sun-spattered, but once my eyes adjusted to the tunnel I saw that the scars were really there – harshly moulded welts that gripped half of his face. They crowded his left eye, forced its corner to travel down with them. I stopped walking.

'Wunderbar,' I said. 'Wo hast du gelernt?'

He didn't change the pace of his playing. Nor did he look up.

'Schläfst du hier?'

No answer. Sunset lanced through the tunnel, cutting our shadows off at the knees. I found my purse, took out a note and let it flutter into his violin case. I liked his indifference. I respected it. He finished his piece and packed up his violin, shaking the money out of the case first. It blew away, but I stomped and trapped it under my foot, still watching him, wondering, I suppose, if he would acknowledge me before leaving. 'If you want to talk to me you can talk to me,' he said, as he snapped his case shut. 'But not here.'

And he leapt to his feet and sprinted away, through the tunnel and across the smooth lawn of the park, through the rose-covered trellises that flanked its gates. He crossed over concrete and, at a mad, desperate dash, through the traffic that whirled along a broad avenue. And I followed, chased briefly by my flying ten-euro note, colliding with pedestrians, knocking handbags off shoulders and newspapers from people's hands. The violinist's hat fell off his head and I picked it up and ran harder, shouting, 'Entschuldigung!' and shaking it joyfully. Near the end of a dimly lit alleyway my quarry knocked on a door in a complicated manner – a series of knuckle raps and open-handed slaps – was abruptly admitted and tumbled inside. I drew the line at that. I approached the door, which looked like any other door, and placed the top hat to the left of it. Then I went off in search of something to eat. The running had made me hungry. I hope he recovered the top hat – it wasn't a cheap one.

I've wondered, I have wondered, what that chase was all about, but I've never regretted leaving the matter at that. I didn't want to follow the violinist into the company of persons unknown to me. So I didn't do it.

I decided that I would not be calling S.J. Fox – there was something married about him. So I left his business card in the back of the taxi. I've left purses and cameras and mobile phones in the backs of taxi cabs and have never once been called back to collect them before the cab drove off. This time the driver called out: 'You've forgotten something, miss,' and I had to go and pick the business card up.

*

I liked to go home. I'd worked hard on the place, repainting a room a month, stencilling bright butterflies in corners, building little galaxies of light with crystal lampshades, pouring gauze over the windowpanes. There was no darkness where I lived.

I let myself in, picked my letters up off the doormat and walked through two weeks' quiet, the floorboards soft under my feet, a gentle path to my unmade bed. It looked storm-tossed, just the way I'd left it, just the way I liked it. I lay down, opened letters, and listened to my answer machine. There were hardly any messages. A couple from my agent, about jobs.

As I listened to the messages I looked at an invitation to a fancy-dress party; really looked at it, held it close to my face. The words were printed alongside a picture of me, looking too silly for words. They'd done my hair up in Victorian ringlets and dressed me up in a grey wolf suit and a red cape. The snarling wolf's head was hung around my neck, sharp teeth and bright gums. In the background there were soft multicoloured lights that were supposed to suggest fantasy and imagination. It was for charity. The party was due to start in an hour, and the venue wasn't far from my flat – not by taxi. I could still go. It seemed wrong not to take a chance to meet people.

There was a shepherd's crook leant up against my bathroom door – I'd got it on the Portobello Road a few months ago. I considered going to the fancy dress ball as a saucy shepherdess. Or Christ. Or I could go as a saucy shepherdess and when people asked me if I was a shepherdess I could say, 'Christ, actually.'

I moved on to the last letter in the heap, the only one

addressed to Miel Shaw. It was a dove-grey envelope addressed in thin dark purple print. Which meant that it was from my father. I had one hundred and twenty-seven other envelopes like it, many of them unopened because they'd arrived on days I knew I couldn't cope. The letters were all in a shoebox under my bed. My hoard. I opened the new envelope little by little, sliding a nail along under its sealed flap, from one corner to the other. It took a long time.

The letter was upsetting, so I'll try to paraphrase it. It had been written by someone else on his behalf – dictated, it seemed, and sent without editing. My father apologised for writing to me – he said he knew that I didn't like him to. But he had been taken aside and told terrible things about what was happening inside his body. He was dying of colon cancer. He had gone through chemotherapy, and he was still dying. There was a smell in the air – a sweet smell that terrified him and was with him always. He thought it was coming from his stomach. He asked me to visit him at the prison hospice. You've never seen such a place, he said. *You couldn't know that a place like this exists. Come and see me. Just quickly, just once.* Or if I telephoned, if I wrote back – just to show that I was there, that there was someone. He said that he'd seen me in a magazine, but that I'd just been paint and porcelain. Are you really there? he asked. Are you?

I folded the letter, put it back in its envelope and added it to the others in the box. *I don't care. I don't care.* He hadn't put my name in the letter, and that made it easier for me to refuse the letter – it had not been written to me.

I thought I heard something in the next room,
a footfall.

I paced through the flat with the reassuring weight of the shepherd's crook in my hand, checking that all the windows were locked. They were. I was alone. Safe, alone.

All the times I've been frightened because of my father. My need for night-lights, my inability to sleep in a room unless I'm able to clearly see all four corners from the bed – and dreams, bad dreams like messengers he sent. All the times he's frightened me. Die, then, I thought. *Die*. And I wondered when he would be gone.

I phoned my lawyer, and I phoned his lawyer, and left messages. Long messages. Part of the reason I changed my name was so that my father wouldn't be able to contact me. Yet somehow he has always been able to find me. His secretary used to send me cheques twice a year, cuts from my father's investment yield that he instructed her to pass on to me. But I've never cashed them, not under any circumstances. When I moved house I left a post-office box as my forwarding address, and I haven't checked it since. You have to be like that when there's a person like my father in your life; when you leave places you mustn't look back or you'll find him there.

'S.J. Fox, psychiatrist,' I murmured. 'S.J. Fox, psychiatrist.' Whilst thinking I was looking at his card. I'd placed it on my bedside table. The card was so plain, so black and white and uncreased, that it made everything around it, the frosted-glass lamp that shone light on it, the framed photograph of my cousin Jonas and me, look insubstantial. I was interested in his work, this St John Fox. Did he know, could he tell, when a fugue state was coming on? The clinic he worked at was in Cornwall, and that was far away. I covered the card with my letters. There was no point invoking psychiatry in this matter. I am sane and it's well documented that my father is sane. He seemed fully aware of what he'd done, and he was sorry, so sorry. My father is eloquent and sensitive, fair-haired and fair-skinned. His facial expressions flow into each other with mesmerising transparency, grief, anguish, scorn. 'He gets so worked up,' my mother used to say. She said it lovingly. Then she took to saying it in a puzzled way, then with contempt.

There was always something strange about the three of us together. Little things that might have been fun, but somehow weren't fun. One sunny morning my father made my mother lie down – she was laughing, and she said she wanted to do it, but she was an actress, can you trust an actress and a sunny day? – he made her lie down in the garden in her bikini and he wrote all over her. I can't remember what he wrote; it was a long poem, in blue ink, an original poem, maybe. I was ten going on eleven. I didn't like what was happening and I didn't know why. He wrote on her back first, kneeling beside her, then he made her turn over and wrote all across her front, pressing hard, and the letters were big and ugly, but she pranced around afterwards holding out her arms and saying things like: 'Am I in the poem? Or is the poem in me?' And he just sat in a deckchair as if exhausted by his work and watched her. I thought, something very mad is going on, she doesn't like this, but she'll never say so.

I was taken to a theatre matinee for my twelfth-birthday treat; that should have been fun, too. We had the best seats possible, because that's what things were like with my father. My mother was playing Juliet, and the first two scenes dragged – blah blah, said one actor – Romeo, I presumed.

Blah blah blah, said a second actor; some relative of Romeo's. Asking him something; merry, but concerned. Blah blah blah blah, Romeo said, looking downcast for a few seconds before proceeding to jump around and climb things. My father stared into space and I felt my eyes begin to close of their own accord. Until Juliet made her airy appearance, soft and slender – 'How now! Who calls?' and suddenly we were listening, Father and I, watching, our heads tilting to take her in, as if we'd never seen her before. The stage makeup exaggerated her eyes, but her mouth was still larger, very much larger. Something from the distant past – a great-grandfather who was an African. She was self-conscious about her mouth and called it her clumsy flytrap, but my Aunt Molly told me that that's how it should be – when a woman's lips are larger than her eyes it's a sign that she's warm-hearted. Her hair was a bright mass of crinkles, a lion's mane. Romeo embraced her and she gave herself over to him with eager, trembling bliss. There were quite a few embraces, and my father became conspicuously still and watched with startled pain. I was uncomfortable because I'd never seen her like this before, but he'd seen her perform plenty of times. It's only acting, I thought. *Is he always like that when she acts?*

After the matinee my parents took me to lunch, and the strangeness was there with us. It was there in the powdery smell of the velvet on the restaurant chairs and it was there in the palm fronds that tickled my head. My mother and father talked politely about things they had read in the newspaper, and changed the subject whenever it seemed they were about to disagree. As usual, my father ordered something that wasn't on the menu, just because. He told me to order whatever I liked, and I did. My mother drank martinis and said sharply: 'Three whole courses! What a pig you are, Miel.' And I was so surprised I almost cried. It was my birthday. And she'd never said such a thing before. My father and I were silently against her for the rest of the meal, sticking to our plan to order ice cream even though she wasn't having anything and was ready to leave.

I wish I hadn't ever been bad to my mother. I see that afternoon again and again. She had acted wonderfully, she had been Juliet, and then we'd met her at the stage door and treated her as if she had done something wrong. We hadn't said 'well done' to her, or much of anything. My father had just pushed a bunch of flowers into her arms.

Just over two years later, my father killed my mother. She was running away from him down some stairs and he seized her by the hair at the nape of the neck – he must have lifted her onto her tiptoes – and he forced a knife through her chest. From behind. Then he called the police, and waited for them. I was at boarding school, and everyone there knew, because it was in the newspapers, and some of my friends went and lit candles in the school chapel. I found that deeply bogus. All the newspapers were kept away from me so I wouldn't see what was being said. I didn't need to read about my mother – I knew her well – we spoke every day until he killed her. She'd moved out of his house and she was living with her new boyfriend, Sam. She went back to the house to get some things. She had his permission, as long as he didn't have to see her. So they'd settled on a weekday afternoon – he was supposed to be at the office. But he wasn't.

He said that she had been turning me against him (this

isn't true: my father always frightened me. If I had been allowed to testify I'd have said so). He had a lot of explanations that I wasn't really able to take in at the time. He said he couldn't take it any more.

'It'.

What is 'it'? Sometimes I think he killed her to show us something, to show us what 'it' is. She was my best friend, and she knew almost everything – if she didn't know she made outrageous guesses. She made me laugh and I made her laugh. When I spoke to my mother I was the funniest, cleverest, most interesting girl alive. Other people's mothers told them to 'be good' or to 'take care'. Mine told me to be bad and wicked and not to worry. While waiting for her to phone me at school I'd feel seconds bursting inside me and leaving clouds. That won't come again – it can't. I'll never have that with anyone else. I'll never even come close.

So. When I say I've been visiting my mother, that means I've been visiting her grave. I bring her foxgloves; her maiden name was Foxe. At her funeral she was hidden away in a closed casket because she was no longer beautiful. He'd done other things before he stabbed her – no one would tell me what. I suppose I could have insisted on seeing her, if I'd really wanted to.

I had counselling, which helped. I discovered cough syrup as an aid to sleep, and that was even better.

*

I didn't go to the charity ball that night. I couldn't face it. I called Jonas instead – he's the closest thing I've got to a brother. His parents took custody of me and paid for the rest of my schooling and my food and clothes. And because I was academically advanced and they thought it would be wrong for me to be kept back, they put me through university at the same time as Jonas – I was a drain on their resources. I kept a tally of the running costs as best I could and paid them back when I got a big enough contract. They were very angry, because they love me, and Uncle Tom tore the cheque up, and we never spoke of it again. They are such good people and I owe them so much that I can hardly look either of them in the eye. Jonas's mother, Molly, is my mother's younger sister – they used to tease each other about their Anglophilia, two American girls who married British men and developed a keen interest in the goings on at Ascot, Wimbledon and the Henley Regatta. Their older sister, Jane, is the one who still lives in America, and the one who had my mother flown out there to be buried. She's an odd one, Aunt Jane. I don't think I like her. Jonas isn't keen on her either. It exasperates him that she uses his name so often whilst speaking to him; it gives the impression that she's trying her hardest not to forget who on earth he is. She does that to everyone. She's always careful to call me Mary, so I find her constant repetition of my name sinister, as if she's reminding me that I'm not who I say I am.

Jonas is a seminarian – in four or five years' time he's going to be a priest. I've never been inside his seminary, only glimpsed the grounds. A silence in the centre of London. The main entrance is a glass door set between grey pillars, and when I wait for Jonas on a Friday afternoon, sexy, soberly dressed men of every nationality pour out onto the street. Sexy because they belong to God and will never more be caressed by human hand. A strange thing, because I remember when we used to French kiss, Jonas and I. We'd French kissed all over the house while his parents went to concerts and galas and dinner parties. It was my idea. He said he'd never kissed a girl, and I felt sorry for him. So I showed him and showed him and showed him. 'This isn't right,' he stammered. 'We're related by blood.' But he liked it, and he was good at it. Very good at it, actually. Gentle, but subtly demanding, too, the way he'd pass his hand through my hair, his lips moving over my mine, slow, savouring. He was talented, at an age when other boys were horrible kissers, just horrible and sloppy. I was fourteen then, and he was sixteen. When Jonas came to the phone I asked him if he remembered that we used to kiss. 'I remember,' he said, tersely. 'Is that why you called?'

I meant to tell him about the letter from my father, and to ask what to do. But I could already hear him telling me that I'd have to go to the prison hospice, that place of marvel my father promised me. So I ended up telling Jonas that someone had died on the plane, and that her name was Yelena. He didn't ask me if I was all right. He listened. He let me tell him what happened again and again, in more detail as the details came to mind.

'Why are you laughing?' he asked, abruptly. It was true, I was – and not quietly, either. I managed to say that I had to go, and hung up. So he was dying! My laughter rose in pitch to equal a scream.

Maybe the letter was a trick, like my father hiding in the house, waiting for my mother to come home without fear. I'd know tomorrow, when the lawyers phoned me back.

Dinner was vodka, such a lot of vodka. And *Swing Time* was on TV, so I watched that.

'Listen,' Ginger Rogers said to Fred Astaire, 'no one could teach you to dance in a million years!'

That dried my laughter up immediately. I turned the TV off and went to bed, to the sleep that I loved.

*

In the morning I Googled S.J. Fox, and found a sad story – a eulogy he'd written for his wife four years ago. It was tender. Very tender, and I stopped halfway through – I had no right to be reading it. There was no mention of the word 'suicide', but it was clear to me that that was what he was getting at. Someone from his wife's family had posted the full order of the funeral service, including the hymns sung and the psalms and Bible passages read, and they, too, pointed to suicide. Oh, you broken, broken soul, they seemed to say. There is a balm in Gilead, etc. I studied the photograph of her. Daphne Fox. She was sitting on a mossy boulder with sunshine all around her, wearing a picture hat and holding on to it at the crown so it didn't blow away. She'd been a PE teacher at the local comprehensive school, and given it up when she'd married him. Like someone from another age. She was a bit plump, and she smiled shyly. Not at all the type I would have expected to see with someone like S.J. She seemed to like butterflies. She was wearing a pair of butterfly earrings and a butterfly pendant. I also made out a butterfly bracelet; the wings closed around her wrist. The life of a butterfly is very short. The German word for butterfly is *Schmetterling*. These were thoughts I had while avoiding the fact that Daphne Fox looked familiar to me. She was a redhead, like me, but that wasn't it. I must have just looked at her for too long.

*

Having ascertained the facts, the lawyers returned my calls. Their voices were serious and low. The letter wasn't a trick. My father was very ill.

Jonas said, Go to him.

Aunt Molly said, Go to him. So did Uncle Tom.

Aunt Jane said, Go to him, Mary.

There was something morbid about their insistence. He was going to die soon, so now his words were important and had special meaning. That's what they wanted me to believe. It was disgusting . . .

I pretended my mother spoke to me. I pretended she said, Don't go to him, he's evil. Don't forget, she said, that he had that folder full of newspaper clippings. Don't forget how he made you look through them. Don't forget that some nights he kept you up until you had read through all the clippings again. He'd test you. He'd watch you wilt.

Why was Fatema Yilmaz buried alive under a chicken pen?

As punishment for talking to boys. She wasn't allowed to.

Who punished her?

Her father and her grandfather.

How deep was the hole they dug?

Three metres.

Three metres? Are you sure?

No – no. Two metres.

Correct. Why was Medine Ganis drowned in a bathtub?

Because she wouldn't do as she was told.

Elaborate, Miel. Elaborate.

Her father chose a man for her to marry and she said she wouldn't do it.

Who was there when she drowned?

143

Her father was there, and her two brothers were there, holding her down. Her mother was there, but she took no part in it.

Where in the article does it say her mother took no part in it? Don't embroider. Silence is consent.

But it doesn't say her mother was silent—

Enough. Why was Charlotte Romm shot to death in her bed?

Because her husband didn't want her to know that he'd spent her parents' life savings. But, Dad—

Yes, Miel?

He shot their children, too. And her parents.

I know. But I didn't ask you about them. Don't answer questions you haven't been asked.

My mother would tell him to stop it – I passed these stories on, with gruesome embellishments, to other kids at school and their parents complained – but he said that the world was sick and that I should know I wasn't safe in it. My mother told me not to listen to him, but it was impossible not to. I kicked open cubicle doors in public toilets, so expectant of discovering an abandoned corpse that for an instant I'd see one, slumped over the toilet bowl, her long hair falling into the water. I saw them in the dark, the girls, the women yet to be found. I counted their faces, gave them names and said the names, as if calling a class register. Here's what I learnt from the clippings: that there is a pattern. These women had requested assistance. They'd told people: someone is watching me, has been following me, has beaten me up before, has promised me he will kill me. They'd pointed their murderers out, and they had been told 'it won't happen', or that nothing could be done, because of this and that, etc. I was jumpy in those days, expecting something terrible to happen to me at any moment, without knowing where it would happen to me, or why, or who would do it.

My father sent press clippings to me at school, from prison. As if to say, your mother wasn't the first and won't be the last. Maybe I could have shown all the clippings to someone and somebody would have looked at his sanity again, tried to get him treatment. But that might have reduced his sentence, or they might have hospitalised him. My father, out in the world again – a thought I couldn't think. Not ever.

*

A box arrived in the post, forwarded from the agency. I signed for it, and sat down on the sofa with it, afraid that it was something my father had sent to me. Then I reminded myself that his letter had come directly to me – he knew my address. Still, my hands shook as I unwrapped a brass-handled magnifying glass and a tiny book about half the size of my thumb. I turned the pages – there were only three, and each had a word written on it in a fine, light hand. Trying to breathe, I held the glass over each page and read:

You
didn't
call . . .

He'd included another card inside the box, allowing me the excuse of having lost the first one. He answered on the third ring, as if he'd been waiting.

'It's me,' I said, stupidly.

I thought he couldn't hear me clearly, and was about to add: 'It's Mary Foxe,' but he spoke just a heartbeat before I did. 'Are you seeing anyone?'

'No.'

'Will you see me?'

His voice in my ear. It did interesting things to me. It curved my back and parted my lips. I felt lazy and feline, and he wasn't even in the room. 'Yes. When?'

'I'm in town next week – I do a couple of days a week at a private practice.'

'Call me next week, then.'

'I will.' He paused. I paused.

'I'm sorry about your mother,' he said, at the same time as I said: 'I'm sorry about your wife.'

I recovered first. 'Thank you for saying that,' I said, without emphasis. He must have found one of those stupid and unnecessary 'she isn't doing too badly for a girl whose mother was murdered' articles. He'd have had to dig deep, though. It was such a long time ago.

'Likewise,' he said.

'I'm sorry I snooped.'

He made no reply. He'd already ended the call.

'Soon, then,' I told the dial tone.

*

I stopped talking to Jonas and Aunt Molly and Uncle Tom and Aunt Jane. It wasn't easy. I missed them. Especially Jonas. I attended foam parties and tube parties and hedge and highway parties. I took every job my agent could get for me. People looked at my contact sheets and told me I was doing my best work yet. I couldn't see what they meant – the pictures looked the same as always.

It was at another charity fundraiser that I remembered where I had seen Daphne Fox. Light hummed in crystal chandeliers. Jonas, decadent Catholic that he was, would have loved the party. Men in dinner jackets and starched white collars, throats pulsing with laughter. Yards of oyster-coloured silk, and diamonds, diamonds, garnets, rubies. One old man had a walking stick topped with an emerald the size of an egg. I holed myself up in a corner with a couple of girls I knew from jobs I'd done, and we listened to the speeches and stood there drinking and looking at everything through our sunglasses, waiting for something to happen. The room was in half darkness, raked by a roving spotlight. Every now and again someone who had only been a silhouette suddenly transformed into a pillar of flashing jewels. I hadn't thought to wear any jewellery, and when the spotlight finally fell on our group, I stepped out of it. It didn't take much to make my head spin just then – the sudden change from blinding light to dusk made my hands clammy. That and the cough syrup and the cocktails and the wine. I excused myself and weaved out of the ballroom, towards the toilets; a crowd of women emerged and momentarily surrounded me. 'Come back,' I wanted to tell them. 'Don't leave me alone in here.'

But they had, and I walked up the row of cubicles, kicking doors and watching the mirror while a tap dripped bleakly and muzak floated in through the speakers. I kicked the last door open and clenched my jaw against a scream – the image of a dead woman flashed fiercely, just as I used to when I was eleven; exactly like that.

It was the same woman I conjured up each time, sprawled in the cubicle with wet, dangling hair, and that bashful, almost apologetic expression – *sorry about this*. The face was Daphne Fox's. That was my last clear impression for a while.

*

Some time went by. A night, a very late night, I think; street lamps spiked the dark, and no one was out. Whatever

I was doing, wherever I was, I was most aware of the grinding of my teeth – the sound and the feeling. The supple clicking was a comfort.

At first I was alone, then I was with S.J. Fox, at a restaurant – potted plants as tall as trees, fancy bread rolls, tapenade, and out of a window I saw Cleopatra's Needle dividing the sky. I was very nervous. Close up his skin was weathered and held frown fractures so fine and deep that he seemed made of them. I still couldn't guess how old he was. I didn't listen too closely to what he was saying. His expressions changed suddenly and completely – a frown would chase a boyish grin midway through a sentence; not even my father had switched masks so quickly. And that was what all the expressions felt like – masks. I didn't believe them. They were too thorough, too nuanced, they were never at odds with his subject matter. He probably had to be like this because of work – he had to show people what normal, balanced emotions looked like. But that's just not how it happens. People move from comic to tragic with the remnants of a smile left on their lips. Natural expressions linger. There was someone behind all S.J.'s masks, someone who stared mockingly and dared me to say that I knew he was there. And that was the one I wanted to meet. The unprofessional.

It took a lot of concentration not to mention his wife. *I never met Daphne, but I've seen her in my head . . .*

We walked out of the restaurant and down the street, to the hotel he was staying in. His arm was around my waist. I moved deeper into the curve of his arm as he collected his messages at reception. In the lift he gently pushed me away and made me stand on my own, facing him. 'You have a gap in your teeth,' he whispered, and he filled it with the tip of his tongue.

He looked at me as he did it, and I looked at him. This was no silver-screen kiss, we were in each other's wide open eyes, and I dared not flinch. It was a long way up – the lift kept stopping, and other people entered it and left – I couldn't see them, only felt them, like clouds drifting around us.

His hotel room was cream and burgundy. He drew the blinds and sat down on the chair by the dressing table. I sat on the bed.

'I loved Daphne,' he said. He studied my reaction – I had opened my mouth, but I said nothing. He went on: 'I did. But in the last few months she was worse than a child. She lit fires on the carpets and she threw coffee tables through locked windows. She always had to be watched.'

I couldn't look at his face any more, so I looked at his long-fingered hands, the way his knuckles jerked as he opened and closed his hand around the room key.

'I see. She was too much trouble—'

'That's not what I was saying—'

'So you killed her?'

There, it was out.

'Do you always talk like this?' he asked, calmly.

'Did you kill her?'

He answered with a smile. The darkest and most malignant I had ever seen, too strong to be voluntary. The door, I thought. The door. But I didn't dare turn to it, in case it wasn't there. His smile stayed. It stayed and stayed, until it became meaningless. It calmed me. So lightheaded I stopped trying to sit straight. I dropped onto the floor, and he watched me approach, on my knees. I didn't stop until I was looking directly into his eyes, deep in their hollows. His face tightened – he was barely breathing.

'Oh, you,' I said. 'You are a man I've been waiting to meet.'

I took his hands. I arranged them around my throat, closed my own hands over them, tight, like a choker. 'Did you kill her and get away with it? How did you get away with it?'

'She killed herself.'

I moved so that they pressed together, the four pairs of hands. I let go, then pressed them together again, made my breathing fold like bellows. It felt good. It felt like forgetting.

'Stop it,' he said. But he didn't move his hands.

'Did you kill her? Did you kill her?'

'I said stop it.'

'And me? Do you want to kill me? Is that why you look at me the way you do?'

'What do you want, Mary?'

I offered my lips to be kissed. He didn't move his head, though he stayed close.

'Kiss me,' I said.

He took a deep, rattling breath. 'You're . . . a strange girl.'

'Kiss me.'

He did. My hands worked at the buttons of his shirt, carefully, slowly. He peeled my dress away from my shoulders. Then we were on the floor together. I was pinned beneath him at first. Our open mouths. Our heat. I hooked my legs around his, drank his skin, strange salt that ran like water; my hair swept across his bare chest; I was astride him by then, and I took him an inch at a time, ('Wait,' I said, 'wait,' pulling away every time he tried to take too much) an aching delay between each movement that brought him deeper. Such pleasure when he finally steadied me above him, his hands where my waist softens into my hips, such pleasure when he filled me.

'I'm sorry I said those things,' I said, when we lay together afterwards. His lips brushed my forehead.

'It's understandable,' he said. 'I understand. The lightning . . .'

I hated the kindness in his voice – where did it come from? It wasn't why I wanted him. I wanted the look in his eyes when I'd asked: 'Did you kill her?' The moment in which he had hated me.

'You shouldn't work out of hours,' I said.

He laughed softly. 'Then don't make me.'

He left me sleeping – when I woke I held out my arms to him and there was nothing, not even a note.

Another day passed, and another night, I think. Without him. Then there were a lot of people, and I didn't know who any of them were. There were so many of them. Why so many? I realised that I was in public. I had to stay there, in public, because I didn't know how to get home. Every direction looked exactly the same to me.

Someone took my mobile phone. Someone else took my purse. It wasn't robbery, exactly – I must have just been sitting there, on a park bench after dark holding out my purse and my phone, my hands like weighing scales, and then they were empty. I didn't worry about it. I thought it was summer. 'It's summer,' I said to myself. And I saw ants troop past my feet in single file. I wondered about ants. I wondered whether within each ant there is another and another and another until finally you reached a cold small chip of the universe, immovable and displeased.

Then Jonas was there. I don't know how he found me. We

went into McDonald's, because it was nearest and I was almost frozen. Ha! Not summer after all. I said I wanted onion rings and he bought me onion rings, which I didn't eat. No, I tried ring after ring on my heart finger. Wedding rings. None of them fitted, but they didn't fall apart, either. Jonas watched me and he rubbed his head all over, as if searching for a thought, then raked hair out of his eyes. His dear face – his thrice-broken nose, his summer eyes. He had bought me onion rings; he wasn't going to take anything from me. I didn't really have anything left, anyway, apart from mascara and my door keys. I was happy when he put his arms around me. I hid my face in the lapels of his jacket and my frame loosened, lava-like, beneath my skin. I don't know how I didn't scald him. Jonas's heart beat steadily, not fast, not slow; its order restored me. He drew back.

'Where have you been?' he said. He was Old Testament angry, calm and wild at once, like a prophet come down from the mountains with a storm under his tongue, holding it until it was time.

'When?'

He stared at me, and I said quickly: 'I went to a party.'

'Are you sure?'

'Yes. A big one. There were probably photos in the paper. It was at . . . oh . . . at—'

'The Athenaeum?'

'That's it.'

'Three nights ago.'

'Three . . . really . . . ?'

'Yes, really.'

'Oh . . .'

He counted days off on his fingers, his face stony. 'So

there was yesterday night. And the night before that. And the night before that. We've been trying to reach you.'

'Have you . . .'

'Roger died on Friday. They were going to cremate him day before yesterday, but we've asked them to hold on until we could reach you.'

'Reach me? Why?'

'So you can see him,' Jonas said, simply. 'If you want to stop being afraid, Miel, you'll do this.' He pulled me up out of my seat. I fought him, but he merely locked his arms around me and contained me. I stomped on his foot and his grip didn't loosen, but his touch became gentler; he brushed his nose against my cheek: 'Sh, sh . . .'

'No,' I said. 'I can't.'

'I'll be there.'

I hoped someone would intervene, but everyone else in the vicinity just stared down into their cartons of fries. They must have thought we were having a lovers' tiff.

*

Jonas took my keys and opened the front door, talking on the phone as he did – he was cancelling my credit cards for me, asking me for information. Jonas is a good boy. I don't deserve him. He unzipped my dress, which had wine all down its front, and dragged the satin down over my waist, my hips – it might have been erotic if he hadn't been so businesslike. He chose a new dress and pulled it over my head, leaving me to wriggle into it. Jonas isn't afraid of me. God knows I've tried to frighten him in my time, jumping out from behind doors and screaming shrilly, prank-calling him when I knew he was at home alone, bookmarking his favourite psalm with a Tarot card – the hanged man. He's never been scared of me, so he'll never run. I'm glad, so glad of that. I've tried to show gratitude. But what can I do for Jonas? Last summer I spent almost an hour blowing dandelions off their stems towards him, so that he had a chance to wish for everything he wanted. He was very polite about it, but it can't have meant much to him. Jonas thinks about eternity and other things that make wishes seem tiny and silly.

*

The morticians had done well with my father. He didn't even look that stiff. There was a waxiness to him, but it was more like that of a new doll's. It was almost eight years since I'd last been in the same room as him, and he looked even younger than I remembered. The sickness had made him small in his suit. I hadn't expected to be able to see that he had suffered. Now he looked cordial; it felt impossible that he could have done anything terrible, could ever have felt or thought or planned . . . if you didn't know, you could believe that this man had never done anything at all but lie there, patiently waiting for whatever happened next. His cheeks so rosy I almost laid a hand on one, for warmth. I have my father's nose. I have his ears. I touched my nose and ears. Soon they would be ashes.

Beside me, Jonas began to pray. I don't know how I knew he was praying, since he didn't speak, and his lips didn't even move. But he was praying. For a moment I tried to see this situation from Jonas's perspective. But I couldn't do it at all. I will never think the way you do, Jonas. You see, my father is a murderer, and yours is not.

Father, in my life I see
(Father in my life I see)
You are God who walks with me

(You are God who walks with me)

I looked back at my father, to see what he thought about Jonas praying. My father was amused, and I followed his lead.

*

I think I'm going to have to go—
I think I'm going to have to go.
'Go where?' S.J. asked. He was at the other end of the line. I phoned him, at home, at 4 a.m., and he answered.
'Where do you think you have to go?' S.J. asked again.
Where indeed . . .
My family was a mistake, I think. The three of us.
I'm the only one left.
I think I'm going to have to go.
'Will you come and get me?' I asked him. 'Please.'
'Now?' We were talking about a seven-hour drive through the dawn, and through rush hour. If he started now, he'd be here at about noon. Anything could have happened by noon. They were going to cremate my father at 9 a.m. It sounds amazingly stupid, but I was convinced I'd burst into flames with him. I'm bound to my father. How did this happen? I've been running from him.
'I'll come,' S.J. said.
'No.' It scared me that he was so willing. I know I'd asked him to, but his 'yes' was impossible to decipher – what was it supposed to mean?
'I want you here. For observation.'
'Haha. I'll take the train,' I said.
'All right. I'll take a couple of days off.'
'You can't. People need you.'
'So do you,' he said. 'Call me when you're on the train.'

155

I nodded, and I very carefully wrote down the address he gave me.

When I sat down at my computer, checking e-mail before bed, I saw that I had opened twelve identical windows, and Daphne Fox smiled coyly at me out of each one.

*

I'm no good at train journeys. Half an hour of scenery (which I try to admire), half an hour of the sound of the train on its track and I have seen and heard enough – my legs begin to jiggle frenetically entirely of their own accord. I began to fall asleep, but the empty seat beside me made me watchful. I didn't want to fall asleep and wake up and find someone sitting there looking at me. Yelena, Daphne, anybody. The dead are capable of creeping up on you when you aren't looking, just as capable as the living are.

I kept myself awake with phone calls – to my agent, to explain that I'd be away for a while.

'What? How long for, exactly?'

'I don't know. My father died.'

'Oh . . .' He didn't say that he was sorry – honest man, my agent: 'Take all the time you need, darling. Call me if you need anything.'

He got off the phone quickly. I called Jonas next, and told him where I was going, in case he was interested. Jonas was suspiciously enthusiastic.

'Sounds promising, Miel,' he said.

'Does it?'

He sighed.

'And it's Mary, by the way,' I said. People shouldn't think that they can call me Miel just because my father has gone, as if I'm a little girl who was hiding from an ogre. Now they're all walking around calling out that I can come out now. Well it's too late.

It took almost as long to get to Brier Moss by train as it would have by car. Six and a half hours later I climbed out of a taxi cab and walked up to a house that stood alone behind a large flat whorl of a garden, almost out of sight of the road. Grasshoppers ticked away in the bushes as I knocked on the front door. S.J. answered, in pyjamas, barefoot, and carrying a towel. Drops of water clung to his lips and ran down his chin, and as I followed him into the house he ducked his head beneath the towel and emerged with his hair standing on end. The hallway smelt strongly of polish and paint; its walls were a very strong and spotless white. No stand for coats and hats, no mat for wiping muddy feet, no carpet, even. The other downstairs rooms were unfurnished and painted the same white as the hallway, until we came to his study, which was walled with shelves that stopped only at the ceiling. There was a ladder attached to the shelves by a wooden claw, the sort of ladder I'd only seen in bookshops – on it you could move around all the books and climb, touch all of them, pluck the exact book you wanted out from amongst the rest yourself. They all looked medical – gynaecology, psychiatry, neurology.

He was watching me. 'What do you think?'

I set my bag down by the door and walked around, looking.

'Cosy.'

There was only one chair, and that was behind the desk, which faced the French doors and the late afternoon. I could see how someone would want to live only in this room and abandon the others. But nobody actually does that. You have to at least have something to look at or sit on in the other rooms, even if only for form's sake. I told myself I would wait a little while and then point that out to him. There was a plate on his desk with three squares of iced cake on it. Each had been firmly and largely bitten into just once, and then left. It seemed a strangely dainty thing to do.

'Wait here,' he said, and disappeared.

I looked out through the French doors and said to myself: 'What . . .' It was such a bare garden. Nothing flowered. There was just green grass levelled low in every direction. It was the sheer effort of maintaining these conditions that amazed me. Because things grow. Wherever there is air and light and open space, things grow. So much cutting and uprooting must be done to keep a place like this bare.

My phone rang in my pocket. It was S.J.

'Have you left the house?' My voice pitched higher than I'd have liked it. But I hadn't heard him leave. And I didn't want to be alone in this house. He tutted.

'I'm on the roof,' he said. 'Meet me up there.'

'How—'

'Go round to the side of the house – not the side where the cedar tree is, the other side. There's a ladder. Climb up.'

I hung up and did as I was told, leaving my bronze pumps on the grass and stepping quickly into the sky – not quite running; there was dew on the soles of my feet, and the iron frame beneath me creaked a little too much for my liking. But I went up with ease, the walk was easy, and I didn't look down once.

He was waiting for me at the top, as he had said. He took my hand and pulled me off the top step and onto the flat tiles. There were two chairs ready, with a single lantern set between them. The chairs faced north, looking out over rooftops and hills and the roads dipped deep in them. The view made me dizzy; the same scene endlessly multiplied. It could have been a trick done with mirrors, vast ones. Dusk was only just falling, and I heard moths stun themselves against the lantern, the hard flicker of their wings as they sprang away again. S.J. poured whisky from a jug into shot glasses and toasted me. 'Here's to visions,' he said.

I drank, and realised it wasn't whisky. It started off like liquid gingerbread, then lingered on the tongue, deep and woody, the way I imagined tree sap tasted.

'What's this?'

'Non-alcoholic. Nutmeg, mostly.'

'Nutmeg? That's meant to be an aphrodisiac, isn't it? It tastes nice.'

'Yes. And in large doses, it's a psychotropic agent.'

I spat my drink back into the glass. I never want visions. They're not fun.

'Mary,' he said, suddenly.

'Yes?'

'I didn't do anything to Daphne.'

'Okay.'

'I tried to take care of her – to help her. And I couldn't.'

His voice was completely steady, but he was crying. 'She slipped through my fingers every time.'

I wiped his tears away with my hands.

'Okay,' I said. 'Okay.'

'I didn't speak to anyone for three days after I found her. I mean I didn't speak to anyone who didn't have to speak to me. Nobody called. They knew what had happened, but they didn't call. I stared at the phone. I understood what was going on – I've done it myself. When someone's bereaved you think they want to be alone, or that they don't want to talk, or that they only want to talk to someone close to them. Someone closer than you are. So you don't phone. You assume that the poor bastard is being inundated with calls from other people, and you don't phone.' His voice grew halting. 'They were – long days. I wanted to talk. To anyone. I didn't want to be alone. I wanted to be with people. But mostly I stayed here. I tried not to go too far from the house, because I thought that if I got too far away I might decide not to come back. And it would be a shame not to come back. The house is all right. It didn't do anything wrong—'

'People should have called,' I said. I was angry. Why wasn't he angry? 'Even if they tried and it was engaged they should have kept trying. They didn't even try. I would have called.'

'Really?'

'Yes. And I'd have said anything that came into my head. I'd have read you the weather forecast. We should have known each other back then.'

There was something childish, something timidly happy about the way he smiled as he listened to me. As if he had been promised something so good that he was trying to manage his hope, trying not to believe it until he saw it with his own eyes.

*

Later he showed me where I would sleep. The room was crammed with a four-poster bed hung with grape-coloured velvet, which I gaped at as I walked around it. I heard the creaking of a rocking chair, but couldn't find the chair itself at first – the space was complicated by folding screens and empty vases and trinket boxes. I began counting the different vases, lost count, began again. At some point this room must have been bursting with flowers. Five foxgloves stood up like spread fingers in one of the vases. There was a dressing table and chair in there too, and a kind of mirror closet – it was a box of mirrors that had a latch and pulled open so that you could stand surrounded by every possible view of yourself whilst dressing.

Daphne's room. Daphne had been gone for four years. This was the state of things, him living in two rooms – just his study and a bedroom, the one next door to this. I tried not to show that it made me sad.

We undressed. He turned the light out and lay down beside me. He kissed me, and parted my legs with the stroke of his hand. He was gentle at first, and rocked slowly, then he pressed all the breath out of me, little by little. At first it was good, and then it wasn't good. Our bodies were cold and it hurt when he moved inside me. I didn't wince or cry out. I kept my eyes firmly closed.

(He'll stop once he feels that it's hurting me.)

But he didn't; he stopped when he was finished.

'I can't stay here,' he said, and he left, stumbling over things – shadows, slippers, whatever was on the floor.

Minutes pricked shallowly, like thorns. I shivered in my chemise. I'd never slept in a four-poster before – my dreams came framed by the purple velvet of the canopy. I kept waking up, or thinking that I did – I couldn't tell. This was Daphne's bed. Daphne Fox had lain here, looking up into this canopy. How had she lain? What had she looked at? Was it here that he had found her? The pounding on the door, the footsteps rushing towards the bed, the sound he made when he found her dead. He'd have shaken her, I imagine, slapped her, tried to revive her, dragged her about, knelt over her with his mouth pressed desperately to hers. Now, in her bed, I tried to find her. I lay on my front, but it was too suffocating, so I changed and lay listlessly on my side, my head on my arm, pretending to be a woman who didn't want to live. Then I turned onto my back, and cold surged all along my body. My hands followed it. How full my breasts were, how soft my stomach; in death everything froze. But my thighs were warm, and the bedclothes were soft against my back, and there was the smell of the foxgloves . . . my bones moved with suppleness under my skin as I pushed my hips upwards, rocking against my fingers . . . it became almost too much. Who is touching me? Me, it's only me, only me. The heavy wetness on my fingers, as if I'd smeared them with honey. When it was over, goosebumps forced themselves up from every patch of bare skin.

And the handle of the bedroom door clicked as it turned from the outside, and the door swung open.

I shot upright and jerked the bedclothes up around me. But no one appeared in the doorway, and when I marched up to it, there still wasn't anyone there. I looked up and down the empty passageway. In a very small voice I said: 'S.J.?'

His bedroom door was closed.

I closed mine, too, and returned to bed, only to be jolted from sleep by the sound of the door opening again. It was not a dream or any sort of reverie. There was something terrible about watching the door come open the second time. It opened all the way, and with such force that I don't know what stopped it from slamming against the wall.

I didn't call out. I closed the door again. There must be

something wrong with the doorframe, or the way the door had been set in it when the place was built. It happened, doors popping open of their own accord, bad builders taken to task. The third time the door opened it felt as if I was being told very sternly to go. But go where? Get out, clear out.

I stood, half asleep, and held the door closed for two hours or so. It began to feel as if I was shaking a small, cold, smooth stump that had been proffered in place of a hand. When I'd had enough of that I sat, then lay on the blue carpet, hardly aware of what I was doing, or where I was. The door opened again as soon as I let go of the handle. Let it stay open then, let it stay open. I heaved myself back into bed as a collection of parts, concentrating on getting my arms up over the edge, torso, legs.

*

The next time I opened my eyes it was very early morning. I put on a pair of slippers that were beside the bed. They were just my size. Which gave me something of a jolt. But they were warm, so I left them on. I went down to S.J.'s study. The plate with the squares of cake on it was still there on his desk, and I wanted to get rid of it. It jarred me. I found it feminine. So I opened the French doors and stepped outside, showering moist crumbs amongst some finches and sparrows who were already pecking at the grass outside. There were seeds in the cake, and it smelt of rum. I hoped the birds wouldn't get too drunk. I wiped my hand on my skirt. Then I stood near the twisted cedar tree, staring. There was just enough light for the leaves to glow. I imagined touching a branch and watching it rise, followed by another branch and another, the trailing leaves parting so that I could step into the space the tree guarded, the secret place it hunched over for safekeeping from the sun.

S.J. came out of the house and stood beside me.

'Morning.'

Tentatively, without looking at me, he held out his hand. I took it and held it clasped to my chest. I didn't look at him either. We were eyeing the cedar.

'Morning.'

'What shall we do today?' he asked.

We went out walking, wrapped round in scarves and jackets. We tramped down lanes and places in the earth that seemed to have been dug and rubbed until granite came through, then abruptly left. We passed signs with names like 'Merrymeet' and 'Tremar' and 'Saint Cleer' written on them, and by the time we crossed a low stone bridge with its feet in a shallow pebbled brook our landscape was three-quarters blue. I began to step gingerly, even though I could see that the ground was firm all around me. There was so much sky that it felt as if we were on a precipice – there was not enough grass to stand on, it was so thin and flat by comparison. We walked around a barrow that rose from the long earth in the shape of a taut shoulder. Every now and again a bird coasted overhead, spreading shadows with the flap of its wings, and I would move uneasily, thinking that it must be coming for us, since there was nothing else for miles but flat tors and, in the distance, a hill so vast that it looked both broken and smooth as the eye tried to absorb its image all at once. I ruined my boots in what felt like an unending series of turf pits that had stored the previous week's rainfall. I struggled in the last pit, thinking I was sinking, and S.J. crooked his arm and stood still on a safe spot, so I could take his elbow and step out. We came to a halt by a lake that seemed to have clouds in it even though it was a clear day. The moor swept on after the water interrupted it, and looking at the other side I felt doubled; without turning I could see what was behind me. S.J. told me stories about the lake. He was a good storyteller; matter-of-fact, convincing. Excalibur had come out of this lake, he said, and I saw no reason to disbelieve him. I saw kites go up. Small figures rushed along up the hill, their wrists and fists leashed to the bright creatures in the sky. I want to stay here, I thought. I want to stay.

In the evening S.J. worked, even though he'd said he wouldn't, sat in the study with huge books opened up all around him, underlining bits of the case studies he was taking notes from. I looked at some cookbooks for a while, then left him and went upstairs, to the blue room. With dramatic bravado, I switched all the lights on and went through Daphne's things, moved them around recklessly, daring her. If I was afraid that something bad would happen, why wait? Why not make it happen now?

Some papers had been folded into a square and pushed into a corner at the back of one of the dressing-table drawers. The words were written in faded, grainy pencil strokes – I had to hold them under the lamp to make them out properly. There was a lot of crossing out. They were the same few sentences, over and over. Different drafts. The last one read:

I've drunk quite a lot of bleach. Enough to kill me, I shouldn't wonder. I did it on purpose.

Daphne

I put my head down on the desk because I felt braver with my head supported. In the corner of the last note, written in small letters and lightly, was *L 11: 24–26*. Without lifting my head, I dragged a King James pocket Bible, covered in white leather, out of another drawer in the dressing table. I set it in front of my nose and looked through it.

Leviticus . . . Lamentations . . . Luke . . . well, it couldn't be Lamentations, because that only had five chapters.

The Leviticus passage was incomplete; the first sentence of it referred to the sentence before it, and the last sentence was an admonition against eating pork and mutton.

Luke said:

When the unclean spirit is gone out of a man, he walketh through dry places, seeking rest; and finding none, he saith, I will return unto my house whence I came out.

And when he cometh, he findeth it swept and garnished.

Then goeth he, and taketh to him seven other spirits more wicked than himself; and they enter in, and dwell there: and the last state of that man is worse than the first.

My gaze snagged on two parts of the passage again and again:

I will return unto my house whence I came out

Seven spirits more wicked than himself.

I read the passage aloud. I couldn't help it. Better that than keep it as a thought.

As I said the last word, the rocking chair groaned behind me.

Exactly as if someone had sat down in it.

And the chair began to rock.

I changed my mind – I didn't want her there. I didn't.

I ran, leaping three steps at a time, coming down so hard I almost turned my ankle.

S.J. looked up when I re-entered the study, breathless.

'What is it?' he asked. There was a note in his voice – as if he knew.

'Nothing.'

I lay down at his feet, my breasts against the rug. I turned the pages of a cookbook and pretended to read, but really I was imagining him walking across my back; his heel grinding into the base of my spine, the next step pushing the vertebrae away from each other; by the time he reached my neck I'd be in pieces. He wouldn't do it, but he could – he had the ability. With his lips and hands he refigured me, coaxed me into moving so closely with him that we disappeared and left a trail of sighs behind us. Not just in the bed. Against walls, across tables, on floors with my heels dancing the same pleading two steps over his shoulder blades. But we didn't go into the blue room again.

'Where's all the downstairs furniture?' I asked him, in the morning.

He looked wary. 'In the cellar,' he said.

There was a little platform immediately inside the cellar door, and a staircase leading straight down. It was gloomy once the door had closed behind us.

'You first,' S.J. said in my ear.

So I went first, sending a torch beam ahead of me with one hand and feeling my way with the other. S.J.'s hands collided with mine, and I heard him breathing behind me. There were a lot of chairs and tables packed into a very small amount of space; it was like climbing out into a sea of brocade and velvet padding. Insects wriggled around between the armchairs, and chair legs fell apart as I moved them out of my way; I picked bits up and saw they were worn through with holes. Woodworm. We stayed down there until we'd identified some pieces that were salvageable, taking turns sitting on each chair and leaning against each table to be sure. It was a slow, airless hour, full of rustling, like someone whispering through cloth. From time to time I trained the torch on S.J. He kept looking at me, looking away, then back at me, quietly surprised that I was still there.

We dragged the whole pieces out and arranged them in the rooms they belonged to. The place began to look less like an austere puzzle. I tampered with his placement of the sofas and armchairs and side tables and vases, and he tampered ceaselessly with mine. When we caught each other in the act we pretended we hadn't seen. Those were the rules of playing house.

*

The next afternoon we went down to a cove in the opposite direction from the one we'd taken to get to the moor. It was only a little cove; it sloped down to the water smoothly. Gravely, as if guiding me into the deep of his secrets, S.J. showed me the markings on the stones he collected. Darkness fell and we stripped down to wetsuits and walked into the sea. When we tired of swimming I just floated and span in the gloss of the water and he bobbed beside me. We were top and tails; he held my ankle so I didn't float away too far.

I texted Jonas: *Happy.*

And he sent the word back to me: *Happy.*

I ignored my agent's phone calls and deleted the threats he left me via voicemail – I was smiling in a way that felt new, so fresh it was like another face, and I didn't want to stop. Not even for the moment needed to take one of those pictures people said were so good, the ones in which a girl with blank and shiny eyes stood on one leg, looked over her shoulder, was an acrobat, was no one.

*

The day S.J. went back to work I dashed around Brier Moss, buying things to cook for a dinner party in the evening. He wanted me to meet some of his friends. Two female friends and two male friends. They were all single, so he was also hoping to set them up. I bought candles and flowers and artichokes and steak and braced myself for a frosty reception from the single female friends. It wasn't unlikely that they had stayed single in the hopes that he might suddenly fall for them. When I came back from town I went into S.J.'s study, to fetch a cookbook. He'd left the French doors open, and in going to close them, I almost trod on a finch. The bird lay on its back in between the doors and didn't take fright at my drawing so near. Its beak and feet pointed at the sky, blackened, as if blasted by flame. It had died with its eyes open and some liquid in them congealing. And there were more just outside. I stopped counting after ten. They were all in the same condition. There were more birds chirping from somewhere, there were still birds, still singing, but I couldn't see them. *They must be very high up.* For a moment I thought I'd be sick, but I wasn't sick. The majority of the bodies were congregated in an uneven half-ring around the cedar tree. *Oh . . .* my eyes flickered closed – for a moment I saw myself standing on the grass, cake flowing from my hand like sand – my eyes opened again. I used a rolled-up magazine to push the bodies towards each other, into a heap. I wanted to dig, so that I could bury them, but I had nothing to dig with. I tried a little with my hands, and it took a long time to make even the slightest pocket in the ground. I had to cook the food, I had to get ready for guests. I didn't want people to arrive and find me here, scrabbling in the earth with my fingernails. I just had to leave the birds where they were.

I went into the kitchen and stood beside the Aga, staring at the wall. It was on; it had been on all morning. I'd laughed at it when I first saw it, but it gave off serious warmth. Dinner would be ready, possibly even burnt, in no time. And then I would have nothing to do.

I think I'm going to have to go.

I grasped gratefully at that thought. I became busy. I chopped the steak and made a marinade for the artichokes. I closed the kitchen door and lined the bottom of it with tea towels. I opened the oven door and knelt down and breathed blue, dancing gas. I coughed, but without urgency. I was dizzy and the heat around me was not unpleasant; it was like being lost in a fog when you had nowhere in particular to go. It didn't matter. I collapsed onto my stomach and looked to the side, not that there was anything to see, apart from grey-coated metal.

I began to choke. I couldn't move. I wanted to, but my head wouldn't do it – the fog was in it.

I heard a distant sound – a dial turning.

The Aga shut down. No more blue, just gaping blackness.

Someone was crouching near me. She put her hand on my leg. My skin shrieked. I can't explain how it felt. There was movement beneath her fingernails.

'You're an idiot,' she said. Her voice wasn't at all the way I'd imagined it. It was clear and firm.

'Nothing's wrong here. Can't you see that? Nothing's wrong. Next time just don't feed the birds with cake that's

170

been experimentally laced with pharmaceuticals. You listen to me, Mary Foxe, or whatever your name is. Stay here. There's a decent man here who will probably fall for you if you don't make a mess of things. He'll take care of you. And you take care of him. No point having any more death.'

My mother. My father. I couldn't speak.

'Yes,' she said. 'I know. But you're what happens next. That's all I wanted to tell you upstairs, but you ran like – like the Hound of the Baskervilles or something.'

'Thank you, Daphne,' I whispered.

'Oh, yes, you owe me one. So you'll tell him?'

'Tell him what?'

'That it's not his fault about me. Because it's not.'

'I'll tell him.'

'Don't just say it. Make him believe it.'

'How—'

'*Make him believe it.*' She squeezed my ankle.

'I will!'

'I'm tired,' she said. 'I'm going now. Be bad. Be wicked. And you should worry. But don't.'

Mary stayed out of my way for a couple of weeks. I was busy with Daphne, trying to get her to like me again and call off the death threats from her friends. I began teaching Daphne to drive. She was fearless – a little too fearless for my taste – and she learnt fast. She'd bought a pair of driving gloves specially, and her hands rested serenely on the wheel when it was her turn to try taking a corner. We drove down to the pheasant farm I used to shoot at when I was coming up – fifteen minutes away, but it took us thirty-five with Daphne driving. She brought a pheasant back with us and cooked it up for dinner – it was the worst meal I'd ever encountered, but I choked it down and appreciated it. She was trying, and I was trying. It'd be wrong to say my wife hasn't got any go in her. On our honeymoon she spent the best part of a morning leaping around a rock garden, bouncing from ledge to ledge like a lunatic and singing some almost offensively sugary song. She slipped, and twisted her ankle, but she didn't howl about it. She bit her lip and she cried a little, because, she said, she didn't want to pretend it didn't hurt. And she hobbled around good-humoredly, taking snapshots and studying the gaudy little paintings for sale on the streets just as solemnly as if they were up in a gallery. Remembering that she'd cried, I got a doctor to look at her ankle for her when we got back to the hotel. It was a sprain. I'd have understood if she'd howled.

Another day we drove down to the state park. It's called the Devil's Hopyard. That was a pretty good afternoon. Close to the waterfall each tree quivers as if trying to shake itself awake from a bad dream without waking the others up. And the stones all around the waterfall itself are half hollowed out – we looked at stone after stone for almost an hour. The hollows were definite, as if someone had come along with a scoop and removed the heart of each stone.

'These are the reason this place is called the Devil's Hopyard,' I told Daphne. 'People round here used to say the devil himself made the marks in the stones with his hooves as he walked over them . . .'

'It's the only explanation,' Daphne said, solemnly. I found myself playing with her hair – just sort of mussing it and walking my fingers down the strands until they fell back into place again.

'How's Mary?' she asked me, almost straight-faced. Almost.

'Mary who?' I asked.

That night, after love, she rolled away from me and sat up in her own bed. I was falling asleep, but she sat in a way that demanded I look at her. She had her hand on the top of her head, as if trying to keep something in.

'What is it?' I asked. I stretched out an arm. 'Come back!' She stayed where she was.

'I've just got to go and – you know.' She was whispering as if she didn't want to be overheard. Even though we were the only ones in the house.

'Oh – okay, honey. Good thing you remembered.' Daphne

sponged with Lysol disinfectant to keep from getting pregnant. It worked, too. She hadn't wanted a kid when we got
married, and I hadn't argued.

I closed my eyes. Daphne didn't move. I felt her weight a
few inches away, warm and still. I opened my eyes again.
She was looking at me and her smile had crumpled.

'What? Have we run out?'

'No.'

'What is it, D?'

'You want me to? You want me to go and – you know?'

'You don't want to.' I was alarmed, and I sounded
alarmed. It wasn't the thought of a baby, per se. It was just
the sudden change; she might as well have pulled the mat-
tress right out from under me.

She smiled. Falsely, brightly. She scrambled out of bed.
'Okay. Thanks for letting me know how you feel.'

'D. Hold on. Hold on just a second—'

She vanished into the bathroom. I went up to the closed
door and heard nothing. The taps didn't turn on. She might
have opened the cupboard and reached for the yellow bottle
that sat between my razor and her set of heated curlers, but
if she had, then she'd done it with infamous and unnecessary
stealth. After a few more minutes I became convinced she'd
climbed out of the window and run off into the night. I
knocked on the door. 'D.'

'Yes, darling.'

'Are you going to come out?'

'Yes, in a minute.'

There are things I should have said to her then, but I
didn't say any of them. I thought I'd tell her when she came
out. She didn't come out. She was still in there when I fell

asleep. I woke up at some point before dawn and she was there in bed beside me, nestled up against me. She'd taken my arm and put it around her. And I was grateful. Pathetically grateful. Next time the matter came up, I would say the things I knew I should say.

Very early the next morning we walked down to Cloud Cove and walked out across the sand to the island; it was accessible on foot when the tide was out, and I wanted to show Daphne the lighthouse. I own it – I mean, I inherited it, and just like my father, who inherited it from his father, I don't know what the hell to do with it so I just make sure it gets a good spring-cleaning from top to bottom three times a year and keep some books there. My great-grandfather won the place in a game of cards. I always think I might go over there to work, but I never do.

Daphne and I didn't talk much on the way over. We picked up bits of driftwood, shells and pebbles, and arranged them on the ground when we felt we'd carried them too far away from where we'd picked them up. The wind nipped us through our clothes.

'Oh God,' Daphne said, as the lighthouse came into view. She said, 'Oh God,' again and again with every step we took towards it. 'It looks *evil*.'

It wasn't evil. It was just a white tower with long slits for windows. Not even a particularly tall tower. She liked it better when we were inside and she saw that it was spick and span and modern. I took her up to the lantern room, and she stared at the lantern through the glass panels. It was the size of a man, and covered in dust. I pointed out the lenses that surrounded it, and explained how they refracted the light from the lantern and made it fly out in all directions the way

175

she'd seen it in movies. When I took her to the watch room she insisted on turning the handles that rotated the lamp lenses. We heard the lenses whirring – not a comfortable sound to have above you – like huge wings flapping in place – but there was no kerosene in the lamp and even if there had been, it was morning, so the whole thing was a pretty pointless exercise.

'You must have loved this place as a boy,' she said, as we came down the spiral staircase. 'It must have been like a four-storey playground.' She'd brought some log books down with her, clutched against her chest, even though I'd warned her that all she'd find written there was times and dates and comings and goings and observations on what direction the wind was coming from.

'Not really,' I told her. 'I didn't see the point of it.'

'All right, well – normal kids would love it . . .'

She'd brought a flask full of coffee and some rolls, and we had those at the kitchen table. She looked over the log books, lost interest after about four pages, as I had predicted, but soldiered on. I left her at the table and went to go and pack up a few books I wanted. I dragged a couple of crates over to the back door, so I could look out at the sea while I searched – the tide was high, and choppy, but not so that I couldn't see across the cove. I looked from my books to the water, from my books to the water – sunlight flashed once, twice, three times on the waves. The fourth time I saw that it wasn't light. It was a hand, raised up at the end of an arm, and it was waving at me. Gradually, Mary Foxe walked out of the sea and paced across the sand towards me. She wasn't smiling. Her hands were behind her back. She looked as if she had a lot on her mind. Once she was standing directly before me, she dropped a curtsey.

'Mary.'

'Yes, Mr Fox?'

'I think I know what we're trying to do with this game of ours.'

'Tell me.'

'We've been trying to fall in love—'

She raised her eyebrows. 'With each other?' she asked, coolly.

'Would you let me finish?'

'With pleasure.'

'We've been trying to fall in love – yes, with each other – but we've been trying to take some of the danger out of it. So no one ends up maimed, or dead. We're trying for something normal and nice.'

Mary folded her arms. 'That is *not* what we're trying to do.'

'Oh. What, then?'

'Your wife loves you. Turn to her. Properly. Stop fobbing her off and being a counterfeit companion. It would be good if, after all this, just once you wrote something where people come together instead of falling apart. Just show me you can do it and I'll leave you alone.'

'But I don't want you to leave me alone.'

She turned to face the sea. The wind whipped her hair around. Her hair is a miraculous color, like autumn leaves shaken down around her shoulders. She looked wild and lovely.

'Mary. If you were real I'd run away with you for ever.'

I went to her; we faced each other. She said: 'You're cruel, Mr Fox.' Her voice, her eyes. She was weary.

My heart was doing that jerking thing it did when I'd thought Daphne might leave me, but worse. Much, much worse. Almost unbearable. I was about to go off like a bomb or something. It actually hurt.

(Please don't let me keel over on the sand at this woman's feet.)

'I would like to have breakfast with you,' Mary Foxe said. 'And I would like to have you defer a little to my tastes and habits – at present I have none, because you haven't given me any. I'd like to go to dinner parties with you and play charades. I'd like to have friends to lend me books and tell me secrets. I would like to have nothing to do with you for hours on end and then come back and find you, come back with things I've thought and found out all on my own – on my own, not through you. I'd like not to disappear when you're not thinking about me.'

She enunciated her words very slowly and carefully. As she spoke I saw that I'd proposed the impossible.

'So if you *did* find some way for me to be real and for me to be together with you, then I wouldn't mind that. I wouldn't mind at all.'

'Honey,' Daphne called out. 'Shouldn't we go before it gets dark?'

Mary wasn't there any more. She'd never passed out of my sight so abruptly before.

I was shaken, and Daphne mustn't know that I was shaken. I'd told her she had nothing to worry about where Mary was concerned. I'd said it wasn't 'like that'. Had I lied? To Daphne? Or just now, to Mary? I'll say anything to get out of a spot. I counted to ten, holding my chest like a fool, like Young Werther guarding his sorrows, then I went to Daphne. She was sitting on the front steps with a paperback. It had to be *War and Peace* – it was thick enough. The title was in Cyrillic, and so were all the contents.

'Is that . . . Russian?' I asked her.

She answered in words that left me stone cold. Russian, I presumed.

'Daphne!' It made her laugh, the way I was looking at her.

She winked. 'Don't worry, I'm not possessed. I said I'm just brushing up. I've been taking a correspondence course. You've got a lot to find out about me, my friend.'

She looked a little cold, so I put my jacket around her shoulders and we strolled down to wait at the post where the ferry came in. And she leaned against me, and it was all right.

hide, seek

Once, in Asyût, east of Cairo, a boy was born to a market-trading family fallen on hard times, a family too poor to keep him unless he had somehow been born full-grown and ready to work. The boy's tiny mother had given birth to five big, healthy, noisy boys before him. But the first thing this particular boy did when he was born was cough quietly, and turn a blind, bewildered glare on his brothers, who elbowed each other and watched him closely. This new boy was far too small. He had to be spanked six times before he proved his lungs to the midwife, and even then, his cry wasn't lusty enough. He was limp and wouldn't cling to a finger when it was placed in his palm. He refused his mother's breast, wrinkling his nose at the knotty brown bud of her nipple with slow bafflement.

Yet his eyes said that he needed something.

The boy's mother saw into the future. Her mind hunkered down in the midst of her tiredness and spread the dead circle of her nerves until it overlapped into her next life, her next fatigue. The boy's mother saw that she wouldn't be able to coax this son, to coddle him, to silently cherish him, to let him fall and find no help, to do all of the things that it would take for this boy to survive into his strength as a man.

(She looked into his eyes – they were like a famine.

180

Seeing them sent hurt and light through her. His eyes kept asking, asking, and she knew that a person could die trying to love him.)

If it hadn't been certain before, the decision not to keep the boy was now absolute.

'He will not be strong,' the boy's father winced, when news of the birth was brought to him at his sand-blown stall. 'He will not be of use.' He didn't tell the other men whose threadbare robes jostled his at market because it was not a good thing to have to send a child away.

'He will not be strong,' the midwife said, averting her eyes from the child's. She left as soon as she could, with promises that she would tell all the doctors she knew about the child, in the hope that they knew of some infertile couple.

Sunset on the outskirts of Asyût brought clarity.

Even from the narrow side-streets where damp sand beads and breathes, any window can tell you why they say here the world began with a brother and sister locked in a beautiful circus trick. In Egypt, like everywhere, the land is made to fit the sky; but here it is more so. Here it is possible to say 'this is land' and point, and 'this is sky', and point, but the eye can't discover the dividing line. Nut cranes her neck over her long lithe blue back to kiss Geb, and Geb cradles her, careful, because she is nothing, less than nothing, but if he should drop her it would be the end of everything. The boy's mother was comforted by sunset, and she closed the shutters and began preparing her new son's cot.

The next day's noon came like a blazing hoop, and the sun spat razorblades through it. People did what they had to to keep from wilting. Slim women waddled; fat women crept close to the ground, barely taking steps. Amongst them came a tall, ramrod-straight woman in pure black; she parted the jostling knots of people in bounding spurts, like a dark thought. She was accompanied by the boy's midwife.

The woman took the market traders' son away with her because, she said, she needed a seeker, and this boy was one.

The woman's voice was soft and you had to listen hard for it, otherwise you thought she was trying to speak to you with her eyes alone. The atmosphere around this woman told of books and fine rugs. The boy's mother cried and held herself, held her leaking breasts as the woman took her son away. But she didn't change her mind.

*

A girl was born in Osogbo, in a small hospital a few feet away from a stone shrine to love. The girl was a heavy baby, with features that were pleasing because they were fluid and made her simple to look at, as if she was carved all of a piece. The girl was very quick learning to walk, speak in both English and Yoruba, eat solids, use her potty, smile in a certain way that brought maturity down like an axe on her face. At six years old, she prostrated herself before her elders unasked. She clambered over her milestones with unassailable, businesslike calm. No cute lisping, no unusual habits. It took the girl's parents a long time to realise that their daughter's docility and sweetness was in fact vacancy, a kind of sleepiness and an instinct for ease that translated itself to her entire body. The girl's hair grew soft and light so that combs flashed through it without tangling, so that it sat well in plaits. Blemishes fell away from the girl's skin with simple soap and water. The same question put to this girl two times in a row would yield two different answers, depending on who asked the girl the question, and in what tone. The day that he saw that it was enough, the girl's father was chauffeuring a sweaty, bearded oil executive to the airport. The girl's father looked away for a moment from the well-fed face, from the firm, confident mouth of his passenger in the rear-view mirror, and saw his daughter following a street vendor home, nodding and smiling in the shade of the bush-lined thoroughfare, a sack of the street vendor's rice piled across her shoulders with a sturdy, troubling grace. The girl's father bundled her into the car without ceremony or apology to his passenger, and at home he thrashed her with a walking cane. He held her head down on the kitchen table as he beat her, and his fingers dug into her scalp, but he did not feel her neck tensing against him, and she didn't make a sound. He kept on hitting her because he wasn't sure whether she was feeling this or not. The neighbours came en masse, some with their fingers entwined in the fur at the scruff of their goats' necks, and they remonstrated with him. Women pulled off their head wraps and wrung their hands. 'It is too much,' everyone told him. The girl's father stopped when he was tired of hammering on her bones. He watched her breathing; her shoulder blades rose and fell with her head turned away from him and into the table. When she lifted her head she said unsteadily, 'Sorry, Daddy.' Blood welled from the space between her lips.

*

The boy grew up with a hard smile and a complicated manner that was at once condescending and eager. He developed a gait that made him seem arrogant. These were attempts to counteract his eyes and their treacherous tendency to ask. He wasn't handsome, or talkative, but his adoptive mother made sure that he dressed well, in English tailoring and American denim. And his sadness was luminous. Girls his age gave him kisses and held his hand even when they shied away from other boys. Women offered him honeyed pastries, confidences, concern. He walked the markets and puffed pipe smoke in corner tea houses, breathed in the spice-pod musk of men and took their advice with throwaway thanks.

The woman who had adopted him was a widow, and it was possible that her bereavement had made her mad. The boy's new home terrified him, because the downstairs was bright and softly pastel-coloured and air-conditioned, but the upstairs was cordoned off. If he looked hard enough, he could make out doors and bare floors, but that was all. At night he slept on a couch beside the woman who had adopted him; the woman herself slept on a boat-shaped chaise-longue, it took to her body in a way that he would never see again, let her sleep with grace although her arms and legs were bunched up and her feet were hanging off the end of the couch. It didn't seem to matter very much that the woman didn't grow older as he grew older, either, though he suspected that something about the woman herself slowed him down, bathed his thoughts in perfume, set his dreams afloat so that his mind was abuzz with stranger things than her age, or her solitude, or the silent upstairs.

The woman insisted on being called mother.

(Which the boy called her, but with a secret hiss that came from a place inside him that he did not understand – inside his head her name became *motherhhhhhhh*, smothered myrrh.)

She was an art collector, but she only collected art that was body pieces, one considered piece at a time, painstaking finds because she was looking for a collection that, when put together in a room, would create the suggestion of a woman, a woman who crammed the room from wall to wall. The boy took telephone calls and messages left for his new mother by her contacts all over the world. He travelled Egypt with her and observed cemetery graffiti as she did, so closely that she almost inhaled it – in hundreds of perfumeries they watched glass-blowers torture air between their hands, force it to become solid.

Always, as they travelled, she pointed and asked him, 'Do you like that? What do you see there?'

He told her the truth, and she always listened to him. She said that he chose well.

But when they got home, the boy did not ever feel anything in the presence of these well-turned ankles and smooth calves, these arms and shoulders captured in shade and the moment of motion. They were a collection, not a woman.

Then the boy and his mother got a face for their collection. The face was a photograph. The photograph was of a girl who had died with her family one night when her neighbours smashed the door down and took an axe to all the living inside that house. The neighbours did this because a radio broadcast told them to. The radio broadcast advised them not to wait for the evil that lived next door to grow and get the better of them. And so it was done. But after killing the family, the neighbours had not touched anything else in the girl's house, which is how the boy and his new mother, picking over this room at the end of a series of devastated rooms, found the girl's picture. At first the boy thought that it would be wrong to take the picture. But it was a picture unlike any other. It had been taken in the back yard of the house, at some point between the sun's disappearance and the illumination of the moon. The girl's smile did not seem to correspond to the presence of the camera, or even to a joke told off-camera. Her smile was unnerving because it had no reason. They took the picture home, even though the boy's new mother complained that it wasn't art. Then the boy's new mother asked him what he thought of their almost complete collection, waved her arms at all the fineness and said, 'You want someone. Is she here?'

He said, 'No.'

'We need a heart,' the boy's new mother said, and when she looked at him, in that moment, she seemed to him so high. It seemed that her feet connected to the ground only tenuously and it was her shadow that bore her up. The boy thought in that moment that this woman must be beautiful, no of course she was; fine eyes, wide-curved lips, and cheek-bones like slanted hooks. But at the same time he thought that his new mother must be a spider.

*

What nobody knew about the docile girl from Osogbo was that her heart was too heavy, and that almost from birth she had felt its weight, a gravitational pull that invited her to her grave. Her heart was heavy because it was open, and so things filled it, and so things rushed out of it, but still the heart kept beating, tough and frighteningly powerful and meaning to shrug off the rest of her and continue on its own. People soon learnt that they could play on her sympathy, and, because she was terrified that one day this unasked-for conscience of hers might kill her, she gave away whatever money she earned, gave away bread and went without. The girl tried, several times, to give her love away, but her love would not stay with the person she gave it to and snuck back to her heart without a sound. What people didn't know about this girl was that the ancestral dead kept her company – they came to find her at bathtime and sat four at a time in the bathwater with her, cooing wistfully and using their wasted, insubstantial hands to wash her hair. The girl urged them to take care of their own children, but they refused. Her head lolled at these times and she was overcome with gratitude. At bedtime the dead took her with them, and in her dreams, she visited their graves.

At first, in rebellion against her heaviness, the girl thought that she needed to be thinner, and she took to reading imported women's magazines on credit from a bookstall owner. The magazines talked about calories and saving calories and keeping some back so that you could have a glass of wine. One day at the dinner table, the girl asked her mother for an estimate of how many calories there were in the fried stew that bubbled at the bottom of her bowl beneath a layer of *eba*. There is no Yoruba word for calories, and so her mother just looked at her and said musingly, smilingly, in English, 'Calories,' as if she was trying to understand a punchline hidden in between the syllables. Then the girl didn't ask any more and just sat looking at the food, which was bottomless and made to sink hunger.

The girl decided that she had to hide her heart somewhere until she was big enough to keep hold of its weight. One night the dead helped her, some stroking her hair and soothing her while others hooked their fingers into her and carefully lifted a strand of steam from her chest. The girl took her heart, and that cool night she was frightened even though she walked amidst a crowd of other people's ancestors. The shrine was a rectangle of stone arches that spoke of other kinds of love – strange, ugly, smoke and choking sort of love, carvings of cruel hands that killed candle flames to break refusal in the dark, women thrusting out hard breasts and genitals. Also in the carvings was the kind of love that wakes you up from nightmares. And also there was a sundial of wise children's faces. The shrine was the kind of place where a Valentine's heart would have trembled and wilted. With her fingers the girl scratched a place for herself in the north wall and slipped her heart through into the dry moss behind the stone.

And she walked away, and she walked away, and that was that, and that was that.

*

Because he had been told to, the boy looked for hearts. He examined unusual playing cards and alabaster chess pieces and went to London with his new mother to examine posters plastered onto the walls of public-transport stations. On the boy's twenty-first birthday, his new mother took him to the west coast of his continent to view a shrine, a shrine where, one of their contacts had told her, you could hear and feel a heart beating when it grew dark. They stood, amidst a small crowd of other curious people, and waited for sunset, which came with a slow earthquake that sent the ground slipping away, until they realised that the sensation was the legendary heartbeat. The boy, now a man, stood a little apart from his new mother, who listened intently, and the heartbeat said things to them both, things that made the boy smile with all of his soul in his face, things that made the new mother suck in her cheeks and look suddenly pinched and old. They stayed long after everyone had gone, and fell asleep at dawn with their heads laid on rocks converted to pillows with thick shawls.

When the next morning came around, the asking in the man's eyes was so powerful that no one could look at him without offering, offering, offering.

*

The girl was lighter without her heart. She danced barefoot on the hot roads and her feet were not cut by the stones or glass that studded her way. She spoke to the dead whenever they visited her. She tried to be kind, but they realised that they no longer had anything in common with her, and she realised it, too. So they went their separate ways. Other people became closed to the girl, and she enjoyed it this way – at the market place she handed over her bread and exacted the correct payment for it with a slight pressure of the hand and an uncaring smile. When the girl moved amongst people, she felt as if she were walking in a public place at an hour of the night when it was too dark to come out, or at noon, when it was too hot to be outside, and all the doors around were closed and barred. The girl felt this solitude to be an adventure. She moved away from her parents and went to live by herself on the ground floor of a tenement, even though this was frowned upon. When she was not working or wandering, she listened to the white noise inside her head, or she sat on her bare floor and listened to people arguing, romancing, accusing, the people all around her, she let their words fall into her body like coins into a bottomless well. Sometimes she thought about her heart, and wondered how it was doing without her. But the girl was never curious enough to go and find out.

Except once, when she almost went back to see.

Except once, when she woke up one morning convinced that she was in love. All over her, her skin felt softer even than her breath, and her eyes felt wider, clearer, dreamy, lashed and lidded with an unknown stuff that had drawn a man in. For a week, she washed and dried and rubbed cream into her body with a special, happy care, and she realised that she was preparing her body for caresses. She found a taste for cold things that released their sweetness slowly – ice cream that slid down her throat before she could taste it, tinned peaches in chill syrup.

But there was no heart there in her chest.

When the girl remembered this, she forced herself to eat a bite of mashed plantain, and the first swallow was hard. But after that, life stepped straight again.

*

The man's new mother told him, 'That heart, that heart in the shrine, it's the heart that we must take for my collection.' And then the art collection, the beautiful woman, the new mother's obsession, would be complete. 'If only we can locate the heart and take it with us,' the man's new mother said, watching her new son closely.

The heart had told him, it had called to him, *Come. Take from me, I am inexhaustible.*

But the man said nothing.

'I know that you know where that heart is,' the man's new mother said, and she bared teeth as sharp as daggers. 'You are a seeker, you find things. Bring it to me.'

The man told his new mother to give him five days. He

ground valerian root into her tea to make her sleep, and the new mother slept with a beauty like rose and earth, and her bitterness was a weed whose roots were scourged by her sleep, and so her bitterness fell away.

The man moved the collection, in carefully packaged batches, to the Osogbo shrine. It was a cry to the owner of the heart, this offering; he would not take the heart from the walls of the shrine until she came. He looked at all the love carved into the stone, and it was a lot of love, and he believed that it must be enough; he had to believe that it was enough. He arranged the fragmented woman as best he could, and sometimes he felt as if unseen hands helped him, propped a canvas in such a way that the light enhanced it. The man was desperate now, and he asked the heart to call to its owner, for she was the strength that he had somehow been born separately from.

The heart called.

The heart called.

The man called.

The gathered woman, scattered across sculptures and glass and photographs and scraps of paper, the gathered woman became complete and almost breathed.

Almost.

The man waited for five days. He thought that he must surely die under the sun and the pain of this disaster. But he didn't die, because the shrine stones protected him.

When on the sixth day the man saw that the heart's owner did not come, he left that place.

I don't think my husband likes me. And I don't know how to make him. I try talking to him about books, and when he replies he won't look me in the eye, and sometimes his voice is muffled, suppressing a coughing fit . . . or laughter. I think it's important to be able to laugh at yourself – I hate people who are always offended. But when you've got to be prepared to laugh at yourself every single time you open your mouth . . . well, that's just depressing. I asked Greta for advice and she gave this tiny scream, as if she'd just heard the funniest words ever uttered, and she said: 'Oh, did you marry him for the intellectual conversation? You didn't even finish college, Daphne.'

I took her point, even though it was unfair of her to bring that up. College was a near-fatal bore. I had some really serious nosebleeds just at the thought of going to lectures. Gush, gush, gush, and afterwards I had to sit still for a couple of hours on account of having lost a lot of blood – doctor's orders. Philosophy! I must have been crazy. I only did it because they told me at school that I was smart, and gave us all these thrilling speeches about the privileges and responsibilities of women in higher education. I can learn things, all right; I don't deny that I can learn things. But I can only learn them when it isn't important. If someone tells me something and then says: 'Well, you'd better remember that, because in three months' time I'm going to make a decision about you based on whether you've remembered or not,' then it's all over and there's nothing I can do about it. Pops says he loves me just the way I am, but not everyone in the world is like my father. Maman, for example. A difficult and dissatisfied woman. She made me learn flower arranging and how to walk properly – books on my head, the whole bit. These things ruined me for life. Now it sets my teeth on edge when I see flowers carelessly flung into a vase, and I'm forever looking at other women in the street and thinking, 'Sloppy . . . sloppy.' And I know I shouldn't care, and I want to poke myself in the eye for caring, but I care anyway, so thanks for that, Maman. I guess most mothers are difficult and dissatisfied, though. I haven't heard of any easy-going ones, unless they're dead and everyone's being nice about them. But even then they don't say: 'She was real easy-going,' they talk about her sacrifice and how she had time to get involved in everyone's business. Anyway. My mind is wandering. I know that's because I'm thinking crazy thoughts and I don't want to be thinking them. I liked St John because he's different from the boys I grew up with. Nothing like John Pizarsky or Sam Lomax; they just shamble around like they always did, only in nice clothes they buy for themselves now. I can't take them seriously. Now St John could have been born into his elegance. It's a dangerous kind of elegance – he doesn't raise his voice, he lowers it. Sometimes he says something funny and when I laugh he looks at me and asks what I'm laughing at, as if he'd genuinely like to know. And he's a solitary type . . . but when he comes back from wherever he's gone he can look so glad to see me . . .

Ordinary life just swerves around him, though, and I run off the sides like an ingredient thrown in too late. I can't stand the way he talks to me sometimes; very simply, as if to a child. The other day I suddenly realised, mid-conversation, that we two had spoken of nothing that morning but the matter of whether we ought to have calling cards made up for ourselves, to be left for friends who chanced not to be at home when we visited. Are calling cards too old fashioned, he wondered aloud. And what is the correct design and texture, and should we be Mr and Mrs Fox or St John and Daphne Fox, our names linked in the middle of the card or printed on separate sides of the card. He told me to consult my Emily Post, but I said I didn't have any of her books. He looked kind of surprised (I have several editions) but I lied because I don't like him thinking that these are the only things that interest me. The way he talks to me. I thought it was just his manner – I didn't mind that he never said anything romantic, not even at the very beginning – I was relieved about never having to wonder whether he really meant what he was saying. But now I'm starting to worry that this simplicity is contempt, that he picked me out as someone he could manage. I don't like to give that thought too much air, though. It'd be hard to go on if I really thought that was true.

I wish there was some level ground I could meet him on. Say he liked baseball, I could educate myself about that quite easily; just hang around while my dad and my brothers are waxing lyrical. That's easier than books. With books you've got to know all about other books that are like the one you're talking about, and it's just never-ending, and it's a pain. But this situation is fifty per cent my fault. When I was a lot younger, maybe fourteen or fifteen, I had ideas about the man I wanted. I remember a piano piece my music teacher played as part of a lesson. It was the loveliest thing I'd ever heard. People talked and passed notes all the way through it, and I wanted to shut them up at any cost, just go around with a handful of screwdrivers slamming them into people's temples. I waited until everyone had gone. Then I laid my notebook on top of the piano the music teacher had closed before he'd walked away, and I wrote his name, wrote his name, wrote his name, and underlined each version. I vowed that I wouldn't have a man unless he was someone I could really be together with, someone capable of being my better self, superior and yet familiar, a man whose thoughts, impressions and feelings I could inhabit without a glimmer of effort, returning to myself without any kind of wrench. Music. Sometimes it just makes you want to act just anyhow. I wasn't in love with the music teacher, I only wrote his name because it was a man's name.

I met St John at Clara Lee's soiree – she was great friends with my mother and at that time I had to keep meeting people and meeting people in case one of them was someone I could marry. Clara Lee basically threw this soiree with the almost express purpose of helping me, I mean, helping my mother. So there were ten or eleven clunking bores, two or three very sweet men who didn't think me sweet and a couple who obviously had something sort of wrong with them and the something wrong was the reason they were still bachelors. And then there was Mr Famous Writer; St John Fox. He must not have had anything else to do that evening. He had a terrible sadness about him. It's highly irregular for that to be one of the first things you notice about someone. I looked into his eyes, and realised, with the greatest consternation, that he was irresistible. He took me out on Sunday afternoons, and it was just calamitous – after about three of those I was done for:

So the simple maid
Went half the night repeating, 'Must I die?'
And now to right she turned, and now to left,
And found no ease in turning or in rest;
And 'Him or death,' she muttered, 'death or him' . . .

I didn't want someone I could understand without trying – I didn't want that any more. I wanted St John Fox. It turned out that he felt the same way about me. Then they lived happily ever after . . .

No. I don't think I was really that naive, thank God. I know I've got to work at this.

He went someplace this afternoon – research, he said. He didn't say where he'd be, but he did say he'd miss dinner – and I kissed him at the door. I wore a jewelled flower clip in my hair. He gave it to me himself a week ago, but today he said: 'That's pretty,' as if he had never seen it before. Oh, I don't know, I don't know. At least the dropped phone calls have stopped. They stopped once I'd told him about them. The last one was such a heavy call. She didn't just drop the receiver when I answered. She made a sound. *Pah-ha-ha-ha.* And I recognised it right away. That's how you cry when you are trying not to cry, and then of course the tears come all the harder. And do you know what I said? 'Don't . . . oh, *please* don't.' And she hung up.

Since then I've just been waiting for him to go off somewhere alone. He told me 'she's not real' – I just smiled and pretended to see what he meant. He's been spending a lot of time in his study with the door locked, but I've been biding my time. She must have written him a love letter or given him some kind of token. And if he's been fool enough to hold onto it, then I'm going to find it, and I'm going to force him to drop her in earnest. We're all better off that way. Things were tough enough without this girl coming between us. And the sound of her crying. Sometimes I try to hear it again. I wonder if it could really have been as bad as it sounded. It made me shudder – my husband is capable of making someone feel like that.

I waited for an hour, to make sure that he was really gone; then I searched his bathroom. An unlikely hiding place, but that could've been just his thinking. Then I searched his bedside drawers – nothing. I looked inside all the books in the drawing room, then went to his study again. He made a big show of not locking it before he left, so I'd know he'd forgiven me for kicking his things around a couple of months ago. I'd already searched his study, immediately after the heavy phone call, but there might have been something I'd overlooked. I sat down at his desk and looked around, trying to see some secret nook or cranny or a subtle handle I could turn. And as I looked I slowly became aware of a hand creeping across my thigh, the fingers walking down my knees.

I pushed the chair back as far as it would go; the legs made ragged scratches in the carpet because I pushed hard. I don't know if I screamed – if someone else had been there I would've been able to tell, I'd have been able to see them hearing it. But I couldn't hear anything.

Then I took my hand off my kneecap. My own hand.

Stupid Daphne. Is it any wonder he feels contempt . . .

I pretended that the past couple of minutes hadn't happened, and while I was doing that I opened his writing notebook – well, the one that was at the top of a pile of them. He'd just started it – it was empty apart from a table he'd drawn on the first page. I saw the letter D and the letter M, divided by a diagonal line. And there was talking, faster than I could follow, all in my skull and the bones of my neck, and I knew I'd found what I was looking for. Proof. But I couldn't understand it yet. I settled down and concentrated.

Under D he had written:

Is real. Is unpredictable. Is lovely to hold. Loves me (says M). Doesn't know me.

Under M he had written:

Is so many things – (too many things?). Is unpredictable. Is lovely to behold. Disapproves of me; wants more, better. There's nothing she doesn't know about me.

I sat with my head in my hands, shaking. Because the situation was so much worse than I thought. My husband was trying to choose between me, his wife, and someone he had made up. And I, the real woman, the wife, had nothing on the made-up girl. We each had five points in our favor. That son of a bitch.

I hate him, I hate him, oh God, I hate him.

I was holding my stomach. I felt sick because I had been a fool, I'd been foolish. I'd stopped using the Lysol after we made love. I wanted to run upstairs and fix that right away, but then I thought: it might be too late. I could already be pregnant. I have a doctor's appointment tomorrow. I thought if I gave him a child—

But he's been making lists. I'm pretty sure I could have him certified insane. But then she'd win, wouldn't she, this

Mary? It'd be the two of them together in the ward. Unbe-lievable. Horrible and unbelievable. I had to laugh. There's no one I can tell, not even Greta. There's nothing I can do about this. I measured my waist with my hands. He must have imagined her smaller about the waist than me. How much smaller . . . I pulled my hands in tight, tighter, this much smaller, this much. She was taking my breath. Taller than I am, or shorter? Taller. So she could look down on him. He seemed to like her looking down on him. I hunched over the desk with my hands in fists and my wedding ring swung from the chain around my neck.

'But it's not fair,' I said. 'You don't really exist. He could take a fall, or hit his head, and whatever part of his brain you belong to, that could suddenly shut you out. You're just a thought. You don't need him.' The sounds I'd heard down the telephone, the awful sobbing, those sounds were pouring out of me now. So many crazy thoughts kept coming – maybe I could make him take a fall – not a serious one, but it might shake him up, and she'd be gone. Or I could ask him, tell him, to stop, just stop, do whatever was necessary, he could kill her or something – what did that even mean, to kill someone imaginary – why, it was nothing at all. He could do it. He should do it, for me.

I had to get out of his study, go and get the Lysol, do something, before I started kicking his things around again. That was no way to win him over. I could see him adding to Mary's side of the list in his cheery handwriting, all apples and vowels: *She doesn't trash my study*. I stood up. And then I sat down again, staring at the floor. I stood up and sat down, stood up and sat down. There was something on the floor. A shadow that stood while I sat. Long and slanted and blacker than I knew black could be. It crept, too. Towards me. 'Oh my God.' I held my hands out. 'No!'

The shadow stopped. What would have been its hair fanned what would have been its face in long wings. The shadow seemed . . . hesitant. I didn't move. The shadow didn't move.

'Mrs Fox?' it asked.

Its voice was faint, but present. Not inside my head, I heard it with my ears.

'Did you hear me?' The voice was even fainter the second time. If I ignored it, it would disappear. But I couldn't ignore it. I looked at the ownerless shadow on the floor and I saw something that was trying to take form, and I felt bad for it. I felt sorry for it.

'If you can hear me, why won't you speak? Do you know who I am?' I really had to strain to hear the last few words.

'You're – Mary,' I said, as loudly as I could.

And she stood up. I mean – she stood *up* from the carpet in a whirl of cold air, and there was skin and flesh on her, and she was naked for almost a second, and then she turned, and she was clothed. I screamed – that time I know for sure I screamed, because she looked so alarmed, and screamed a little herself.

'You're real,' I said. I don't know why it came out sounding accusing; I just wanted to establish the facts.

She held her arms up to the light and looked at them exultingly, as if she'd crafted them herself. They were nice arms. Nicer than mine, that was for sure.

'Stay back,' I said, when she took another step in my direction. 'Stay back.' I picked up St John's stapler. It was a big stapler, about the size of a human head. If I had to, I'd staple her head.

'Okay, okay,' she said, wide-eyed. She must not have wanted anything to ruin all that peachy skin. He'd said she was British, but her accent was just as New England as mine – maybe even more so.

The doorbell rang, and she scattered. That's the closest word to what happened to her when the doorbell rang. I want to say 'shattered', but it wasn't as sudden as all that.

It was John Pizarsky at the door. Before I let him in I looked hopefully through the spyhole for Greta. Maybe I could tell her after all. What else are friends for?

I could tell her: St John's in a bad way. He says he's fine and he acts as if he's fine, but he's in a bad way. I don't blame him for not being able to tell; he doesn't do sane work for a living. And I have been sleeping with him, eating with him, we took a bath together last Tuesday – so I'm in a bad way too. I've seen and heard a woman he made up. I know what this is a called – folie à deux, a delusion shared by two or more people who live together. It was such a strong delusion, though. Like being on some kind of drug. Nobody warned me how easily my brain could warp a sunny morning so fast that I couldn't find the beginning of the interlude. One moment I was alone, the next . . . I was still alone, I guess, and making the air talk to me.

Those opium-eaters . . . Coleridge could have said something; he could have let the people know that it could happen this way, without warning. De Quincey could have found a moment to mention this, for God's sake.

Greta wasn't with J.P., but I opened the door anyway. I

had to have company. If I didn't have company now, right now, I didn't know what would happen or what I would do.

'What the hell took you so long?' J.P. asked.

'St John's out,' I said. 'And I don't have a number you can reach him on. So beat it.'

(Please stay.)

J.P. stood on the doorstep, looking at me. He looked until I twitched my nose, thinking I had something on my face.

'Say . . . did you ever play croquet?' he asked, finally.

'Never,' I said. 'Come inside and tell me about it.' He stepped back onto the driveway.

'Get your coat,' he said, 'Come outside and play it.'

I had my coat on before J.P., or anyone, could say 'knife'.

It turned out to be the nicest afternoon I'd had in a long time. Greta was at some luncheon or other, so it was just me, J.P., Tom Wainwright and his wife Bea, who's just the right side of chatty and very nice; never has a bad word to say about anybody. So relaxing – we played on the Wainwrights' front lawn. I was terrible at croquet, kept forgetting the rules even though J.P. tried to help and whispered them in my ear. But Tom and Bea just turned a blind eye when I did my worst. And there was sunshine, and cucumber sandwiches, and champagne, and I swung up high on it, higher than heaven, and forgot all about what was waiting for me at home.

my daughter the racist

One morning my daughter woke up and said all in a rush: 'Mother, I swear before you and God that from today onwards I am racist.' She's eight years old. She chopped all her hair off two months ago because she wanted to go around with the local boys and they wouldn't have her with her long hair. Now she looks like one of them; eyes dazed from looking directly at the sun, teeth shining white in her sunburnt face. She laughs a lot. She plays. 'Look at her playing,' my mother says. 'Playing in the rubble of what used to be our great country.' My mother exaggerates as often as she can. I'm sure she would like nothing more than to be part of a Greek tragedy. She wouldn't even want a large part, she'd be perfectly content with a chorus role, warning that fate is coming to make havoc of all things. My mother is a fine woman, all over wrinkles, and she always has a clean handkerchief somewhere about her person, but I don't know what she's talking about with her rubble this, rubble that – we live in a village, and it's not bad here. Not peaceful, but not bad. In cities it's worse. In the city centre, where we used to live, a bomb took my husband and turned his face to blood. I was lucky, another widow told me, that there was something left so that I could know of his passing. But I was ungrateful. I spat at that widow. I spat at her in her sorrow. That's sin.

I know that's sin. But half my life was gone, and it wasn't easy to look at what was left.

Anyway, the village. I live with my husband's mother, whom I now call my mother, because I can't return to the one who gave birth to me. It isn't done. I belong with my husband's mother until someone else claims me. And that will never happen, because I don't wish it.

The village is hushed. People observe the phases of the moon. In the city I felt the moon but hardly ever remembered to look for it. The only thing that disturbs us here in the village is the foreign soldiers. Soldiers, soldiers, soldiers, patrolling. They fight us and they try to tell us, in our own language, that they're freeing us. Maybe, maybe not. I look through the dusty window (I can never get it clean, the desert is our neighbour) and I see soldiers every day. They think someone dangerous is running secret messages through here; that's what I've heard. What worries me more is the young people of the village. They stand and watch the soldiers. And the soldiers don't like it, and the soldiers point their guns, especially at the young men. They won't bother with the women and girls, unless the woman or the girl has an especially wild look in her eyes. I think there are two reasons the soldiers don't like the young men watching them. The first reason is that the soldiers know they are ugly in their boots and fatigues, they are perfectly aware that their presence spoils everything around them. The second reason is the nature of the watching – the boys and the men around here watch with a very great hatred, so great that it feels as if action must follow. I feel that sometimes, just walking past them – when I block their view of the soldiers these boys quiver with impatience.

And that girl of mine has really begun to stare at the soldiers, too, even though I slap her hard when I catch her doing that. Who knows what's going to happen? These soldiers are scared. They might shoot someone. Noura next door says: 'If they could be so evil as to shoot children then it's in God's hands. Anyway I don't believe that they could do it.'

But I know that such things can be. My husband was a university professor. He spoke several languages, and he gave me books to read, and he read news from other countries and told me what's possible. He should've been afraid of the world, should've stayed inside with the doors locked and the blinds drawn, but he didn't do that, he went out. Our daughter is just like him. She is part of his immortality. I told him, when I was still carrying her, that that's what I want, that that's how I love him. I had always dreaded and feared pregnancy, for all the usual reasons that girls who daydream more than they live fear pregnancy. My body, with its pain and mess and hunger – if I could have bribed it to go away, I would have. Then I married my man, and I held fast to him. And my brain, the brain that had told me I would never bear a child for any man, no matter how nice he was, that brain began to tell me something else. Provided the world continues to exist, provided conditions remain favourable, or at least tolerable, our child will have a child and that child will have a child and so on, and with all those children of children come the inevitability that glimpses of my husband will resurface, in their features, in the way they use their bodies, a fearless swinging of the arms as they walk. Centuries from now some quality of a man's gaze, smile, voice, way of standing or sitting will please someone else in a way that they aren't completely aware of, will be loved very hard for just a moment, without enquiry into where it came from. I ignore the women who say that my daughter does things that a girl shouldn't do, and when I want to keep her near me, I let her go. But not too far, I don't let her go too far from me.

The soldiers remind me of boys from here sometimes. The way our boys used to be. Especially when you catch them with their helmets off, three or four of them sitting on a wall at lunchtime, trying to enjoy their sandwiches and the sun, but really too restless for both. Then you see the rifles beside their knapsacks and you remember that they aren't our boys.

'Mother . . . did you hear me? I said that I am now a racist.'

I was getting my daughter ready for school. She can't tie knots but she loves her shoelaces to make extravagant bows.

'Racist against whom, my daughter?'

'Racist against soldiers.'

'Soldiers aren't a race.'

'Soldiers aren't a race,' she mimicked. 'Soldiers aren't a race.'

'What do you want me to say?'

She didn't have an answer, so she just went off in a big gang with her school friends. And I worried, because my daughter has always seen soldiers – in her lifetime she hasn't known a time or place when the cedars stood against the blue sky without khaki canvas or crackling radio signals in the way.

An hour or so later Bilal came to visit. A great honour, I'm sure, a visit from that troublesome Bilal who had done nothing but pester me since the day I came to this village. He sat down with us and mother served him tea.

'Three times I have asked this daughter of yours to be my wife,' Bilal said to my mother. He shook a finger at her. As for me, it was as if I wasn't there. 'First wife,' he continued. 'Not even second or third – first wife.'

'Don't be angry, son,' my mother murmured. 'She's not ready. Only a shameless woman could be ready so soon after what happened.'

'True, true,' Bilal agreed. A fly landed just above my top lip and I let it walk.

'Rather than ask a fourth time I will kidnap her . . .'

'Ah, don't do that, son. Don't take the light of an old woman's eyes,' my mother murmured, and she fed him honey cake. Bilal laughed from his belly, and the fly fled. 'I was only joking.'

The third time Bilal asked my mother for my hand in marriage I thought I was going to have to do it after all. But my daughter said I wasn't allowed. I asked her why. Because his face is fat and his eyes are tiny? Because he chews with his mouth open?

'He has a tyrannical moustache,' my daughter said. 'It would be impossible to live with.' I'm proud of her vocabulary. But it's starting to look as if I think I'm too good for Bilal, who owns more cattle than any other man for miles around and could give my mother, daughter and I everything we might reasonably expect from this life.

Please, God. You know I don't seek worldly things (apart from shoes). If you want me to marry again, so be it. But please – not Bilal. After the love that I have had . . .

My daughter came home for her lunch. After prayers we shared some cold *karkedeh*, two straws in a drinking glass, and she told me what she was learning, which wasn't much.

My mother was there, too, rattling her prayer beads and listening indulgently. She made faces when she thought my daughter talked too much. Then we heard the soldiers coming past as usual, and we went and looked at them through the window. I thought we'd make fun of them a bit, as usual. But my daughter ran out of the front door and into the path of the army truck, yelling: 'You! You bloody soldiers!' Luckily the truck's wheels crawled along the road, and the body of the truck itself was slumped on one side, resigned to a myriad of pot holes. Still, it was a very big truck, and my daughter is a very small girl.

I was out after her before I knew what I was doing, shouting her name. It's a good name – we chose a name that would grow with her, but she seemed determined not to make it to adulthood. I tried to trip her up, but she was too nimble for me. Everyone around was looking on from windows and the open gates of courtyards. The truck rolled to a stop. Someone inside it yelled: 'Move, kid. We've got stuff to do.'

I tried to pull my daughter out of the way, but she wasn't having any of it. My hands being empty, I wrung them. My daughter began to pelt the soldiers' vehicle with stones from her pockets. Her pockets were very deep that afternoon, her arms lashed the air like whips. Stone after stone bounced off metal and rattled glass, and I grabbed at her and she screamed: 'This is my country! Get out of here!'

The people of the village began to applaud her. 'Yes,' they cried out, from their seats in the audience, and they clapped. I tried again to seize her arm and failed again. The truck's engine revved up and I opened my arms as wide as they would go, inviting everyone to witness. Now I was screaming too: 'So you dare? You really dare?'

And there we were, mother and daughter, causing problems for the soldiers together.

Finally a scrawny soldier came out of the vehicle without his gun. He was the scrawniest fighting man I've ever seen – he was barely there, just a piece of wire, really. He walked towards my daughter, who had run out of stones. He stretched out a long arm, offering her chewing gum, and she swore at him, and I swore at her for swearing. He stopped about thirty centimetres away from us and said to my daughter: 'You're brave.'

My daughter put her hands on her hips and glared up at him.

'We're leaving tomorrow,' the scrawny soldier told her.

Whispers and shouts: *The soldiers are leaving tomorrow!*

A soldier inside the truck yelled out: 'Yeah, but more are coming to take our place,' and everyone piped low. My daughter reached for a stone that hadn't fallen far. Who is this girl? Four feet tall and fighting something she knows nothing about. Even if I explained it to her she wouldn't get it. I don't get it myself.

'Can I shake your hand?' the scrawny soldier asked her, before her hand met the stone. I thought my girl would refuse, but she said yes. 'You're okay,' she told him. 'You came out to face me.'

'Her English is good,' the coward from within the truck remarked.

'I speak to her in English every day,' I called out. 'So she can tell people like you what she thinks.'

We stepped aside then, my daughter and I, and let them continue their patrol.

*

My mother didn't like what had happened. But didn't you see everyone clapping for us, my daughter asked. So what, my mother said. People clap at anything. Some people even clap when they're on an aeroplane and it lands. That was something my husband had told us from his travels – I hadn't thought she'd remember.

My daughter became a celebrity amongst the children, and from what I saw, she used it for good, bringing the shunned ones into the inner circle and laughing at all their jokes.

*

The following week a foreigner dressed like one of our men knocked at my mother's door. It was late afternoon, turning to dusk. People sat looking out onto the street, talking about everything as they took their tea. Our people really know how to discuss a matter from head to toe; it is our gift, and such conversation on a balmy evening can be sweeter than sugar. Now they were talking about the foreigner who was at our door. I answered it myself. My daughter was at my side and we recognised the man at once; it was the scrawny soldier. He looked itchy and uncomfortable in his djellaba, and he wasn't wearing his keffiyeh at all correctly – his hair was showing.

'What a clown,' my daughter said, and from her seat on the cushioned floor my mother vowed that clown or no clown, he couldn't enter her house.

'Welcome,' I said to him. It was all I could think of to say. See a guest, bid him welcome. It's who we are. Or maybe it's just who I am.

'I'm not here to cause trouble,' the scrawny soldier said. He was looking to the north, south, east and west so quickly and repeatedly that for some seconds his head was just a blur. 'I'm completely off duty. In fact, I've been on leave since last week. I'm just – I just thought I'd stick around for a little while. I thought I might have met a worthy adversary – this young lady here, I mean.' He indicated my daughter, who chewed her lip and couldn't stop herself from looking pleased.

'What is he saying?' my mother demanded.

'I'll just – go away, then,' the soldier said. He seemed to be dying several thousand deaths at once.

'He'd like some tea . . .' my daughter told my mother. 'We'll just have a cup or two,' I added, and we took the tea out onto the veranda, and drank it under the eyes of God and the entire neighbourhood. The neighbourhood was annoyed. Very annoyed, and it listened closely to everything that was said. The soldier didn't seem to notice. He and my daughter were getting along famously. I didn't catch what exactly they were talking about, I just poured the tea and made sure my hand was steady. *I'm not doing anything wrong*, I told myself. *I'm not doing anything wrong.*

The scrawny soldier asked if I would tell him my name. 'No,' I said. 'You have no right to use it.' He told me his name, but I pretended he hadn't spoken. To cheer him up, my daughter told him her name, and he said: 'That's great. A really, really good name. I might use it myself one day.'

'You can't – it's a girl's name,' my daughter replied, her nostrils flared with scorn.

'Ugh,' said the soldier. 'I meant for my daughter . . .'

He shouldn't have spoken about his unborn daughter out there in front of everyone, with his eyes and his voice full of hope and laughter. I can guarantee that some woman in the shadows was cursing the daughter he wanted to have. Even as he spoke someone was saying, May that girl be born withered for the grief people like you have caused us.

'Ugh,' said my daughter.

I began to follow the conversation better. The scrawny soldier told my daughter that he understood why the boys lined the roads with anger. 'Inside my head I call them the children of Hamelin.'

'The what?' my daughter asked.

'The who?' I asked.

'I guess all I mean is that they're paying the price for something they didn't do.'

And then he told us the story of the Pied Piper of Hamelin, because we hadn't heard it before. We had nightmares that night, all three of us – my mother, my daughter and I. My mother hadn't even heard the story, so I don't know why she joined in. But somehow it was nice that she did.

*

On his second visit the scrawny soldier began to tell my daughter that there were foreign soldiers in his country, too, but that they were much more difficult to spot because they didn't wear uniforms and some of them didn't even seem foreign. They seemed like ordinary citizens, the sons and daughters of shopkeepers and dentists and restaurant owners and big businessmen. 'That's the most dangerous kind of soldier. The longer those ones live amongst us, the more they hate us, and everything we do disgusts them . . . these are people we go to school with, ride the subway with – we watch the same movies, root for the same baseball teams. They'll never be with us, though. We've been judged, and they'll always be against us. Always.'

He'd wasted his breath, because almost as soon as he began with all that I put my hands over my daughter's ears. She protested loudly, but I kept them there. 'What you're talking about is a different matter,' I said. 'It doesn't explain or excuse your being here. Not to this child. And don't say "always" to her. You have to think harder or just leave it alone and say sorry.'

He didn't argue, but he didn't apologise. He felt he'd spoken the truth, so he didn't need to argue or apologise.

Later in the evening I asked my daughter if she was still racist against soldiers and she said loftily: 'I'm afraid I don't know what you're referring to.' When she's a bit older I'm going to ask her about that little outburst, what made her come out with such words in the first place. And I'm sure she'll make up something that makes her seem cleverer and more sensitive than she really was.

*

We were expecting our scrawny soldier again the following afternoon, my daughter and I. My daughter's friends had dropped her. Even the ones she had helped find favour with the other children forgot that their new position was due to her and urged the others to leave her out of everything. The women I knew snubbed me at market, but I didn't need them. My daughter and I told each other that everyone would come round once they understood that what we were doing was innocent. In fact we were confident that we could convince our soldier of his wrongdoing and send him back to his country to begin life anew as an architect. He'd confessed a love of our minarets. He could take the image of our village home with him and make marvels of it.

Noura waited until our mothers, mine and hers, were

busy gossiping at her house, then she came to tell me that the men were discussing how best to deal with me. I was washing clothes in the bathtub and I almost fell in.

My crime was that I had insulted Bilal with my brazen pursuit of this soldier . . .

'Noura! This soldier – he's just a boy! He can hardly coax his beard to grow. How could you believe—'

'I'm not saying I believe it. I'm just saying you must stop this kind of socialising. And behave impeccably from now on. I mean – angelically.'

Three months before I had come to the village, Noura told me, there had been a young widow who talked back all the time and looked haughtily at the men. A few of them got fed up, and they took her out to the desert and beat her severely. She survived, but once they'd finished with her she couldn't see out of her own eyes or talk out of her own lips. The women didn't like to mention such a matter, but Noura was mentioning it now, because she wanted me to be careful.

'I see,' I said. 'You're saying they can do this to me?'

'Don't smile; they can do it. You know they can do it! You know that with those soldiers here our men are twice as fiery. Six or seven of them will even gather to kick a stray dog for stealing food . . .'

'Yes, I saw that yesterday. Fiery, you call it. Did they bring this woman out of her home at night or in the morning, Noura? Did they drag her by her hair?'

Noura averted her eyes because I was asking her why she had let it happen and she didn't want to answer.

'You're not thinking clearly. Not only can they do this to you but they can take your daughter from you first, and put her somewhere she would never again see the light of day.

Better that than have her grow up like her mother. Can't you see that that's how it would go? I'm telling you this as a friend, a true friend . . . my husband doesn't want me to talk to you any more. He says your ideas are wicked and bizarre.'

I didn't ask Noura what her husband could possibly know about my ideas. Instead I said: 'You know me a little. Do you find my ideas wicked and bizarre?'

Noura hurried to the door. 'Yes. I do. I think your husband spoilt you. He gave you illusions . . . you feel too free. We are not free.'

*

I drew my nails down my palm, down then back up the other way, deep and hard. I thought about what Noura had told me. I didn't think for very long. I had no choice – I couldn't afford another visit from him. I wrote him a letter. I wonder if I'll ever get a chance to take back all that I wrote in that letter; it was hideous from beginning to end. Human beings shouldn't say such things to each other. I put the letter into an unsealed envelope and found a local boy who knew where the scrawny soldier lived. Doubtless Bilal read the letter before the soldier did, because by evening everyone but my daughter knew what I had done. My daughter waited for the soldier until it was fully dark, and I waited with her, pretending that I was still expecting our friend. There was a song she wanted to sing to him. I asked her to sing it to me instead, but she said I wouldn't appreciate it. When we went inside at last, my daughter asked me if the soldier could have gone home without telling us. He probably hated goodbyes.

'He said he would come . . . I hope he's all right . . .' my daughter fretted.

'He's gone home to build minarets.'

'With matchsticks, probably.'

And we were both very sad.

*

My daughter didn't smile for six days. On the seventh she said she couldn't go to school.

'You have to go to school,' I told her. 'How else will you get your friends back again?'

'What if I can't,' she wailed. 'What if I can't get them back again?'

'Do you really think you won't get them back again?'

'Oh, you don't even care that our friend is gone. Mothers have no feelings and are enemies of progress.'

(I really wonder who my daughter has been talking to lately. Someone with a sense of humour very like her father's . . .)

I tickled the sole of her foot until she shouted.

'Let this enemy of progress tell you something,' I said. 'I'm never sad when a friend goes far away, because whichever city or country that friend goes to, they turn the place friendly. They turn a suspicious-looking name on the map into a place where a welcome can be found. Maybe the friend will talk about you sometimes, to other friends that live around him, and then that's almost as good as being there yourself. You're in several places at once! In fact, my daughter, I would even go so far as to say that the further away your friends are, and the more spread out they are, the better your chances of going safely through the world . . .'

'Ugh,' my daughter said.

I've grown a beard or two in my time. Long, full, Moses-in-the-wilderness – that type of beard. Mainly as a way to relax, hiding my face so I can take it easy behind my beard. A while ago I went to London, to see a play they'd cooked up out of one of my favorite novels – I couldn't wait the eight months it would take to cross the Atlantic. And in the weeks leading up to the visit I must have just quietly left shaving out of my mornings, so quietly I didn't notice I was doing it, because when I got to London the beard was so bushy it distracted me from the sights. Big Ben and my beard. Buckingham Palace and my beard. The Tower of London and my beard. Caw caw, said the ravens. (Were they making reference to the beard?) I had a great time. No one bothered me that entire trip. Funny to do something and then realise the reason for it afterwards – I'd grown the beard so that no one would bother me. Time to start another beard. If only I could remember how long it took for the last one to grow.

I want to be on my own for a spell. But there's nowhere I can be on my own. I went to the library in town, thinking, it's such a nice Saturday, so fine out, no one will be there – but it was full of bespectacled girls 'studying'. The bluestockings of today. Dressed up just to go to the library, making eyes at a fellow across a room, bold as anything. I like to look, but I don't like it when they look back. All you're doing is taking

an appreciative moment, maybe two or three, if she's a serious matter, and she's staring back and thinking, *I've caught
his eye. Good. Now what I'd really like to do is keep it until
his dying day.* It's some kind of God-awful whim she has.
This isn't just talk; I know this type of girl, the type who
looks back. I know her all too well. She's the type who's
really trying to start something. Rousing at the beginning,
the heated command, until you realise she can't get enough
attention, and she needs all of yours, every last scrap of it.
And then come the ugly scenes. And I don't mean con-
frontations, but hissed exchanges, half-hours of being kept
waiting for her in some lobby or other for no good reason,
parties where she bestows one freezing cold glance upon you
and then spends the rest of the evening holed up in some
cosy corner with someone else; that kind of scene fixes the
equivalent of a jeweller's loupe to your eye. You examine
your diamond, and find her edges blurred with tawdry
cracks; stay involved for a few more months and you'll find
she worsens over time. Rapidly, too. All these tactical
attempts at mind control; I'm not kidding. It sounds like an
exaggeration until someone tries it on you. It's hard to find a
woman without tactics. That'll be why I made one up. Then
she started a game, had me pursue her through Africa. She
cast me as a desperate spinster with an antique sword.
She cast me as a fellow who ditched his woman out in some
foreign country because he couldn't handle her. Mary Foxe
has really been taking a few liberties. So I'll correct my
statement. It's hard to even imagine a woman without tactics.

When the third pretty bluestocking made eyes at me, I
left. Libraries always make me feel covered in ink, anyway.
Ink on my clothes, ink in my eyes. Terrible. All the body

heat in there is bound to make the pages mushy. My parents
met in a library. My mother was a junior librarian, and my
father's books were always overdue. He asked my mother's
best friend what her favorite books were, and he took them
out, one by one – *La Dame aux Camélias. Thérèse Raquin.*
Madame Bovary. Tess of the D'Urbervilles. Anna Karenina.
He couldn't make head or tail of them – 'Hasty women,' he
told me, shaking his head, 'Hasty women.' But he told my
mother how much he enjoyed them, and when he got around
to asking whether she objected to his calling on her at her
family home some Sunday afternoon to continue their dis-
cussion, she didn't say no.

I thought briefly about going to see my mother, in her tiny
apartment two hours' drive away, but I know she doesn't
want to see me, and I know it's not because of anything I've
done or failed to do. She doesn't want to see anyone. She's
happy like that, I think. Always relieved at the end of a visit.
I think she's too old to want to talk any more; she doesn't
mind listening, but she's got a radio set for that. She's still in
good health, she's still got her wits about her. She had a lot
more to say for herself before my father passed away, but
then he was a fine man, great company – really great company, actually; let you have your opinions and talked about
his own in a way that never put your nose out of joint. And
now he's gone she'd rather not talk to anyone else. Solitary
people, these booklovers. I think it's swell that there are
people you don't have to worry about when you don't see
them for a long time, you don't have to wonder what they do,
how they're getting along with themselves. You just know
that they're all right, and probably doing something they
like. Last time I saw my mother she kept nodding and

saying: 'Everything's just fine, dear. Everything's just fine.' This was before I'd even made an opening remark – she was in such a hurry to get her part of the conversation out of the way. If I went to see my mother, what would I tell her, anyway?

I drove around instead, just drove around, trying to decide where to stop. As I drove I tried to think of a word, a single word to sum up the way Daphne's been behaving lately. Inscrutable. The woman has become inscrutable.

Take yesterday morning. Daphne was right outside my study, watering the flowers in the window box, warbling to herself – a pretty little racket, and I was somehow enjoying it and getting a little work done at the same time. Then suddenly, she stopped, and said: 'Well, St John . . . you know what Ralph Waldo Emerson says . . .'

I waited quietly, held my pen still to show I was paying attention, braced myself for some cloying scrap of verse she'd just remembered from her high-school yearbook. But she didn't finish her sentence. Nor did she continue with the singing. So I said: 'Go on, D, I'm all ears.'

She made a little moue with her mouth, blowing a couple of stray curls out of her line of vision so that I felt the full force of her stare. 'What do you mean, go on? I don't know what Emerson says.'

'Oh, you don't?' I asked, and I laughed. She didn't laugh with me.

'*You* know what Emerson says, St John. That's why I said, "You know what Emerson says." '

Her sleeves were rolled up and her voice kept going from flat to sharp. I got the distinct impression that she was steaming mad at me for failing to supply her with an Emerson quotation.

'Can I ask – would you mind telling me – where you got this idea that I know what Emerson says? Have I ever mentioned in passing that I know what Emerson says?'

She yawned at me. 'Come on, St John. Don't be shy. Tell me something Emerson said.'

I dropped my smile.

'Did someone tell you that Emerson's a great friend of mine? Did the ghost of Ralph Waldo Emerson call one day when I was out and leave a message for me – *Well now, Fox, my boy – you know what I always say*?'

'I really think you ought to know what Emerson says, that's all,' she returned, without batting an eyelash.

I stood up and went to the window. When I got close to her she looked down at her watering can. 'Mrs Fox,' I said. 'You're a horror today.'

To which she replied: 'Why don't you write a book about it?'

Why don't you write a book about it?

Why don't you—

Speechless, I gestured for her to stand away from the window, then I closed it. We looked at each other through the glass – she had this cool, triumphant smile on. She really felt she'd said something extraordinarily cutting. God knows what I looked like. Then she moved on to the next window box. What the hell am I supposed to make of a conversation like that?

Then there was the picnic D and I went to last weekend – neither of us wanted to go, but my publisher was hosting, and it seemed necessary to show my face. Some of the women had brought their little kids along to run around the meadow, singing their nonsensical songs and making daisy chains. There was this one girl with a pair of angel wings on – she actually had quite a lot going for her. She could whistle around two fingers, and she showed some of the little boys how to skim stones off the stream, and she didn't scream when water splashed her. I wouldn't mind having a kid if she turned out to be like that. Daphne was watching her too, and scowling. At one point the girl with the angel wings bumped into Daphne and said sorry real sweetly. Daphne just ignored her, looked straight ahead, tight-lipped. I told the child there was no harm done, but if I could have gotten a million miles away real fast, I would have. Then my publisher's wife, a new mother, offered to let Daphne hold her little boy, and Daphne looked at me with these eyes of mute suffering as if asking: *Do I have to? Do I really, really have to?*

I don't know what's got into her. Well, I guess I do, but it doesn't justify—

On the other hand, it was presumptuous of Ellen Balfour to think that every woman in the world wants to hold a three-month-old baby just as soon as she catches sight of one. Daphne's right, it was presumptuous. Daphne held the kid, her arms really stiff, as if he could roll out of her arms and bounce off the grass and she wouldn't care. I chucked the boy under the chin a couple of times, and said he was a little prince, and he cried his head off. Then Daphne gave him back to his mother. Mrs Balfour seemed to think Daphne was just overcome with delight and kept saying: 'Oh, bless you, bless you. You'll get one of your own soon, Daphne – may I call you Daphne?' English manners.

Daphne whispered to me: 'That's the ugliest child I ever saw.'

'Bad stock,' I whispered back, less because I actually thought so and more because I've been thinking that Daphne and I should be allies, I want us to be allies even when she's misbehaving. I got a laugh out of her, anyway. Nothing's even happened to us yet – we haven't had a broke spell yet, or watched each other lose people, lose our looks, face down sickness. But D seems to be holding out on me, refusing to go all the way into this thing unless there's a child too. Once I think my way past a lot of stuff that hasn't got anything to do with anything, the thought of being called 'Dad' doesn't give me the jumps – well, not as severely as it used to. I didn't used to think about these things. I must be getting older. Daphne could be onto something, but I won't be hustled into it.

The other day I went on an urgent mission to retrieve my wallet from a jacket pocket before D sent our stuff out to be cleaned. D had left a book on top of the laundry basket: *Happy Husband*, that was the title. And underneath, in smaller letters: *Make him happy, keep him happy!* An advice manual. I took it away, read a few pages, chased them down with a couple of despairing drinks. There are real books all around the house, everywhere. She could pick one up and in mere seconds she could be involved in something that makes her laugh and feel nervous and hot and cold and forgive the world its absurdity – Pushkin, maybe, or Céline. Instead she's spending her time reading up on what to do about me. It got me down. The book itself was useless, too – all the advice it offered about the timing of meals and affecting a cheerful disposition and trying to take an interest in the husband's doings even when they're fearfully boring and never saying 'I told you so', these aren't the reasons a person looks with favor upon another person, these aren't the reasons someone stays in love. I put the book back before she knew I'd seen it. If I said anything about it she'd tell me I was taking it too seriously, that she was just looking at it for amusement.

As for Mary, I'd been trying to get her to show up, but she wouldn't. I don't know what that means. Am I drying up? My book about the killer accountant is going as well it can be considering that I hardly know what I'm writing; I'm just jogging along behind the plot like a carthorse, ready to drop it as soon as Mary shows up and it's time to get out of here. But no sign of Mary. She could be staying away deliberately (if so, I didn't know she could do that) or my brainpower's getting weak. Maybe once I'm alone in my beard things will be the way they used to be with her – friendly, I mean. I wrote her name in the steam on my bathroom mirror, as a kind of invocation, and after a couple of slow minutes I added a middle name for her. A kind of incentive, a step towards reality, bait. I wrote Jane. A good, plain, sensible name. Mary Jane Foxe, I wrote. Before my eyes the letters changed; the name grew longer. 'Aurelia'. Mary Aurelia Foxe. This is what it's come to.

I pulled up outside a bar I'd been to a couple of times. I knew I could be kind of alone there, especially during the day, when the social drinkers are waiting for the clock to strike a respectable hour before they start. There were a few guys inside, spaced well apart, one of them sitting at a corner table. He was groaning into his hat, but no one else in there even looked at him. I took another corner table, set down my scotch, lit my pipe, opened my copy of *Metamorphoses* and pretended to read. The other guys started giving me the eye then, including the one who was wailing into his hat. 'Gentlemen,' I said, from behind the cover of my book, 'it's a free country.' That had no effect, so I told the bartender to get them drinks, on me – there were only five of them in total. They left me in peace once they got their drinks.

It was quiet until a bunch of youngsters swept in and started shouting their orders all over the place. I raised my eyes from the line I'd been staring at for the past fifteen minutes or so and watched them. They used long words and called each other by nicknames that alluded to the classical world. Castor was present, and Pollux, and Patroclus and Achilles. College men, in town for the weekend. Three of them had a muttered dispute amongst themselves before heading over to where I sat. They drew out chairs, turned them around and sat on them. Usually it annoys me when people do that, but I wanted to know what they had to say. They asked me if I was S.J. Fox and I said, Yup. They named a few of my books and said they liked them. I said, Thanks. They called their friends over and announced my name. Looking round at the faces I could tell that some of them had no idea who I was, but they did an impressive job of pretending that wasn't the case. There's something to be said for good breeding. You get hypocrites out of it, but you get the odd respectful youngster, too. They called me sir, and boss, and wouldn't hear of me buying my own drinks. I put my book aside and answered their questions as well as I could. These boys all had names like Toby and Jed – their real names, that is. They didn't try to get me to call them by their Greek names. They reminded me of Daphne's set, kids who had never been poor and never would be, spouting cheerfully lopsided theories. Men of the world who didn't live in the world – not properly. Me, I'm a farmer's son. These boys reckoned the Europeans were about to get into a scrap over Czechoslovakia, and that there'd be war again, and we'd be in it again. They wanted to know what I thought about that. I reminded them that Germany had had its balls cut off – land taken, no army to speak of, no money – there wasn't going to be any war. I told them they weren't going to have to do what I did, that if they were looking for glory they'd better find another way. 'I hope you're right, Mr Fox,' Jed said, earnestly – or was it Toby? Blue sweatshirts and ears that stuck out. 'I hope you're right, but I don't think you are. Things are really boiling over – the Germans are saying all kinds of things, and France and England are running around trying to get promises—'

'Didn't you hear? We aren't promising anything. Roosevelt said we're staying neutral. What's Czechoslovakia got to do with us?'

Toby – or Jed – stared at me. 'What's Czechoslovakia got to do with us? Well, what's independence got to do with us? Liberty? The pursuit of happiness?'

All I could think of were a couple of lines someone else had recited to me a long time ago, in France. *To goodness and wisdom we only make promises; pain we obey.* That's Proust, y'know, the guy had told me. (Daphne should have said to me: 'You know what Proust says . . .' If she had, that little exchange of ours wouldn't have happened, or would have happened differently, maybe, would have ended without me having to shut the window in her face.) The boys went quiet, which means I'd said the lines aloud. They were all

squinting at me, as if I was some figure in a fading photograph and each of them was vying to be the first to identify
me. A pox on the young. I left without saying goodbye, just
walked out.

I heard voices as I headed from my driveway to the front
porch. Daphne and a man. She was laughing. She sounded
drunk. It was only three o'clock. I slowed my steps with a
corner still to turn; hedges, luckily, so they couldn't see me.
I heard the porch swing creak – the two of them were sitting
on it. It was Jonas Pizarsky she was with, and they were talking about fairy tales, of all things. D had a pair of scissors,
and a vaseful of water, and was arranging some flowers –
whether she'd bought them, or he'd given them to her, I
was sure the flower arranging was unnecessary – she always
did it, stem by stem, even when presented with a bunch of
flowers that already looked all right.

'Why have husbands got to keep themselves all locked
up, that's what I want to know,' Daphne complained.

'Not all of them do,' Jonas told her. He wasn't drunk at
all. I didn't like that – those two sat together, his voice measured and sober, and her saying just anything that occurred to
her. He was going to remember the entire conversation and
she would remember a quarter of it at the very most. Unfortunate.

'Oh, it's only the cold ones that do it, isn't it?'

'I don't know about cold, Daphne . . .'

'No, you don't know about cold. Because you're not cold,
are you, J.P.?'

He didn't answer. Too busy trying to think of some phrase
that would make her see him as ardent, I'll bet.

'You're not Bluebeard? Or Reynardine?' I caught flashes

of Daphne through the brambles; she was examining her arrangement of the flowers from a number of angles. She didn't ask his advice, and I was glad she didn't. She always asked my advice – not that I ever give a response she can make use of.

'Nor Fitcher, no.'

'Fitcher?'

Just what I was wondering. Pizarsky seemed to know his stuff, though. He'd told me himself that he'd been studying for a doctorate in anthropology until his father had demanded he help steer the family's jewellery business. A diamond mine in Africa and a gold mine in Nevada. Opal fields in Australia, and more. I don't like to think about how rich Pizarsky is. He doesn't seem to like thinking about it either. It's awkward that he has so much. What's left for him to want?

He told my wife a bizarre story. It started out almost too screwed up to even be a fairy tale. It was all about a magician called Fitcher who went around with a basket, begging for food. And any woman who pitied him and gave him food was compelled to jump into his basket and go home with him and be his wife.

'Yes,' Daphne said, laying down her scissors. 'I felt so sorry for him at first . . . all I wanted to do was make him happy . . .'

'Yes, well, Fitcher did this with three sisters in a row. He set each of them the don't-look-in-the-locked-room test – the first two sisters failed, of course. The only way for Fitcher's final wife, the third sister, to survive her danger was by becoming insane. If you think about it, it was inevitable. That woman went through a lot. She found her sisters all chopped up and sunk in blood, and she collected the parts and she joined them up. Only a very, very young child would think of a solution like that, and only an insane person would actually try it. It worked, though; they came back to life and she sent them home. On a clear afternoon in an empty house she covered herself in honey and rolled around in a barrel's worth of feathers, and a skeleton sat by in a chair the whole time; it was meant to take her place, and she didn't hesitate or falter because she'd gone nuts. She was scared right out of her mind. She had to be – to rescue herself. So she stopped working to make sense of things – we don't always realise it, but it's hard work we do almost every waking moment, building our thoughts and memories and actions around time, things that happened yesterday, and things that are happening right now, and what's coming tomorrow, layering all of that simultaneously and holding it in balance. She cut it out and just kept moving. She was nobody, she was nowhere, doing nothing, but doing it as hard and fast as she could. And once she was fully covered with honey and feathers she walked out into broad daylight and used the only words she hadn't forgotten, *I'm a bird, I'm Fitcher's bird.* If she'd ever been anyone other than Fitcher's bird, she didn't know a thing about it. What did she look like, all sticky with quills? What did her eyes say? Did she even understand the words she was saying? Never mind; her mouth said: *I'm a bird, I'm Fitcher's bird.* And nobody who heard her could doubt her. She met the bad magician; she met Fitcher himself, on her way home. *I'm a bird,* she told him. He didn't recognise her. I mean, she was gone. He looked into her eyes and there was no woman there. And he never caught her again.'

Daphne must have had a look on her face that made him stop talking. Neither of them said anything for quite a while.

'She went insane because of him,' Daphne said. 'I think that's happening to me.'

The swing creaked again. I looked out from behind the hedge; I had to see what they were doing. If they saw me, they saw me. But if I saw that he had his arms around her, or even just his hand on her arm, I was going to bust his head open. The conversation itself didn't matter. She was drunk. And he – I knew what he was doing with apparent idleness; using his halting, mysterious European accent to feed her a story that he knew she'd like because she could place herself in it, be the victim, be the heroine. I withdrew before either of them saw me.

'You don't have to go insane,' Pizarsky told Daphne. It doesn't have to go like that.'

'What shall I do, then? What shall I do?' She didn't sound as if she was especially interested in the answer to her question.

Her arms were bare and freckled, her eyes were closed, her head was resting against the back of the swing. Mine. I wanted to lift her up into my arms and carry her around with me, our bodies together, my neck her neck, her hands my hands. He wasn't touching her, he wasn't even sitting close to her, and I could only see the back of his head. But he was very still, hardly seemed to be breathing, and he was looking at her. That was bad.

'Daphne – what's going on?' he asked, eventually. 'What's wrong?'

'I wish I could tell you,' she said.

'You can. You can tell me anything.' He waited, but she

didn't say anything. 'Maybe some other time. I think you should know, though, that there are other ways – apart from going crazy. Do you know the story of Mr Fox?'

'No.' Her voice was languid, reluctant. 'What happens in that one?'

'The usual – wooing, seduction, then – the discovery of a chopped-up predecessor. But the heroine, Lady Mary—'

'Lady Mary?' Daphne asks. I didn't need to look to know that she'd sat up.

Mary Foxe put a soft hand on my shoulder. 'Come away, Mr Fox,' she whispered. I shrugged her off. She was wearing what Daphne called her signature scent. I disapproved – and not just because the scent costs enough per ounce for me to momentarily consider asking the shopgirl to leave the price tag on so Daphne can realise how spoilt she is. Mary was Mary – she's been with me a long time, maybe even before I'd gone to France. She's handled a sickle at haymaking time, stacked and tromped the hay, helped me feed it to the cows and horses. She's stood dressed top to toe in mud, and she's braced herself against the barn beams when she's been too tired to stand. Mary Foxe shouldn't have anything to do with bottled fragrances.

'That farm stuff was before my time,' Mary said. 'Come away with me, Mr Fox.' There was a hard smile on her face. 'You said that Mrs Fox couldn't stop us, remember?'

Suddenly I was getting to be a little tired of Mary Foxe.

'Drop it,' I said to her. 'Just be quiet. In fact – you can't speak. You've just lost your voice, Mary. You're real hoarse today.' And I closed her voice up in my hand.

Mary's lips shaped words, a fast and furious stream of

them, but none of them sounded. She clasped her throat, horrified. She'd been forgetting who was boss.

Undo this, she mimed, furiously.

In time, I mimed back.

But the damage was done. I'd addressed her too loudly; Daphne and Pizarsky had heard me, and they'd stopped talking. I couldn't stay where I was a second longer. I strode round the corner and stepped up onto the porch, car key dangling from my hand. 'Hi there, D. Afternoon, Pizarsky. Thanks for bringing her home. Had a nice time at—?'

'The Wainwrights',' they supplied, quickly. Oh, sure. The Wainwrights'.

Daphne got up and went into the house without kissing Pizarsky goodbye. It bugged me that she didn't kiss him goodbye, as if now even a simple kiss on the cheek could mean something between them. Pizarsky's leave-taking was good, quiet, neither hurried nor laboured – good in that I didn't really even have to say anything to him, or look his way. I thought that if our eyes met I'd have to take a swing at him.

Daphne went upstairs, but not into our room. She went into one of the spare bedrooms and put her flowers on the bedside table. I followed her in; the predominant smell was mothballs. We haven't had an overnight guest for a long time.

'Hi,' I said.

'Hi,' Daphne said. She fluffed the pillows, pushed all the blankets onto the floor and jumped onto the bed.

'Like the flowers?' She flung out an arm in their direction.

'They're okay,' I said.

'First prize for this afternoon's croquet. Pizarsky won

them, but he doesn't care about flowers, so he let me have them.'

'Good of him.'

'I'm hot,' she said. 'Could you bring me some ice?'

'Just ice?'

'Just ice . . .'

'What are you going to do with it?'

'Look at it. Feel cool. God, St John. Does it matter what I do with the ice?'

'I'll get it in a second. What's going on? Why are you taking a nap in here? Don't you like your bed any more?'

'Oh – don't let's fight,' she said. My right hand was still closed up tight, to keep Mary quiet, and Daphne looked at that hand for a couple of seconds, then at my face. I guess she thought I was making a fist at her.

I wanted to ask her if she meant to spend the night here as well, but I didn't want her to say yes. It could be that she was in some kind of mood and just wanted a nap and my question might force her to adopt a stance. She does that, I've noticed; she lashes out when she thinks she's been given a cue.

'Is it okay if I host a luncheon for some under-privileged inner-city girls next Wednesday? Not too many; five or so.'

'Fine by me. Got your under-privileged inner-city girl bait? Want me to drive you down to the city so you can catch them?'

'Be serious. I want to join Bea Wainwright's Culture Club, and the luncheon is kind of an audition for me.'

'That's fine. Just don't let them into my study. I mean it – that's off-limits.'

'Of course.'

She stood up before I could go and get that ice she'd asked for. 'I'll get it myself, okay?' She went up on her tiptoes and kissed my forehead. Quite sadly, I thought.

On my study desk I found a brand-new notebook open on my desk, neatly placed in the centre. There was a list written on the first page. I looked at the list for a minute or two. Points in favor of 'D' and 'M'. It was almost my handwriting, so close that for a second it seemed to me that I'd made the list and forgotten about it. But I hadn't written it. These weren't even thoughts I recognised.

So Mary was writing things down now.

I looked up and she was laughing. Soundlessly, of course. She was even more appealing as a mute. Like an image my eye was chasing through one of those flick books – she wasn't moving, I was. I beckoned her.

'You wrote this,' I said. Mary came closer, gesturing helplessly towards her mouth.

'Just nod or shake your head,' I said. 'You wrote this, didn't you?'

She folded her arms.

'Did Daphne see this?'

No visible response. I closed the notebook and laid my fist on top of it. It was starting to ache, vaguely, but with a throbbing that promised to get stronger.

'This is childish, Mary. Don't do anything like this again.'

She curtseyed wickedly, and left me.

I tore the list out of the notebook and ripped it to shreds – I needed both hands for that. Even if Daphne had found the list and taken any notice of it, she must know that I couldn't write a thing like this in earnest and leave it somewhere she'd find it. But Daphne knew something, or thought she knew something. That tiny kiss on my forehead – why had she given me that? It stayed with me unbearably, like ashes at the start of Lent, the slap on the hand I got whenever I went to brush them away as a kid.

I must have been twenty-five years old when I realised Christ never came back from the dead. Some people would say it wasn't a big deal, it was just that I wised up. But I'm talking about something I'd always believed until then. I damn near knocked myself flat with these new thoughts. I mean, the resurrection could be true – it could be, I wasn't there so I can't say for sure. But it probably isn't true. So that means Christ was killed and that was the end for him. He'd gotten mixed up with some pretty intense people in his lifetime, though, and those people thought he was too important to let go. And they made themselves important with this idea that their friend couldn't be killed, told everyone all about it. And hundreds died because they believed Christ couldn't be killed, and thousands more suffered, I mean, the martyrs, think of all the martyrs, and – I was walking down a street in Salzburg, eating an apple when these thoughts came to me, and I just kept right on chewing and swallowing, chewing and swallowing, since it was something to do.

Love. I'm not capable of it, can't even approach it from the side, let alone head on. Nor am I alone in this – everyone is like this, the liars. Singing songs and painting pictures and telling each other stories about love and its mysteries and its marvellous properties, myths to keep morale up, maybe one day it'll materialise. But I can say it ten times a day, a hundred times, 'I love you,' to anyone and anything, to a woman, to a pair of pruning shears. I've said it without meaning it at all, taken love's name in vain and gone dismally unpunished. Love will never be real, or if it is, it has no power. No power. There's only covetousness, and if what we covet can't be won with gentle words – and often it can't – then there is force. Those boys at the bar downtown, coming round talking idly about more ideas to die for. Something terrible's coming, and everyone in the world is working to bring it on. They won't rest until they've brought it on. Mary, come back – distract me. No, stay away, you're the problem.

31 rules for lovers (circa 1186)[1]

From *the art of courtly love* by andreas cappelanus

1. *Marriage is no real excuse for not loving.*
2. He who is not jealous cannot love.
3. No one can be bound by a double love.
4. It is well known that love is always increasing or decreasing.
5. That which a lover takes against the will of his beloved has no relish.
6. Boys do not love until they arrive at the age of maturity.
7. When one lover dies, a widowhood of two years is required of the survivor.
8. *No one should be deprived of love without the very best of reasons.*
9. No one can love unless he is impelled by the persuasion of love.
10. Love is always a stranger in the home of avarice.
11. It is not proper to love any woman whom one would be ashamed to seek to marry.
12. A true lover does not desire to embrace in love anyone except his beloved.

[1] Rules of particular interest to Daphne Fox, Mary Foxe, and St John Fox have been highlighted by those persons in the order mentioned.

13. When made public love rarely endures.
14. The easy attainment of love makes it of little value; difficulty of attainment makes it prized.
15. Every lover regularly turns pale in the presence of his beloved.
16. When a lover suddenly catches sight of his beloved his heart palpitates.
17. A new love puts to flight an old one.
18. Good character alone makes any man worthy of love.
19. If love diminishes, it quickly fails and rarely revives.
20. *A man in love is always apprehensive.*
21. Real jealousy always increases the feeling of love.
22. Jealousy, and therefore love, are increased when one suspects his beloved.
23. He whom the thought of love vexes eats and sleeps very little.
24. Every act of a lover ends in the thought of his beloved.
25. A true lover considers nothing good except what he thinks will please his beloved.
26. Love can deny nothing to love.
27. A lover can never have enough of the solaces of his beloved.
28. A slight presumption causes a lover to suspect his beloved.
29. A man who is vexed by too much passion usually does not love.
30. A true lover is constantly and without intermission possessed by the thought of his beloved.

31. *Nothing forbids one woman being loved by two men or one man by two women.*
That nails it – I like this Cappelanus fellow! M.F.
Ha ha ha . . . indeed – S.J.F.
HMMMMM – D.F.

I stayed in bed almost all day Monday. To see if St John would notice, and if he did notice, to see what he would do about it. But he didn't notice, didn't even come up to ask me about dinner. Too busy with his book, I guess. It can't be easy killing people off the way he does, especially since each death has got to be meaningful. I heard him on the radio, once, before I even met him – a fan of his called in, ever so earnest, asking him why some character or other had died in such a meaningless way. St John's answer: 'I was going to say that the meaninglessness of her death has a meaning in itself, but the truth is, I missed that one. So thanks. I'm going to work harder.'

While he worked, he played a symphony I liked – he played it very loudly, but it was good that way, rising through the floorboards and welling up around me. I was lying on music, my arms and legs flopping down over a pillar of the stuff, my back the only straight line in me. If only my old dance teacher could have seen me; she'd have had a fit. I was always the girl who was 'just so'. It was the easiest thing in the world back then – if I felt as if taking too deep a breath would make me fall flat on my face that meant I was 'just so'.

There was housework to do, things to dust and scrub and polish and move around and fret over, work that has never been visible to anyone else, and I took great pleasure in not doing any of it. I spent a few hours looking at a book of watercolors that just happened to be lying around, but they began to make me feel weepy. They were so faded, the land-scapes, and they reminded me of some I'd started and put up in the glasshouse, half-finished, because painting them made me yawn so much, and I didn't suppose that anyone who came out there for a cocktail on a summer evening would care enough to ask if they were supposed to look like that. They've been there two summers and no one's asked yet.

When it got dark, Mary Foxe came and sat by me with a candle. I'd gone so dead in my senses and my brain that I'd been expecting her, and it was actually nice to have a change. She closed the door, so we'd have some privacy. I didn't protest. 'He won't be coming up,' Mary Foxe said. 'He's probably going to go to sleep in there tonight.'

'Again. I know.'

She was naked, and not a bit self-conscious about it. She didn't need to be. What I saw by candlelight made me sure that this was really going to happen – St John Fox had dreamed himself up a nice little companion who wasn't going to get old, and he was going to drop me and live with her. She looked younger than me, a lot younger than him—

'For God's sake, put some clothes on, will you,' I told her.

'I don't know where they've gone. I think I've annoyed him and he's trying to punish me. I'm sorry if I'm making you feel uncomfortable. Give me any old thing to wear and I'll put it on,' she said, in a very simple way. No guile, no false concern, just honesty. I couldn't really be mad at her when she spoke to me like that.

I got out of bed. 'Come on.' We went to my dressing room

and I gave her a lilac shirtwaist to put on. I didn't tell her, but it was my favorite thing to wear. I'd worn it in Buenos Aires, on the first day of our honeymoon. There it was all over again, the first day, the first day, the first day, his hand in mine, all that woven into a dress. And there was no denying that Mary Foxe looked as cute as a button in my dress; its shade brought out interesting hues in her hair, or vice versa. I was glad we were the same dress size. It was something of a consolation to know that I'm nowhere near as fat as I sometimes think I am.

Mary Foxe sat in the chair at my dressing table and I stood beside the chair and she stared at me and I stared at her. It was just interesting to see what St John wanted in a woman. Her hair hung over her shoulder in a wispy plait, clumsily done. Someone should show her how to plait her hair. I wondered what would become of me. I didn't see him turning me out, not exactly – but I might be too proud to stay. He'd make me some sort of allowance, I suppose. I couldn't go back to my parents, though. Pops would forbid Maman from giving me a piece of her mind, and she wouldn't – not while he was there. But she'd give me that resigned look – *Messed up again, Daphne? Just what I expected.* The look I got when I stopped going to college, only ten times worse. I should fight this, make some kind of threat. Greta would fight like a hellcat. Twice now, some girl has tried to get Pizarsky to fall in love with her, and each time Greta's seen the girl off. She's not above fighting for her man. How do you threaten someone like Mary Foxe, though?

'I've never seen you this close up,' Mary Foxe said. 'I like looking at your face; it's a good face.'

I couldn't help laughing at her formality. I wanted to say

I thought the same about her, but I couldn't make myself do it. Greta would have risen up in my mind like a ghoul, sneering. *That's right, pay her compliments while she replaces you.* I was always weak in the head – that must be it. I can't seem to care any more about what I'm supposed to do. This is not a typical scenario.

'What are you thinking about, Mrs Fox?' Mary Foxe asked. I laughed again.

'You're thinking of something funny?'

'He said you were British.'

'Mrs Fox,' she said. 'I think I'm more like you than not.'

'How can you know that?' Anger began to kick in. 'How can you know that?'

Mary Foxe looked up at me with big, thoughtful eyes. 'I'm glad there isn't a stapler around.'

Abruptly, I asked her if she knew whether I was pregnant. I'd cancelled my appointment with the doctor. It'd be a bad scene if I was pregnant and a bad scene if I wasn't.

'You don't look pregnant,' Mary Foxe said.

'Do you mean you don't know? If you don't, just say so.'

'I don't know. Of course I don't know. How could I know that? I'm not a doctor.'

'I thought you were . . . magical or something. Like a spirit.'

She opened her eyes very wide, wondering at me. 'No, I don't think I am.'

'Okay. Not magical and not a doctor. Got it.'

She was really too amusing. Now that I'd asked if she was magical, I could see her wondering whether she might be magical, after all. What was this, me finding myself wanting to look out for this girl, thing, whatever she was?

'What do you want, Mary Foxe? My husband?'

'I believe in him,' she said, slowly. I wondered if she'd ever told him that, and if so, what he had to say about it. Someone you made up turns around and tells you they believe in you – what response could you possibly make? The scenario is just plain weird. And really kind of impertinent on her part, too. If it happened to me I think I'd be speechless for the rest of my life.

'I love him,' she added. That simple tone again; she thought this was something that was all right to say to me.

'That's nice. So do I.' We sized each other up again.

'Mrs Fox.' Mary put a hand on my arm, and we jumped away from each other in a hurry. The static, the awful static of her touch, it was exactly the way I imagined I'd feel if I ever brushed against an electric fence. My knees knocked together in a frenzy.

'That caused an unpleasant sensation and I won't do it again,' said the little comedian across the room.

'Good. Well, you were about to say something. Go on.'

'I wondered if you had eaten today.'

'No, I haven't. What's it to you?'

'I wondered – I wondered if we could go out to dinner together. Someplace fancy. And if I could wear a nice hat.'

She wondered if we could go someplace fancy for dinner and whether she might wear a nice hat. One of mine, I suppose, since there weren't any other hats to hand. For all her shapeliness, this wasn't a woman I was dealing with. This wasn't the M I'd pictured when I'd looked over that list of things in her favor. She seemed a girl barely in her teens, mentally speaking. What if I worked on her a little, taught her a difficult attitude and sent her back to her master with it?

'I know a place,' I said. 'Let me just get dressed.'

She turned her back while I dressed. Then we tried all my hats on and I got caught up in the excitement of taking someone new – a brand-new person, almost – out to do something new. She got the giggles and so did I, so loudly that I thought St John was going to hear from all the way downstairs and come up to see what was going on. He didn't. She decided on a hat. Then changed her mind. And changed her mind and changed her mind. Very indecisive about hats, that Mary Foxe. Maybe she'd tire of St John and slope off somewhere. Maybe she'd vanish the moment I set foot in the restaurant and asked for a table for two. How foolish I'd look. But I was prepared to risk it. I wanted to see a smile on her face – some people make you want to see them smiling. And I like a project. I do like to have a project.

After about twenty minutes of hat changing, I'd insisted she stick with the black cloche hat she had on. She pinned on a brooch of mine and moved this way and that so it glinted at her in the mirror, eager magpie of a girl. We rang for a taxi, and I let her give our address – she recited it carefully, and looked so excited. She waited out on the porch, hopping, though she said she'd try to be patient, and I knocked at the door of St John's study.

'Daphne?' he called out. But not at first. He had begun to say 'Mary' and stopped himself. I went in, stayed near the door. He dropped his pen and stood up, strangely gallant. What for? It was only me.

'You're really something, you know that?' I told him. That wasn't what I'd meant to say, it just came out. It was the audacity of what he was doing, and the fact that I couldn't fathom how the hell he was doing it.

'Oh yes? Well, so are you,' he said, and looked admiring, turning his reply into a comment on the way I looked tonight. Our exchanges always seem to turn into whatever he wants them to. I don't think any woman can get the better of him. Keep things brief, Daphne, keep things brief, and you'll get out with your head still on your shoulders. This man is a deadly foe.

'I just wanted to say I'm going out to dinner at the Chop House.'

'Great. We haven't been there in a while, have we? Let me just finish my sentence, and—'

'Oh, no, you take as long as you need. I'm going with Greta.'

'Oh, then don't worry about *my* dinner, I don't need feeding at all. I get by on liquor and flattering notices in the newspapers,' he said, evenly. A dark man, my St John, tall and broad-shouldered and full of force he doesn't exert. I'm only just starting to see him clearly.

'Stop it. She asked me centuries ago.'

He inclined his head, to show that he had heard. He mumbled something. Against my better judgement, I asked him what he'd said.

'Just Greta?'

'What do you mean, "just Greta"?'

St John sat down again, scanning the page he'd just been working on. As he read he began to look baffled, as if someone else had snuck in and scrambled his sentences while he'd been talking to me. 'Wondered if she'd make Pizarsky tag along, that's all.' He attacked his page with short, exasperated scratches of his pen; crossing out. He didn't seem to like a single word he saw.

'Oh, J.P. – such a funny little man, isn't he?' I said. 'So short and squat. And I hardly know what he's talking about half the time.' St John didn't stop crossing things out, but his lips twitched; I think he was happy I'd said that. But I felt terribly guilty, because that isn't what I think about John Pizarsky at all. I honestly think he rescued me yesterday, and showed a sweet side I didn't know he had. And while it's true I'm not quite sure what he meant to tell me, it helped. It did help, and I'm grateful to him. I'd let J.P. down; I knew it in the pit of my stomach, but I told myself he'd never know that I'd talked about him like that. I'd make it up to him. I'd read that book he lent me six months ago, and I'd discuss it with him, and pretend it had changed my life.

That thing he'd told me about Lady Mary conquering Mr Fox just by telling him what she'd seen in his house . . . telling him right to his face in front of all the guests at that ghastly betrothal breakfast. And all Mr Fox could do was stand there denying it, his denials getting weaker and weaker as her story got more detailed. *I know what you're doing – I know what you are.* She had power after that, the knowing and the telling – power to walk away, or stay, save his life, order his death. I don't know what I'd have done in her place. It's easier to picture Greta in that kind of situation – Greta would've blackmailed him, for sure. Just for fun, and pocket change.

*

Mary caused quite a stir at dinner, and I was glad to be there. She was a little sad to have to take the hat off indoors, but she ate and drank and touched the knives and forks and spoons and her wine glass with such delight, you couldn't help but watch her. And she watched everyone, and told me

247

what she thought of them. A group of four men moved tables so that they were in our line of vision, and whenever Mary looked over at them they toasted her. She got quite mischievous about it, and made them drop their cutlery at least ten times as they scrambled to lift their glasses. 'It's kind of like a Jack-in-the-box,' she said. She was blushing because of all the attention, her cheeks a gorgeous shade of pink, and I said, quoting something I'd read: 'Modesty is more effective than the most expensive rouge.' Then I realised I hadn't read it anywhere and I'd just made it up. 'Modesty is more effective than the most expensive rouge,' I said again.

'Hey, you should put that in your book,' Mary said, with a smile of approval. Two couples St John and I knew, the Comyns and the Nesbits, came over to say hello and get an eyeful. I introduced Mary to them as 'a second cousin of St John's', which seemed to satisfy them, and they shook hands with her without any difficulty, though I was very worried that there would be. Mrs Nesbit is the yelling kind, and alarming her in any way is a sure-fire route to notoriety. The Nesbits and the Comyns were as nosy as they could be in a few brief minutes, and Mary told them she'd just come out of finishing school in Boston. She was a fluent liar, and really warm with it, really personal. If I hadn't seen her come to life before my very eyes I'd have believed her.

'You must come to dinner next week,' Mrs Nesbit said, before they left the restaurant. And Mary said she'd absolutely adore to. I began to foresee a disgustingly sociable future, then tried to see the three of us out for the evening; Mary, St John and I, and that jarred me out of my speculation.

'Mary . . . what was that about a book? What do you mean, my book?'

Mary poured us both more wine, fixed me with a suddenly keen gaze. 'Aren't you going to write one?'

I'd won a couple of prizes for essays and things at school, and a prize for a short story. But that was all so long ago. And it wasn't hard to shine at that sort of thing at my school; no one really studied hard because it was so unnecessary when you were going to marry well. Even so, maybe I would try. It could well go the way of the watercolor paintings, and the clay pottery, and the botany. But there would be many lonely hours ahead for me, and I thought it would be good to give them purpose.

'Did you put something in my wine, Mary? I'm just wondering how I'm keeping my temper. You just swan in, take my husband with one hand and offer me a hobby with the other . . .'

Mary's hand hovered over mine. 'We're going to be all right.' She flexed her fingers, closed her eyes ecstatically, and breathed in and out. It was embarrassing and I told her to stop making herself conspicuous.

'Sorry,' she said, not sounding sorry at all.

I had a lot of questions for her. Whether she and St John could read others' thoughts, what her first memory was, things like that. The first thing she remembered was a shilling with King George of England's head on it. It had been very well taken care of, polished and kept clean, and it shone in St John's dirty hand down where he crouched in the trench. He'd swapped something for it – she couldn't remember what he'd swapped, but she knew he'd wanted the shilling because it was bright. She told me about the first job

249

St John took after the war. He'd been a bill collector, but he doesn't say much about those times. It was fascinating listening to her.

'He was one of the best,' Mary said, wolfing steak down as if she'd heard there was going to be a shortage. 'He hounded debtors door to door, plucking away the false names and new addresses they tried to hide behind. He developed a method. Firstly, he paid no visible attention to the poverty or misery of the people on his list. Secondly, once he caught up with them he'd only ever say one sentence, demanding what was owed. That was it, his method. He repeated that one sentence over and over without changing the formulation of it, until he was paid. You should have seen him, Mrs Fox. He was really kind of magnificent. Sometimes he'd get punched or interrupted or outshouted while he was saying his sentence. And, well, he'd just wait until the interruption was over. Then, rather than starting his sentence again, he just went on as if nothing had happened, picking up from the precise syllable where he had been forced to stop. It drove people nuts. His collection rate was outstanding. It doesn't take much to horrify people who are already frightened.'

She frowned. 'He was good at being a bill collector, but it wasn't good for him. For days at a time he hardly talked to anyone but me. And sometimes at the end of his work day he'd walk into walls and closed doors. He saw them up ahead but he just didn't stop walking.'

I asked her about the first story he wrote, and she told me about the crummy boarding house he was living in back then, just a bed, a desk, a chair, and a few easels, which he placed open books on, to look at. Art monographs and cookbooks, poetry, a guide to etiquette, a dictionary, a Bible.

He'd get back from work and walk from easel to easel, picking up fleeting impressions. Mary turned the pages for him. *Gentility is neither in birth, manner, nor fashion – but in the MIND.* Next: *And what if excess of love// Bewildered them until they died?* And: *A woman is always consumed with jealousy over another woman's beauty, and she loses all pleasure in what she has . . .* After that: *Be careful that the cheese does not burn, and let it be equally melted.* Then he'd spend the night bent over his notebook, writing in zigzags, his pace irregular.

She was very reluctant to answer my other questions, about the war, and I thought it must be because of terrible things he'd done, or because he'd been a coward. But she said it wasn't that. 'If I answered the questions you're asking me,' she said, 'you'd wish I hadn't told you, because you wouldn't know what to say. I think he worries that people sneer at him for coming back safe and sound, or think that he must have been taken captive and put to work tending enemy vegetable patches. But just trust me. Mr Fox was decent in those times. He did what he could, and he was as decent and as brave as he could be.'

We changed the subject. Mary told me she had been doing some reading of her own. *Hedda Gabler*, and *The Three Musketeers*, so far. 'The women in these books are killers!' she said, her voice escalating with each word so that by the time she reached the last one the diners around us were looking around for the killers.

'Did you think they couldn't be?' I told her about one of my favorite villainesses, a flame-haired woman called Lydia Gwilt, who died changing her ways.

'Of course she did,' Mary said, frowning. 'This is worse than I thought. If you make the women wicked then killing them off becomes a moral imperative.'

My first thought was, *But they're not real,* and my second thought was, *Under absolutely no circumstances can you say that, you'll hurt her feelings.* So I devised a title for the book I was going to write – **Hedda Gabler and Other Monsters**, and she cheered up at the assurance that everyone would survive.

She wanted to experience things; she had a list. She planned to attend a big-band concert, and she planned to walk through a field of yellow rapeseed, and she planned to get an injection, and anything else I might recommend. She promised me she'd settle down soon, and I found myself telling her to take her time. Growing up I was glad to be the only girl, with big brothers who teased me and acted with unerring instinct to keep the heartbreakers away from me. But it might have been nice to have had a little sister, and to have helped her out from time to time, with advice, and chaperoning, etc.

Mary said she was going to sleep in St John's lighthouse, on Cloud Island. I told her I wouldn't hear of it, I wouldn't sleep for thinking of her all alone in that weird old place. But she'd already stolen the keys from him, and she said she thought it was nice out there. She said she liked to look at the sea, that it made her sing. 'The first time Charlotte Brontë saw the sea – she was about seventeen or eighteen, I think – she was utterly overcome . . .' she told me. She didn't seem to notice she'd slipped into a British accent, and I didn't point it out to her, I just listened. '. . . after all those years on the moors. She'd imagined what the sea was like, over and over, of course, how could she not – but when she saw it, it was more than she imagined. Didn't someone write that nothing's greater than the imagination? I think that's nonsense, don't you?'

She said all this to me in the back of the taxi that was taking us home. She was sort of panting, then she was out and out sobbing, and to hell with the static, I held her and smoothed her hair and pushed the dimple in her cheek until she was able to smile. 'You're very kind,' she said. 'I'm sorry. It's just taken such a lot for me to get here.' I saw what she meant. All I could do to help was treat her as if she was ordinary.

Still – I had to know. I mean, it was a hell of a thing. 'How *did* you get – here, Mary?'

'We were fooling around with stories. We put ourselves in them,' she said flatly, as if she didn't even believe herself. Too much awe. Like someone explaining a house fire that burnt down their whole block: 'we were playing around with matches and gasoline.'

'What – where are these stories? Can I read them?'

She leaned forward and told the taxi driver to drop us off by the dock at Cloud Cove.

I told her that the last boat must have gone an hour ago. I told her to come back with me. I told her that St John would have to know what was going on sometime. That she was real now, that she ate steak and talked to the neighbors and was probably going to have everyone in town, men, women, children, trying to get next to her before the week was out.

'I'll swim over,' she said. 'I like having a secret from him. I'll be all right, honestly. Come and see me tomorrow, and you'll see I'm perfectly cosy out there.'

I looked back as the taxi drove away from the dock – she fiddled with her hair, seemed to be tying the lighthouse keys into a tight knot in her hair. That would be hard work to comb out in the morning. She peeled off my shirtwaist, my favourite lilac shirtwaist, discarded it, and dived into the water. The taxi driver saw her too. He raised his eyebrows, but not too high. He was a taxi driver. He'd seen a lot of things. 'Well, it *is* summer. And she's from out of town.' That's all he said.

*

St John came out of his study as soon as I opened the front door. Very quietly, he told me that Greta had phoned for me.

'Oh – what did she say?' I asked. Then I remembered that I was supposed to have been at dinner with her. And I shivered, a chill in my back that made me feel as if I was falling even though I stood quite still. He shivered, too. Much more noticeably, as if tugged by strings.

'She said she'd call back tomorrow.'

'Okay.' I switched a lamp on. It was frightening to be with him in the dark, seeing him shiver like that and listening to him speak so impassively. When I saw his expression I wanted to switch the lamp back off again. Anger. It was etched all over his face, the lines drawing up into a snarl.

'Why did you lie?'

I looked at him and didn't say anything. He took a step backwards, and I don't know how I didn't scream – he seemed to be readying himself to spring at me.

'Are you going to tell me who you were with?'

I don't think I could have managed a single word, even if I'd wanted to. I knew it looked bad. And it was going to look even worse if I told him who I'd really been with. It would look like mockery, throwing something he'd told me back in his face.

'I think I'm going to knock you down,' he said. 'If you just keep standing there like that I'm really just going to knock you down. Go – upstairs, to hell, get a room somewhere with your damn Pizarsky, just get out of here.'

That stunned me; I don't know why I laugh when I'm hurt. 'Oh, Pizarsky! Oh, you'd like that, wouldn't you? Then you could put another plus in Mary's column – doesn't run around with John Pizarsky.'

I turned towards the front door – but where, as a rational adult, did I mean to go? Did I mean to swim over to the island, as Mary had? Burst in on Greta and J.P., or the Wainwrights? I slid past him and went up to the spare room. I dragged a chest of drawers over to the door; it was just the right height for me to lodge a corner of it under the door handle, which turned ten minutes later, to no avail. Then he must have rammed a shoulder against the door – it shuddered and my heart hammered in my ears. He did that just once, without saying a word. Then he went away.

I sat up late, late, looking out over our garden. There was lightning, and rain battered the ground, and I thought of Mary Foxe, miles away, watching the storm through the lighthouse window. I thought of the things she knew about St John. I saw a shiny shilling and a dark-haired young man with eyes like stains on glass. Alone in a big city, walking into walls. Everyone hurts themselves in the city, then they just pick themselves up so as not to get in anyone else's way. And then he went home, to company devised for him alone, he went home to a girl who wasn't there. I envied Mary for being what she was, for being so close to him; I was so jealous it burned, and I knew I had to let it alone or I'd break something inside me.

The night changed me. I built a scene in my head, better than that line I'd come up with about modesty and rouge. I pictured a woman alone at her dressing table, getting ready to go onstage. She's exotic-looking – maybe dark-skinned, maybe an Indian – she's had hecklers before, guys saying really filthy things, and now she's really going at it with the makeup, just plastering it on, drama around the eyes, making herself look like a woman from another world so the audience will just sit there with their mouths open and let her sing her song and get out of there in peace. And while she's getting ready this woman is talking to someone sat behind a screen – I'm not sure who that someone is yet. Anyway, the woman at the dressing table – her heart's breaking. It breaks three times a week on account of people treating her so badly, and she knows that all you can do is laugh it off. She's saying: 'Let me tell you something, kid. Love is like a magic carpet with a mind of its own. You step on that carpet and it takes you places – marvellous places, odd places, terrifying places, places you'd never have been able to reach on foot. Yeah, love's a real adventure! But you go where the carpet goes; after you've stepped onto it you don't get to choose a goddamned thing. Well . . . there'd better be a market for magic carpets. 'Cause from tonight, mine's for sale.'

And that's how I plan to begin *Hedda Gabler and Other Monsters*. I think I'll cut the part about the magic carpet being for sale, though. It might come off as tacky.

I moved the dresser away from the door at about four in

the morning. I had to go to the bathroom. Then I went into our bedroom, mine and St John's. He wasn't there. I went downstairs and found him in his study, asleep at his desk, drooling a little on some newly written pages so that the ink ran. I pulled the pages out from under his arms and put them aside without looking at them. He woke up, but he didn't open his eyes. 'I can explain about dinner,' I said. 'In the morning. Just come out to Cloud Island with me, and I'll show you.' He made no answer, and I pinched him. He opened his eyes, then, and gave me a sulky look.

'How's the book going?'

He winced.

'Will you read me some? Please?'

'It's not ready.'

'Just a little.'

He read a couple of pages aloud, very quickly. Then he saw that I wanted to hear more and he slowed down. He writes beautifully but without hope. Odd that he could be responsible for a little dancing cinder like Mary. He reached a particularly stressful part of a chapter and I came to crisis and said, 'Oh, Lord,' before I could check myself. He looked up from the page. 'Bad things are going to happen, D.'

'To the two of us?' I held out my hand to him. He took it and touched his lips to my wrist. Pins and needles, as if all my blood was rushing back into me.

'Yes, to the two of us. It's inevitable.'

'But good things are going to happen, too.' He opened his mouth, seemed to think better of it, closed his mouth. 'Were you going to say I sound like Mary?'

'Or Mary sounds like you . . .'

I came to him without substance, and six years later I'm

still the same. Sometimes I say terrible things to him because I don't want him to know I'm sad, sometimes I fly off the handle to hide the fact that I don't know what I'm talking about. And other times – too often, maybe – I don't dare have an opinion in case it upsets anyone. I'm too stupid for him.

Have you ever heard a note in someone's voice that said 'This is the end'? I heard it in the next words he said to me, and I stopped listening. Have you ever wanted to try and cross an ending with some colossal revelation – 'There's something I never told you. I'm a princess from the kingdom atop Mount Qaf', for example, 'my family live in eternal youth, and if you abide with me, you will, too. I kept this secret from you to see if you would cherish me for who I am.' Have you ever wished, wished, wished . . .

My head got so heavy, it sank down onto my chest. So say whatever it is you think you've got to say, St John. That you're not in love with me. That you need to be alone. Say it. I'm not going to like it, no, I won't like it at all. But I'll be all right.

I told him that I loved him. I've never, ever, said that to him before, because I just don't know how he'd take it. *I love you.* I mouthed the words because there didn't seem any point in interrupting him just then. I don't know if he saw. I hope he did, because I don't believe it's the sort of thing a woman can tell a man more than, say, three times in their life together. It's only really appropriate in the event of a life-threatening emergency, 'I love you.' It means a different thing to us than it means to them. God knows what it means to them. God knows what it means to us.

'. . . start again, D. Let's start all over again,' my husband said. He rested his hands on my shoulders for a moment, then took them away. 'Can we?'

Start again? Nice in theory, but what was he really trying to say? How far back would we have to fall? All that undoing . . .

Show you're game, Daphne.

'Sure,' I said. I held out my hand. 'Shake on it.'

We shook hands. He held on to my hand; his grip was tight, and our palms were sweaty. I looked up at him, he looked down at me, and I had absolutely no idea what was on his mind just then. I decided to wait. But after a few more speechless seconds I figured he must not know what to say next. Maybe he was scared of saying the wrong thing.

So I took the initiative. I broke the handshake and introduced myself. I said I was glad to meet him, and I asked him what his name was. I heard myself, all bubbles and sparkle. I'd had to drop my gaze to be able to pull off the playful act, though, and I felt him looking at me, still looking. I heard him stifle a yawn. Then he lifted my chin with his thumb, his lips grazed my cheek, my spine melted down my back, he murmured: 'Okay, but I was wondering if we couldn't go a little faster than that—'

I slid my hands up under his shirt, my fingers spread across the bareness of his chest, shaking as I felt the depth of the breaths he took. It felt nice, of course, but really I was just stalling him, trying to think of a way to give in without letting him think he could always get his own way. I needed some phrase that was simultaneously encouraging and disparaging.

'Well?' he said, and he was so close, smiling just a little, his lips not quite touching mine. I just couldn't find that phrase I wanted, so I gave his nose a good, hard, tweak – all the better for being sudden. He gave a pretty satisfying squawk after that, so I kissed him.

And, laughing a little, he kissed me back. He kissed me like ice cream, like a jazz waltz, the rough, gentle way the sea washed sand off my skin on the hottest day of the year. And the whole time there was that little laugh between us, sweet and silly.

*

We rode the ferry across to the lighthouse in the morning, having slept too late to walk across. Mary Foxe wasn't there. But she'd left us a note on the kitchen table, with the keys to the lighthouse on top of it.

Gone travelling! To Mexico via Mississippi. Met a beachcomber who said he'd take me as far as Virginia – not bad, huh? Don't know how long I'll be gone.

*Mrs Fox – I'll send you a forwarding address when I know it, so you can send me pages of **Hedda Gabler and Other Monsters** – don't forget to write it. And don't talk yourself out of it – you can do it, and it's going to be really good. (Maybe I am slightly magical after all.)*

Mr Fox – don't worry. I'll come back to you. Maybe you'll be nicer to me once you've missed me a little. And hey, now you can do whatever you want. For a while.

I'm dying to know what it'll be like when I come home – the three of us(!) I almost wish I was there and back again already . . .

Take care of each other, okay?

M.F.

We'd found my shirtwaist by the dock, just where she'd

left it, crumpled and ruined by the rain, so I could only hope she had some clothes on.

St John read the note over and over, his lips moving silently. He looked both stricken and relieved. I suspected that in the next few minutes he was going to start quizzing me pretty hard.

As for me, I'd noticed just how similar Mary's handwriting was to St John's and was thinking that perhaps a break from Mary Foxe wasn't such a bad idea after all.

some foxes

I

The little girl feared the fox cub, and the fox cub felt exactly the same way about her.

The woods went on for many miles, and a few foxes lived at the heart of it and didn't encounter people if they could help it. Yet the girl and the fox cub had been pointed out to each other – the girl's mother had used a picture book, and the fox cub's mother had brought him to peer in at a window once, when everyone in the girl's house was sound asleep – and each had been told: *That is your enemy.*

They grew up a bit. He learnt things, and so did she. They didn't unlearn their fear of each other.

The girl was pretty, though . . . and stubborn and strange.

And the young fox was curious and courageous and clever . . .

It was only natural that they would find each other.

The young girl was in love with mystery and secret knowledge. She learnt the names of demons, and summoned them. They never materialised. She didn't take offence. She wouldn't have bothered either, if she were them. The girl lived with her mother and her elder sister at the mouth of the woods – only a few steps away from town – less than ten steps, probably. Still, they didn't get many visitors. In the evenings the elder sister studied and studied, but our girl set up lanterns in her room and performed puppet shows with marionettes she had made herself. During his long illness the girl's father had shown her how to make puppets. Then he'd died. 'Come away from the window,' the elder sister would say, sharply, whenever she saw what the girl was doing. 'Don't draw attention to us. Who knows what's watching from the woods?'

But their mother intervened and told the elder girl to leave the younger be.

Our girl sang songs to accompany her performances, and the puppets cast shadows on the leaves and the grass outside her window. Our young fox observed all this from a distance; he stood stock-still, his narrow eyes just a faint shimmer amongst the shrubs. He heard the singing. The sound meant nothing to him, though it did not displease him. The fox knew about fox business. By now his mother had moved on somewhere and he didn't much miss her. His paws were swift, and he wouldn't let his eyes confuse his mind, so he was good at catching rabbits and squirrels. He slept late and woke early and travelled the whole wood wide, tasting the weather. He knew where the bees went to make their wild honey. He saw when cuckoos visited the nests and knew which birds were going to get a nasty shock come hatching time, and he waited for the spoils. The fox fought no one; he took things easy. When it was time to run away, he ran. But not this time.

What can it mean for a fox to approach a girl? Foxes are solitary. A fox that seeks out human company is planning evil. Or it has something the matter with it. Rabies, or something worse. The fox watched the girl at play, and he didn't understand what she was doing – it certainly wasn't fox business. Still, it interested him, and he gazed and gazed at her as she sat surrounded by all that greedy, dangerous fire that she kept in jars. He gazed and gazed though it served no purpose to do so, gazed without feeling satisfied and with the sensation of a deep scratch in his side (this was an awareness of time and its disappointments, the certainty that the girl would put out the lamps before he had looked his fill). And it was through observing the girl at play that our fox learnt to recognise beauty elsewhere in the wood. Whenever he became caught up in useless looking, he knew. Moonlight on the water brought rapture. Think of a fox, dipping his paws in silver, muzzle dripping. He didn't want to drink the water, only to touch it while it looked like that. Another fox came by and laughed at him. But our fox didn't care.

As for the girl, she looked into the darkness of the woods, and she saw very little. Occasional motion, perhaps, but nothing definite. Our girl developed a distaste for fact. She stopped going to school. Her mother kept a shop in town, selling food, books, toys, linen, and anything else she could think of, and she did very well out of it. The girl joined her mother at the shop counter. She refused to sell people things she didn't think they needed, and argued with them until they saw her point. The elder sister grew more wan and studious, folding herself into her textbooks because she didn't like to live in the mouth of the woods, where things she couldn't see crept and shuddered all hours of the day and fell deathly still when she turned to look at them. The elder sister wanted to get away and go to a city, and be unknown and kick up her heels and have fun. All in time. She needed to get top marks first, and go away on a scholarship. 'What's to become of you?' the elder sister asked the younger, who shrugged and laughed and looked out of the window and dreamed.

Have you forgotten our fox?

The one who now had an eye for beauty, and an inclination to set it apart from other things . . .

The fox wished to thank the girl.

(The fox wished to know the girl.)

It took him a long time to make his mind up. He wasn't happy about it, but he didn't have a fever and he slept well and his appetite was fine, so he thought he must be well and that everything was all right, and that maybe just this once the things the elder foxes had said were wrong.

So the fox brought the girl berries. Plump, rust-red berries wrapped in the largest, greenest leaf he could find. He left the leaf out overnight first, so that it sparkled with dew. How to give them to her?

He watched and waited. The evening puppet shows had become less frequent; this was because the girl was becoming interested in young men and had begun dressing up to go out to dances with her sister. Their mother had previously refused to let the elder sister go alone. 'Young men are animals,' she said. So there were dances, and blushes, and letters written and exchanged, and sighs of longing and – the woods didn't seem quite as real to the girl any more. They were just some trees behind her house. A great number of trees, to be sure, but only trees. Men were quite interesting. They were new puzzles to work at, at least. And if she solved one of them she won a new life, and a new surname, and a companion who wouldn't tell her off for buying too many music scorebooks and new hats. These days the girl only tended to put on a puppet show when she'd fallen out with a suitor. Then a richly gowned female puppet berated a threadbare male puppet for half an hour at a time.

The fox didn't like the new tone that the puppet shows had taken. Something about it . . . anyway, here were the berries, and there was the girl and the lantern light. The time was right. He leapt up onto the windowsill with the leaf in his mouth, dropped it and retreated, farther than a stone's throw, but not so far that they were unable to see each other.

The young woman saw a streak of grey, saw a tail brush the windowpane, saw a green parcel fall. And her puppets fell from her hands with a clatter and lay on the ground with their knees bent as if they meant to spring up again on their own. The lantern flickered. The girl saw a fox a little way down the corridor of trees. The creature was watching her. She moved to the right and its gaze moved to the right. She moved to the left, far left, almost out of the window's frame, and the fox's head moved with her. It appeared to be smiling, but that was just a meaningless expression created by the look of its muzzle. There was an unfaltering clarity to the animal's gaze; thought without emotion. And yet. The fox was quivering. It had brought her something and it had stayed to see what she would do, and it was quivering. So the girl didn't draw the curtain, and she didn't turn away. She opened the window and slowly, very slowly, closed her hand around the bulky leaf. The fox did not approach – if anything, it drew further back. The girl opened the leaf. Berries, but they looked more like jewels. She tasted one, and it was delicious. She ate another and another, and she beckoned the fox. 'Come here, come here,' she said in a syrupy voice she used with very small children. The fox did not approach. The fox looked desperately from the girl's eyes to her berry-stained mouth. She didn't like the gift. She was angry. What was she saying, what was she saying . . .

'Won't you come closer? You're the one who sought me out, you know,' the girl said crossly, in her own voice.

The fox had had enough for one night, and fled.

Now the girl wished to thank the fox.

(The girl wished to know the fox.)

She wrapped herself in a shawl, took a lantern in her hand and slipped out of the house, thinking that she would follow the fox to its den and see how it lived. Our girl raised her lantern as she followed the paths between the trees. She ducked under the bigger branches, but the smaller ones raked her hair; she gasped at first, but then the pull became so frequent that it was caressing, a ceiling of hands. She stepped across shallow, pebbled brooks. Her skirt dragged in the water – the hem would be ruined, she thought, distantly. The fox was nowhere to be seen. The girl stopped beside a fallen log and swung her lantern around behind her, trying to remember the direction she had come from. She couldn't remember. She was lost, and she didn't know what to do. She sat down on the log and cried. Unfortunate girl – her tears were beautiful. From his hiding place, the fox watched her weep. All he could think was that she was doing something with her eyes; something that shone. He watched her until she fell asleep, and he kept watch over her while she slept.

This happened in winter. There was ice in the earth. When the sun was down, skin and clothing were of no use outside. You needed fur, or feathers, or you needed to be indoors. The girl caught a chill. A bad chill. Her breath cracked in her chest; she took a fever because her body needed the warmth. Her teeth chattered. She reminded the fox of leaves blown in the wind. When she woke up, she was weak, and, much to the delight of the fox, she lay on her log and wept again. Without knowing it she had walked a long, long way into the wood. Sunrise dazed the redwoods – birches wept, and so did the girl. Eventually she chose a direction and began to walk – the fox followed her, wondering where she was going. Home – her home, was the other way. Discreetly, he rattled some branches. She noticed him, and then he ran, too fast for her to catch him, but slow enough for her to keep up. The girl could hardly believe that she was following a fox again – it could be taking her anywhere. To her death in a deep pool; to a shallow pit crammed with tiny bones. Perhaps it didn't even mean for her to follow it, perhaps it was just bounding along enjoying its morning. The fox never looked back at her. A different fox?

She heard the search party before she saw them. The air rang with the sound of her name. The fox swerved and dashed past her, back to the heart of the wood. She put out a hand just in time and felt its warm fur against her palm.

There were no more puppet shows after that. Snow fell. The girl sank, and the girl shivered, and the girl raved, and the girl died. The cause of death was twofold – the extreme chill she'd taken alone in the night, and the berries, which were poisonous. The fox didn't know what was happening. He dared much, so he returned to watch the house. All the curtains were drawn. Steady lamplight escaped from a gap at the top of one pair of curtains, the pair in the girl's bedroom.

He lost interest after a few nights of that view, and returned when he next remembered. There was no light that night. The whole house was dark. It was the same the next night, and the next. The fox was philosophical. From the moment he had recognised loveliness he had known it couldn't last. And he returned to fox business.

II

Now I will speak of another kind of fox. The other fox was a grey fox; this one is red. I am speaking now of a fox who had been hunted, a beast of the chase who was only alive because of luck and cowering and grim fighting – grim and miserable and low. This fox wasn't innocent – he had turned hutches into bloodbaths purely to divert himself. But he also knew wounds and weariness, had crawled into holes and lain like a rag wadded deep into the ground. He killed hens because they were there to be killed, and he understood that the hunters sought to do away with him for the same reason. The fox had started his life in a den heaving with cubs, but they had all been hunted down almost as soon as they were grown. A few times he had hidden alongside foxes who had been bred in captivity, but they never got away. Their wits were dull. The horizon made them run around in circles, confused.

This fox had no one. I've said that foxes are solitary, but there's a difference between having no one because you've chosen it and having no one because everyone has been taken away. I'm not saying that I myself know what the difference is. But our fox knew.

One afternoon the fox jumped some fences and walked

straight up to a farmhouse. He didn't want to be a fox any more. He didn't want to be anything. His head was down, so he didn't see the farm dogs, looking askance. They bristled and growled, but they didn't attack, not even when the farmer's wife came out and commanded it. The farm dogs knew a sick fox when they saw one. The farmer's wife went inside, but she left the door half open – she was coming back with something. The fox looked at the ground. He appeared to be smiling, but that was just a meaningless expression created by the look of his muzzle. The fox had no plan. Something might happen soon. Or it might not. Either way he was here, at the end of his nature.

A human form appeared near him – the dogs jumped at the sky and bayed in a way that wolves do sometimes when the full moon draws them. The fox didn't look. This person had been following him about for days. He couldn't remember when she had begun. He had been badly hurt and she was there, she was just there. She had sticky stuff that he had permitted her to smooth over his wounds. The wounds were just scars now; they'd healed fast. He had been too sore to move and she had dug up voles and snapped their necks and scraped at them and fed him. With her five fingers and her funny, flat palm she had placed food in his mouth. At night, when he was in too much pain to rest, she counted stars and whispered into the hollow of the tree he lay in, telling him how many she could see, until he fell asleep. There was no reason for her to do such things. He didn't know what this person wanted from him, and he hadn't come across anything like her before. So she probably didn't exist. The fox ignored her as best he could. Now she crouched down beside him and she touched him. She rubbed his neck.

She spoke into one of his ears, and he understood. Whenever she spoke, he understood. Her voice had all sorts of sounds in it – the flow of water against rock, an acorn shaken in its shell, a bird asking for morning. Her voice wasn't loud, but he heard it throughout his body.

—Listen . . . that woman is looking for a gun.

A gun? Good . . . even if the fox had been able to reply, he wouldn't have.

—She's found the gun. Quickly: why did you come here?

The dogs became braver and crept close – she put out a hand and sent them away.

—It's true, then, fox? That you want to die?

He couldn't tell her the truth; he lacked the language.

She sighed.

—Very well. It is your right. Goodbye.

She stroked his back. She strolled away. The sound of the shotgun shattered the air and sent him after her, as hard and as fast as he could go. They both ran, but he overtook her. All things considered, two legs, etc., she wasn't a bad runner. 'Live,' she laughed, breathlessly. 'Live, live, live.' And when it was safe to stop, she collapsed against a stile in a fallow field and held her face between her hands and made noises that sounded like 'Hic, hic, hic.' He began to pay attention to her. Her eyes were set quite far apart. He had never been so close to one of his hunters, had never been this close to harm.

She told him that she had looked after him because of the white hairs on his forehead that grew into the shape of a star. Sometimes you see that someone is marked and you're help-less after that – you love. She wanted to tell him that, but she decided it was better not to. He hadn't known that there were

271

such hairs on his forehead, or that such a thing could be of significance. She sat and he lay near her, and a little time passed, quiet and bright. Then they had to go, in case the farmer had been told of their trespass and decided to look for them.

They parted outside her hut. It was a ramshackle thing beside a stream. It had a heavily dented tin roof and its windows were coated with dust. All in all, it looked cross, and as if it had plenty of things to say to its inhabitant about having been left alone for so long.

'Come inside,' the woman said to the fox.

The fox demurred. Sadly, the woman watched him go his own way again.

Days went by. The woman made her peace with her hut. She gave it a thorough sweeping, built herself a new roof, washed the windows, plaited rugs. The woman picked herbs and grasses and boiled and bottled various concoctions. Sick people and their relatives sought her out in the forest; she took their money and they took her bottles away and were cured. 'Where have you been?' she was asked, again and again. 'Weeks we've been looking for you.'

And she answered. 'I fell in love.'

'Congratulations! Where is he?'

'I don't know. I don't know if I'll see him again.'

And her pupils grew vast as she spoke, as if her eyelids had been opened while she was still in the first stage of sleeping. Women like her are very serious once they have chosen. To everyone who saw her she said: 'If you see him, tell me. He wears a white star on his forehead.' She didn't tell anyone that he was a fox.

One of the village women went into labour, and our

woman served as midwife. The days were full of screaming, and the nights were hoarse, and there were three of each until the baby was born. This happened in summer. When our woman came home, she jumped into the stream and washed; the blood and sweat whirled away and afterwards she sat outside until the sun dried her. She watched lizards and felt humming in her skin; tiny creatures bit her; they were alive and they wanted her to know. Her pulse slowed to its lowest ebb, and sped up again, flashed through her wrists, in her head. She was happy and unhappy. 'The fox has forgotten you,' she told herself. Yet all around her she saw white stars . . .

Because of a fox?

Because of him.

The woman went into her hut to find clothes to wear and found that she had been robbed. Bottles and picture frames were broken, her table and chairs were overturned, her papers had been rifled through, matches were scattered on the ground. The woman searched the hut for missing things. She wasn't aware of all her possessions, so really she was just looking for a gap. She found it on her bookshelf. The thief had taken a dictionary. Nothing else. She stood, looking at the gap, and thinking. Then thinking turned to wonder and she smiled into her hand.

Now think of a fox in his den, wrapped round a book. His front paws are resting on the pages, and his eyes are very close to the text. These shapes! They're useless. They frustrate him. The more he looks at them the more they mock him. He nudges the book into a sack and drags the sack along by its drawstring, through the forest. In the bushes by the village nursery, he listens to children saying their ABCs.

273

He can see the blackboard. The teacher taps it with a ruler, going from letter to letter. His mind wanders . . . he bites his paw. Look and listen. His mind wanders again . . . he nips at his paw again, savagely this time. And again, and again, until his paw is bloody and he is learning.

First light finds the fox at his stolen book. No one else knows, no one sees what he's doing. But words are coming. The fox doesn't hunt any more – he doesn't hunt! He eats easy meat, forest rats. He stays near his den or he goes to the nursery school, he listens carefully, he connects pictures with words, he eavesdrops, he steals newspapers, he stumbles in his understanding and snarls and shreds the newspapers to pieces . . . but he will know this language, he must have this language.

Because of a woman?

Because of her.

The day came when the fox had words. Only a few, but enough to begin to talk to her. He went to the woman's hut. Her hair was grey, and there were lines on her face, but otherwise, she was the same. She had not been young when they'd met, and two years had tipped the balance. He wasn't young himself. The woman smiled and touched his forehead. So it was still there, this shape that she liked. Good.

—Come inside, the woman said, in that way that he heard from head to toe. One day he would ask her how she could do that.

The fox entered the hut.

The fox had brought the dictionary back. She'd long since bought a new one – just as well, since the stolen one was falling apart. He had also brought words. He had chewed them out of newspapers; long, patient work, and anxious work too, double-checking that each word meant what he thought it meant. If he had got it wrong, all wrong . . . if she laughed at him . . .

The woman settled in a chair and watched the fox sort through scraps of paper. She was holding her breath. She believed – she didn't know what she believed. It could not be. The fox looked lean and crazed. In her mind she ran through a list of concoctions that might do something for the beast . . .

Words began to spread at her feet.

Hello.

The fox looked up at her and panted. He curled his tail around his leg in an apprehensive 'L'.

The woman raised her hand and let it fall. 'Hello,' she said, aloud. She couldn't see clearly. All these tears. She brushed them away.

Can you help me.

He was very intent as she spoke. She answered three times, to be clear. 'I'll try. Tell me what you need.'

Quickly, remembering the afternoon at the farmhouse, she added: 'I can't help you die.'

The fox shuffled scraps of paper, chose two.

Not die.

He chose three more.

Please change me.

He thumped his paw on the last two words, his eyes on hers. Change me. Change me.

'Change you how?'

Not fox any more.

He'd had to tear the word 'fox' from the dictionary. It was tiny.

'No,' the woman said, slowly. 'No, I don't think I can do that. I haven't the skill.'

The fox lay down and closed his eyes. This lull, after all his striving, was enormous. It was like pain. The woman fell down beside him – her pity made her do it. The woman and the fox faced each other, nose to nose. Then he stood, nudged her aside, chose more words.

Stay with you.

I with you.

Please.

The fox applied himself to living as the woman lived. He ate at the table with her, and slept alongside her in her bed, and scrabbled around with soap in the stream. He read voraciously. He read more than she did. And as more words came to him, he told her of the hunt, of the horses and the hounds behind, and sometimes there were falcons, like a rain of beaks and claws. The woman listened, and as she listened, she realised that she was hearing him – that he was saying words instead of showing her. She made no remark, and treated it as normal. She asked him which would he rather be, if he could change – a horse, a bird, or a hound? None of those, he said. At night he suffered himself to be held, a thing that was unthinkable in the first days of their acquaintance, even when he had been very badly hurt. He had less and less trouble sleeping upright each night. Together they built a bigger hut, and a bigger bed. She saw that his claws had become thin and brittle – they were more like fingernails. Very long nails, it was true, but they weren't claws any more.

*

But what teeth he had. So:

The pleasure of biting. Or letting him. And afterwards the

feel of a long wet tongue light against a hot wound. The different ways:

the hidden bite
the swollen bite
the point
the line of points
the coral and the jewel
the line of jewels
the broken cloud.

*

One medicine-making day, as they carried fresh water back to her hut in wooden buckets, he asked her: 'How old are we?'

And she answered: 'I have forgotten.'

She put down her bucket and tried to count years on her fingers. He watched until she gave up, then put his arms about her – he stood a head higher than she did.

'What's so funny?' she asked him.

And he said: 'Nothing.'

III

I almost forgot to mention another fox I know of – a very wicked fox indeed. But you are tired of hearing about foxes now, so I won't go on.

Thank you:

Cathy

Bolaji

Ali

Tracy

Maria

Jin

Kate

Antosca

Tate

Piotr.

And thanks to Amy, Vito, Jess, Denise and everyone at Hedgebrook, including & especially my amazing fellow fellows, Neela, Robin, Tina and Katy, who listened to the first few pages of Mr. F.

When I first started thinking about Bluebeard, I read and watched every interpretation I could find – all of them valuable, but some sank in especially deep: Marina Warner's *From the Beast to the Blonde*, Margaret Atwood's essay *Fitcher's Bird*, and Anne Sexton's *Transformations*. These were wise and excellent guides.